Agrarian Transformation in Egypt

About the Book and Author

The role of agricultural mechanization in the labor process in rural Egypt is the focus of this book, the first major anthropological study in Upper Egypt in a generation. Based on data gathered from a large village, the book portrays population trends, land-tenure patterns, irrigation practices, agricultural labor, mechanization, and marketing, and examines their implications for religion and local politics. The author emphasizes the changing role of the household and the relations between households, particularly the role of women and children. Especially important is Dr. Hopkins's interpretation of the process of differentiation, where class is seen as a dynamic outgrowth of the labor process rather than simply deduced from ownership or control of property. The paradox of his Egypt study is that while objective differentiation is present, class consciousness is not. Patterns of social control based on hierarchy and deference are still strong and ensure the reproduction of the social system.

Nicholas S. Hopkins is professor of anthropology at the American University in Cairo.

Agrarian Transformation in Egypt

Nicholas S. Hopkins

Westview Press / Boulder and London

Westview Special Studies in Social, Political, and Economic Development

This Westview softcover edition is printed on acid-free paper and bound in softcovers that carry the highest rating of the National Association of State Textbook Administrators, in consultation with the Association of American Publishers and the Book Manufacturers' Institute.

Published in 1987 in the United States of America by Westview Press, Inc.; Frederick A. Praeger, Publisher; 5500 Central Avenue, Boulder, Colorado 80301

Library of Congress Cataloging-in-Publication Data
Hopkins, Nicholas S.
Agrarian transformation in Egypt.
(Westview special studies in social, political, and economic development)
Bibliography: p.
Includes index.
1. Egypt—Rural conditions. 2. Agricultural innovations—Egypt. 3. Agriculture—Economic aspects—Egypt. 4. Agriculture—Social aspects—Egypt. I. Title. II. Series.
HN786.A8H66 1987 306′.3 86-32479
ISBN 0-8133-7342-5

Composition for this book was created by conversion of the author's word-processor disks.
This book was produced without formal editing by the publisher.

Printed and bound in the United States of America

The paper used in this publication meets the requirements of the American National Standard for Permanence of Paper for Printed Library Materials Z39.48-1984.

6 5 4 3 2 1

Affectionately dedicated to my father

Contents

Illustrations

Tables

Figures

Acknowledgments

In a process that began in 1979 and continues to the present, I have received the support and encouragement of many people. Most of all there are the people in the village of Musha itself, who tolerated my presence and made the experience enjoyable.

I was introduced to Musha in 1979 by the Catholic Relief Services (CRS) office in Cairo, which was looking for someone to conduct a survey on the social aspects of animal husbandry. I am grateful to the CRS and especially to its director, Mr. Andrew Koval, for providing this initial contact and for continued support over the years, especially through the CRS Asyut office. Engineer Ahmed Bahgat was most helpful at different times, as were the directors of the Asyut office.

I am grateful to a number of organizations for their help in making this research possible. The funding for a year of research in 1980–81 was provided by the American Research Center in Egypt and the Middle East Awards Program, administered by the Population Council office in Cairo. The American University in Cairo granted me a year of leave for the research and also a sabbatical leave two years later that allowed me to make the first draft of the results. While on sabbatical in 1982–83, I was appointed to the Center for Middle Eastern Studies at Harvard University. I am grateful to the Center and its then director, Professor Edward Keenan, for accepting me there as a visiting scholar.

My local support was provided by Asyut University, thanks to the good agency of Professor Mohammed Helmi el-Gibali of the Faculty of Agriculture. Dr. el-Gibali also helped me locate a research assistant. Moreover, I profited from my contacts with many faculty members at Asyut University, notably Professors Bahgat Abdelmaksoud and Ragaa Amir.

Much of my time in the field was spent with my chief field assistant, Mr. Sabr Imam, and with my village guide, the *dallal*, Mr. Ahmed Mahmoud. Without their patient help, this research would not have been possible.

I am indebted to the people of Musha, particularly the late Mr. Abdelmajid Mohammed Tammam, the Umda of Musha and former deputy in the Egyptian parliament, for his hospitality and friendship. I also owe a large bouquet of thanks to Mr. Salah Abdin, President of the Local Popular Council and my immediate host in the village, for support and advice. Too many people in

Musha gave me hospitality and help in the course of my stays there for me to single out only a few. But I want to mention three families where I found a home-like atmosphere: the Adolf Jabra Jirjis family, the Mustafa Mohran family, and the Ahmed Mahmoud family.

A team of field assistants from the American University of Cairo took charge of interviewing the women: Jehan Attia, Maha Adly Guindi, Suzan Ahmed Lutfi Mubarek, and Nadia Adel Taher. They were enthusiastically assisted by a quartet of young women from Musha. In June 1981 Afaf al-Bassam accompanied me to the field to inquire into matters of local administration.

Substantial help with the data analysis in the early phases was provided by Lina Hediah, Maha Adly Guindi, and Maha Fathallah. The final preparation of the manuscript would not have been possible without the intelligent and critical help of Hanan Hosni Sabea.

Without in any way implicating them in the result, I would like to thank many friends for conversations in various contexts over the years: Donald Cole, Robert Fernea, Saad Gadalla, John Gerhart, Laila el-Hamamsy, Iliya Harik, Allen Hoben, Robert Hunt, Rick Huntington, Sohair Mehanna, Soheir Morsy, Cynthia Nelson, Alan Richards, and Lucie Wood Saunders. Many of these conversations were only made possible by the concerned and knowledgeable intellectual atmosphere at the American University in Cairo.

Finally, I wish to express my gratitude and devotion to my family.

Let me turn now to the orientalist's revenge, transliteration. Arabic words written in italics are written in a simplified transliteration based on the system of the *International Journal of Middle East Studies.* Grammatical plurals required by English are written by adding an "s"; "Shaykh" and "Omda," written as ordinary words, are used to refer to particular individuals, as the context will make clear. Place names are based on those used in the *Survey of Egypt* maps. Measures are treated as English words. Personal names are all pseudonyms and are written in the way common in Egypt. This approach makes for some inconsistency but should aid comprehension in other ways.

Prices are given in Egyptian pounds (LE), divided into 100 piasters (PT). At the time of field work, an Egyptian pound was worth US$.83.

Nicholas S. Hopkins

Agrarian Transformation in Egypt

"C'est un lieu commun qu'en Egypte toutes choses sont immobiles et immuables. Il nous semble au contraire qu'il est au monde peu de pays où les modifications économiques, géographiques et historiques soient à l'heure actuelle aussi profondes et aussi rapides. Dans le domaine des irrigations, que de transformations depuis Mehemet Ali! Et nous pouvons même dire, que de transformations depuis quinze ans!" (Brunhes 1902:418)

It is a commonplace that in Egypt everything is unchanging and unchangeable. It seems to us on the contrary that there are few countries in the world where the economic, geographic, and historic modifications are at the present time so thoroughgoing and so rapid. In the area of irrigation, how much transformation has there been since Mohammed Ali! We could even say, how much transformation has there been in the last fifteen years!

"Cependent on perçoit, dans l'économie du pays et dans la condition de ses habitants, certains symptômes d'une évolution profonde. Cette vieille terre n'est plus cultivée comme autrefois; ses paysans ne sont plus tous des esclaves de la glèbe; la plupart d'entre eux ont conquis la situation de petits propriétaires. A côté des récoltes traditionnelles, d'autres comme le coton, le bersim et le mais occupent de vastes espaces dans les champs; ils imposent de nouveaux assolements; ils créent de nouveaux besoins en eau; ils exigent plus de travail au cours de l'année. . . . C'est en moins d'un siècle que ces changements se sont accomplis, laissant prévoir pour les prochaines générations une transformation de plus en plus profonde des conditions du travail agricole et de la vie sociale." (Demangeon 1926:155).

One can notice, however, in the economy of the country and in the state of its people, some symptoms of a profound evolution. This ancient earth is no longer farmed the way it was; its peasants are no longer attached to the soil; most of them have achieved the status of small landowners. In addition to the traditional crops, others such as cotton, berseem and maize occupy tremendous areas in the fields; they impose new rotations; they create new water demands; they require more work in the course of the year. . . . All these changes have taken place in less than a century, foreshadowing for the future generations an ever deeper transformation of the conditions of agricultural work and of social life.

1

Anthropology and Agricultural Change in Egypt

Rural Egypt

Rural Egypt in the 1980s is a complex place, full of contradictory trends and images. One would be tempted to postulate that the Egyptian countryside is in a phase of rapid and unprecedented change, leading perhaps to a qualitatively different type of social organization inserted into the national and international economic and political systems in innovative ways—except that in a sense, this was already the judgment of such observers as the French geographers Jean Brunhes (1902:418) at the turn of the century and A. Demangeon a generation later (1926:155). Demangeon further noted that rural Egypt was rapidly being assimilated into the world capitalist system, arguing that "the penetration of European civilization has oriented towards market production an agriculture long restricted to domestic production." In the spirit of his times, he welcomed this as progress.

It would thus be more appropriate to characterize rural Egypt as being caught up in a perpetual whirl of change than to postulate its unchanging nature. It is not the fact of change that has to be justified, but the nature of that change that has to be specified. Change in rural Egypt is continual, and it has been proceeding in the current direction without respite for at least the last century or century and a half. Among the major aspects of this transformation are commoditization, the penetration of capital, irrigation, transportation, mechanization, education, migration, the growth of cities, government policy towards agriculture, and rural development. None of these is necessarily consistent with another, although they combine to produce the "change" we perceive.

At present we can observe a situation marked by the rise of the part-time farmer, reliant on non-agricultural sources for a substantial part of his income, and tied into emergent capitalist structures as far as agriculture itself is concerned. In other words, the agricultural sector is not fully separated from the other sectors of Egyptian economic life, for the life histories and strategies of individuals link the rural communities to the rest of the country. This is reflected in such processes as education, which touches an ever-larger proportion of young people in the villages, and migration abroad, which is a fact of life in virtually all Egyptian villages. Migration abroad supplements the long tradition of migration within Egypt, particularly rural-urban migration. Work abroad, and work outside the agricultural sector in Egypt, both generate streams of income into the villages which make them more prosperous in many cases than one would judge from the success of agriculture alone. This same openness makes it harder for the traditional processes of social control to operate. Formerly based on the control of village wealth and access to resources through large and powerful families, they are now gradually shifting to other bases.

Materially speaking, there are also many new features in Egyptian agrarian life. We can note the almost universal acceptance of agricultural machinery for certain tasks, notably plowing, field preparation, and harvesting, with water lifting and transport rapidly shifting over to mechanized forms. How this shift towards mechanization affects the organization of agricultural production will be a major theme of this book. Equally important is the improvement of the road network and the burgeoning of a new transport industry based on the small and medium-sized truck, the Toyotas and the Daihatsus. Access to many villages is now by paved road, and there are relatively few settlements that are more than 10 kilometers from the nearest paved road. Most villages now have electricity and piped water, although not all households are hooked into the village system.

The arrival of electricity has made a major difference in the quality of village life. It means that lighting is available now for all nighttime events, from social gatherings to religious sessions. It means that people can now listen to radios and cassette tape recorders, and that the religious brotherhoods and mosque-based Koran-readers can amplify their proceedings and so broadcast their practices and ideas to a wider population. Most of all, of course, it means access to television (and more recently, to videos). Many rural households have television, and many more people visit their neighbors to watch the shows. A television set is usually one of the first items a household will buy with the income earned outside agriculture. Through television, people (and especially women and young people) have access to the ideas and life styles of the wider world.

The physical environment in rural Egypt is also undergoing change. As the comment by Brunhes suggests, one important aspect of this change is the transformation of the irrigation system, particularly now since the completion of the Aswan High Dam in 1964. Since the late 19th century, canals have been dug, abandoned, and relocated. New crops have presented new water needs. In the village, houses are more likely to be made of fired brick than they were a couple of generations ago (Lozach and Hug 1930), and the new areas of houses on the edges of most villages are laid out on more of a grid pattern.

Before the overthrow of the monarchy by the free officers in 1952, rural changes were led and to some extent controlled by the rural upper class—the estate owners and the large farmers. They introduced the major technological innovations, and they represented the rural areas in the Parliament and other national councils. After the 1952 revolution, the new government became more systematically concerned with the well-being of the rural population—and of course somewhat hostile to the rural upper classes who were considered to be the de facto allies of the royal family. Particularly during the 1960s, the government of Gamal Abdel Nasser made a major effort to equip the villages with schools, clinics, cooperatives, and other government institutions and programs (Harik 1974). The current generation of young adults are the first to have benefitted by all this attention, and the children continue to do so. The inadequacies of the educational and health systems have often been decried, but it is equally correct to note their contribution to the awakening and the opening up of rural society.

Nevertheless with all this change there are some continuities. Even though their functions have changed, the family and the household continue to be major institutions for organizing the population, providing the context for much of the work and a ready-made structure for organizing work. In urban Egypt, the household has often become primarily a unit of consumption and no longer of production (cf. Rugh 1984), but in rural Egypt the dual function is still evident. Similarly, although their environment keeps changing, the major families in each village have managed to retain a leading role in village economic and social life. Relationships based on vertical links are still the most common and provide a major organizing principle for rural life.

As long as this is so, it is not surprising that religion continues to play a significant role at the village level. Egyptian villages have often witnessed a debate between different interpretations of proper Islam, and the present is no different in that respect. So far there is no evidence for a substantial shift in the nature of rural religion (although that may be just our ignorance), but it is still very much an issue whether one or another set of practices is licit, and there is still a variety of religious experiences available even in the villages. As the material underpinning of life in the rural areas changes, so presumably will the predominant religious expression of the resulting society.

A generation ago, Ayrout (1963:89) noted that "Nothing is more like one Egyptian village than another Egyptian village," a statement which is in fact disproved by his own book. There is much variety in the world of Egyptian villages, whether we think of population (the average is around 6,000 to 7,000, and most villages are between 2,000 and 16,000), geographical location (on the river or a major canal, next to the desert, near or far from a city), history, economic diversity, cultural sophistication, or internal political structure (Hopkins and Mehanna 1981). We can also distinguish between the reactions to the process and direction of change characteristic of each village in terms of alternative "paths of rural transformation" (Keyder 1983).

One such path is the capitalist path, based on the ability of a stratum of large farmers (though not as large as those who existed before 1952) to acquire machinery and other means of production and to accumulate funds. Since there are limits on the investability of these funds in agriculture, capital escapes to the urban areas in the form of real estate purchases, a pattern that was also true before the agrarian reform. These capitalist farmers rely on machinery (tractors, motorized pumps, trucks, telephones, etc.) and on hired labor, thus reproducing capitalist relations of production in the villages they dominate. Musha, the site of the analysis presented here, is such a village.

A second path is that of the petty commodity producers. These small-scale producers for the market, although they may control several feddans of land, have less access to the other means of production than the large farmers. They typically rely on family labor to some extent, but most also hire labor to supplement the household labor supply. Most petty commodity producers also hire private tractors and pumps to complete their work. In a paradoxical sense, this amounts to labor hiring capital rather than vice versa (cf. Marglin 1982:290). Yet at the same time, the small farmers are losing both some of their power of decision-making over the agricultural process and they are being "deskilled." In sum, the petty commodity path exists, but the producers are to some extent falling under the influence of the capitalist farmers. In villages where petty commodity producers are common, agriculture may appear an increasingly marginal activity.

A third path of agrarian transformation revolves around the role of the state. This is most obvious in agrarian reform areas, or on the so-called New Lands, reclaimed from the desert since 1952, and which have been the subject of much policy debate in Egypt (Meyer 1978; Springborg 1979; Gotsch and Dyer 1982; Johnson et al. 1983). In these areas, the state is omnipresent, whether through cooperatives or state companies, and it controls both the land and water. Villages here have a "man-made" quality to them. The size of holdings is larger, but the dependence on government policy is also higher. The population was imported from elsewhere, typically according to categories such as "smallholder," "graduate" or "official," which are more important than the vertical relations of the older villages. Finally, there are also villages that live predominantly from labor outside the village, such as the Nubian village of Kanuba (Kennedy 1977; Fahim 1983) or the Delta village of el-Suiwini, analyzed by El-Messiri (1983), many of whose people work on organized migrant labor gangs (*tarahil*).

Individual villages are often dominated by one or another of these paths of agrarian transformation. Many of the older villages of the Central Delta, for instance, are clearly dominated by the petty commodity producers. An index of such a village would be a relatively low average land-holding size; say around one feddan (cf. Zimmermann 1982a; Glavanis and Glavanis 1983:54–72). Other villages throughout Egypt, such as Musha, are clearly dominated by the capitalist path of agrarian transformation. However, even such a village contains within it many petty commodity producers—even if they rely on the capitalist farmers for access to the mechanized means of production (cf. Stauth 1983). Even more importantly for the class structure of such a village, it contains many people who depend on daily wages for their living. They may possess a small parcel of land, or none at all; in either case they work for daily wages. But they do not always work in agriculture. In virtually every village, whether capitalist or petty commodity producing, a substantial number of people earn their living by working outside the village. They thus are no longer really included in the agrarian class structure of the village—except that they continue to be present, and so have their weight in village-level social and political processes. Also increasing in virtually every village is the number of people who work for the government, in every capacity from common laborers to clerks to professional-level officials (Commander and Hadhoud 1986:177).

Musha is not typical, but its problems are exemplary. It has a relatively greater concentration of landholding than most Egyptian villages, it is larger in area and population than most of them, and it has a relatively high degree of mechanization. But the effects of this mechanization on the organization of labor are pretty much the same as elsewhere in Egypt, and the problems of labor organization, class formation, the role of the household are comparable to rural Egypt in general. The cropping pattern, the effect of the government-imposed rotation, the kind of technology involved are also all representative of rural Egypt. Thus, although Musha is relatively more "capitalist" than many Egyptian villages, and cannot be considered "typical" in the sense that it stands as a sample of one, with all findings directly transposable, it falls within the general pattern. The difference is in the proportions rather than the elements involved, and most other Egyptian villages will combine the same elements.

The Social Organization of Agricultural Production in Egypt

This book deals with an aspect of the contemporary situation in rural Egypt. It is an analytical study of the labor process in Egyptian agriculture based on the detailed field study of the social organization of agriculture in one village. This involves the understanding of the institutions of agriculture such as property rights and dispute settlement, the place of the household in the organization of hired and family labor, and the role of mechanization and irrigation. The growing interest within economic anthropology in systems of production stands behind the direction of this book and its theoretical options (cf. Meillassoux 1975; Seddon 1978; Hart 1982). The detailed analysis of systems of production at the local level provides an essential complement to the economic studies of development which attempt by careful extrapolation to argue from aggregate data to reach local systems and individual decision-making. While sensitive to the questions of economists and development specialists, I undertake in this book an investigation and analysis based on a certain anthropological tradition and approach.

The goal of this study is to delineate the present social organization of agricultural production in rural Egypt, based on a case study of one village. The emphasis is on the household and the family as a unit of production and one way to organize the productive work of agriculture. Agricultural mechanization, which stimulates changes in the organization of the labor process in agriculture, is a major new element in the situation. By fragmenting the labor process, mechanization transforms it. All this occurs in the context of a village social order which organizes land tenure and access to economic resources. The book traces the interaction between individual strategies and strivings on the one hand, and the constraints of the system itself on the other. A major contradiction exists between the accumulation of capital in the form of agricultural machinery on the one hand, and the equilibrium of the traditional village social order on the other. This also raises issues of equity and equality. The mode of production changes because capital penetrates the village instead of being merely externally imposed on it, and because the level of the productive forces is increased, both the labor process and the social formation in general are also transformed.

There has been much recent interest in economic anthropology and in economics in the structure and organization of village production systems. The Egyptian case deserves attention because it concerns a country with a fully irrigated agriculture, a long history of substantial state intervention, an equally long history of involvement in international markets, and a process of mechanization which is considerable yet not complete. An analysis of agricultural production in Egypt is distinctive from most other cases analyzed in anthropological studies of production, for it evokes problems otherwise scarcely treated in the literature, in particular the problem of the role of machinery in the labor process.

In Wallerstein's terms, we are dealing with the semi-periphery, yet with a semi-periphery that has been one for over one hundred years and is characterized not only by commoditization but also by a reorganization of the structures of production. This is qualitatively different let us say from an African economy linked into the world market in the last generation or two through the market economy, but where the structures of production retain precapitalist features (Meillassoux 1964). Even the very rich literature on India does not present too many analogous cases, for apart from the Indian Punjab the level of mechanization appears rather low (cf. Leaf 1983). The implications of mechanization are, however, spelled out for the inhabitants of an irrigation scheme in Malaya by Scott (1985).

Egyptian agriculture is daily debated in the Egyptian and foreign press. Because of Egypt's rapidly growing population (roughly increasing by a million people every nine months), national food production is supplying an ever smaller percentage of Egyptian needs. The general level of Egyptian agriculture is high, but there is room for improvement. A sophisticated understanding of the social forces present in agriculture is thus relevant for any explicit or implicit policy intended to assist Egyptian agriculture. The majority of the many recent good studies of Egypt have dealt with the country as a whole, though they frequently contain assumptions about the organization of agriculture derived deductively from data aggregated at the national level.

This study was carried out in a village. There are both tactical and theoretical reasons for this. Tactically, working within the relatively restricted compass of one village is a precondition for collecting certain kinds of data that represent the main contribution of this book. Theoretically, one of the goals of this study is to go beyond an analysis of production in terms of households alone. This entails seeing the relationships that form between households. The arena in which this is possible is the community. At this level, too, it is possible to detect relationships between more abstract entities, such as "social organization," "politics," and "ideology." Finally, the labor process has to be seen at the level of the community or of the entire system and not just as a matter of individual choice and decision-making because the processes of social control are best perceptible at the wider level. However, this preference for the village as a field for researching the problem at hand should not be confused with an effort to consider the village as an isolate with a discrete social and cultural system of its own, protected from outside influences. Indeed, the way the village fits into the wider national and international spheres is a recurring theme of the book.

I am concerned with the role of the household in the labor process in agriculture. The basic unit for work in the village is now, as it probably has been throughout the past, the household. The household represents a group of people organized to carry out the tasks essential for the survival of its members, given the environment, the technology, and the agricultural system in general (cf. Netting, Wilk, and Arnould 1984). The most convenient definition of a household, however, starts not from production but from consumption: a household is a group of people who eat together. If the basic unit is the household, the community can be seen as an agglomeration of households. These households have some structural similarities even though their resource base may vary. The household incorporates the sexual division of labor, while the community reflects a different kind of division of labor based on the specializations of the men.

At the present time, when rural Egypt has been largely integrated into the money economy, the household must share the stage with other social forms and institutions including principally the state as the organizer of the national economy. While the household remains an important institution, it has to some extent changed because of the different context in which it finds itself. Analytically, the problem emerges of trying to determine the current nature of the household economy and its relationship to the national and world economies. This again brings us to consider the village as an intermediate level. If we accept the ideas of Sahlins (1972) and Meillassoux (1975) that there is such a thing as the domestic mode of production, then what is the relationship between this domestic mode of production and the encapsulating capitalist mode? The current study takes the problem of the role of agricultural mechanization as the starting point for an answer.

The analysis here starts from the "givens" of the situation—demography, land tenure, imposed crop rotation, institutional structure—in order to suggest the framework within which the individual farmers and others in the village must act. The framework provides constraints on action, and also constraints to action—i.e., it both precludes certain possibilities and encourages others.

Change is an incremental process in which there is a gradual accumulation of individual changes in behavior which eventually amounts to a change in the system of constraints on all behavior. My concern here is with process in everyday life—the insignificant individual decisions and interactions that add up to a significant shift. There is a contradiction between the incentives to certain kinds of actions (or inactions) by individuals and what the system needs to reproduce itself. As people are led to seek education, to migrate, or to mechanize, their actions may conflict with the conventional behavior and systemic requirements of their environment. In John Bennett's terms (Bennett 1969:14), what are successful adaptive strategies (for individuals or households) may not be beneficial adaptive processes (for the group or system). There is a dialectic between individual and household strategies on the one hand, and the system they constitute (the framework for action) on the other. Within such a framework, individuals acting to preserve their interests are the ones most likely to cause change.

Plan of the Book

The organization of this book reflects the argument on agrarian transformation in Egypt. After a presentation of a set of theoretical concepts,

I examine data on the social organization of agriculture in the light of that theory and then attempt to draw conclusions relating specifically to the Egyptian case. The general approach is therefore inductive, for it moves from a field study of Egyptian agriculture to general conclusions about the transition from peasantry to petty commodity production, and from there to observations of class formation and the political process.

Through an analysis of the labor process, we can understand the present organization of agricultural production. One very important dimension of this is the changing role of the household, and in particular the changing pattern of relations between households. The analysis of the labor process suggests a new interpretation of the process of differentiation, where class is seen as a dynamic outgrowth of the labor process rather than simply deduced from ownership or control of property, or inferred from the comparative literature. The "Agrarian Transition" model and the "Labor Process" model are presented in Chapter 2. Both these models have been used to explain or understand cases such as the one I am presenting here. Without abandoning the interest in differentiation inherent in the agrarian transition model, I prefer the more inductive labor process model.

The argument concerning the evolution of the labor process requires certain kinds of data on demography, land tenure rules, the structure and organization of the household and in particular on the role of women inside the household and beyond. Thus in Chapter 3 I move to a description of the setting, the village of Musha, in its Upper Egyptian regional context. This general description is then followed in Chapter 4 by a presentation of the demographic and institutional setting for agriculture, through an analysis of people and land as productive forces seen in terms of their historical development. It is important not only to know how many, but also what kinds of people, and thus I also discuss education and occupational structure. The analysis of land covers the land tenure system and the landholding pattern, which together determine access to land. This material is intended as a contribution to the documentation on Egypt and as background for the analysis of the social organization of agriculture.

The descriptive analysis of the social organization of Musha begins in Chapter 5 with the household. The changing role of the household plays a key role in the analysis, although finally the household is subordinate to the emerging capitalist mode of production. After presenting some data on household composition and organization, and on occupation and marriage, the chapter raises the issue of the variety of household strategies, and gives some case studies of Musha households. Chapter 6 extends this analysis by focussing specifically on women. This chapter is based on the results of a survey carried out among village women, and includes some information on women's work, on the role of women in organizing consumption and in managing the household, and on leisure, education, and marriage.

The next three chapters provide a detailed analysis of the organization of agriculture, showing the place of mechanization and the role of marketing in the labor process. Through an analysis of the social organization of water lifting and tractor use, Chapter 7 treats the role of mechanization in the labor process in Musha agriculture. The following chapter, on the role of labor, begins with household labor and then moves to hired labor and the labor market. It makes the point that the maintenance of the household allows for the decentralized control of labor. Chapter 8 also includes information on the significance of migration both within Egypt and abroad. Chapter 9 is a descriptive analysis of marketing. It contrasts government purchasing and private trade, and establishes a distinction between centralizing merchants and arbitragers. A complete analysis of the labor process cannot stop with the harvest, but must include the consumption or sale of the crop.

Finally the social and political organization of Musha is the subject of the last two chapters. This organization is presented as an outgrowth of the labor process, but also as part of the process whereby the reproduction of that labor process is ensured. Chapter 10 covers formal and informal politics, the processes for dispute settlement, and the relevance of the organization of the religious brotherhoods in village life. Chapter 11 raises the issue of inequality in Musha, and shows that this inequality is not yet locally considered in class terms. Thus class does not appear to be a major axis of social organization in the village despite the evident pattern of inequality and hierarchy generated by the labor process in agriculture. The book closes by evoking some implications of this study for agrarian transformation in Egypt.

Methodology

In order to help the reader evaluate the analysis that follows, I present here some comments on the methodology according to which data was gathered or generated. The principal method used was participant observation, supplemented by two simple surveys and by some other systematic data gathering in the field and by library research for the historical background.

The choice of the village came about by accident. In 1979 I was asked by the Cairo office of the Catholic Relief Services to conduct a sociological survey of small farmers in two villages in Egypt, in preparation for a project to improve animal fodder (cf. Hopkins et al. 1980). One of these two villages was Musha. No one could ever explain to me why Musha had been chosen by the Governor of Asyut for this project, but it was suggested that he made the choice because it was fairly close to the governorate capital and had the reputation of being a secure village (i.e., without feuding).

Participant Observation

Participant observation is the anthropological method par excellence. During the period of the field research (September 1980 through June 1981) I lived in the village of Musha slightly more than half the time. I spent the remaining time in Cairo with my family. Because Musha was about 8 hours by car from Cairo, I adopted a rhythm of spending around 12 days at a time in Musha, followed by 9 days in Cairo. This was a somewhat different experience for me than the other two major field experiences I have had, in Kita, Mali (1964–1965) and in Testour, Tunisia (1972–1973), when I lived full-time in the village with my family. Although I was not in the field continuously, I think that my experiences in Musha were more intense. It is worth noting that since I was over forty years of age at the time of this field work, having relationships with the village power elite came somewhat more naturally, while it was harder to relate to the young men. As a professor at the American University in Cairo, I had a fairly well recognized position in Egyptian society.

When I was in the village, I resided in the *duwwar al-'umda*. This building had been built in the 1940s as a residence for the Umda of Musha. Around 1950 it was superseded by a grander structure built by the last Umda. Downstairs the building had several reception areas both indoors and outdoors; upstairs there were several private rooms. I used the upstairs rooms as my headquarters. The reception areas downstairs were occasionally used for various public purposes, either for the 'Abdin lineage itself or for the wider community. The building was under the control of the President of the Local Popular Council, a junior relative and associate of the Umda. This man was my host and provided me with my meals.

In the village, the *dallal* (village "agent" charged with keeping records and settling disputes concerning the division of property, both farm land and houses) was more or less assigned to be my guide. His house was nearby, and I visited it frequently. He was not always available because of the press of other business. I gradually developed a circle of friends whose houses I could visit. For formal interviews and general assistance I had a second helper, a recent graduate of the University of Asyut from another village. He lived at home and came to Musha every day. We would sometimes make visits together to places that we knew, but we would rely on the agent to show us new places, both in the village and in the fields. However, many times, especially in the late afternoons and evenings, I would go out by myself, especially to explore what was happening in the threshing grounds and other working areas around the edge of the village. It was usually possible to find some men lounging around or working with whom I could start a conversation.

There were also various kinds of situation that I could enter, here more as an observer than as a participant. For instance, it is very common in

Musha for men to gather in the evenings at the house of one of the powerful village leaders. Some of these are men who work for the leader, some are favor-seekers, some are friends and neighbors, and some are members of his lineage who express their acceptance of the leader's position by these evening visits. The conversation at such times is sometimes desultory and casual, sometimes very focussed on particular political and economic issues. Agriculture is a frequent topic of conversation. The tone of the conversation may also change as people enter or leave. I frequently sat in on these evenings, especially in the reception room (*mandara*) of my host, the Hajj, and at the "rest house" of the Umda. Men would come to both these places because of disputes or problems, and so this was one way to learn about them. Seeing who called on the agent for help was another. For somewhat the same reasons, I would go to call on the President of the Village Council, a government official, in his office in the mornings. There again I might be lucky enough to chance upon something interesting. Such sessions are essentially open, and so the presence of a foreign anthropologist was no threat.

Dispute settlement is a formal activity in Musha, requiring lengthy negotiations between the parties involved and a team of mediators. Here again, people did not mind having a foreigner around, and indeed even took pride in showing me how their system worked. Another type of activity that I was able to witness involved the religious brotherhoods, or rather one particular chapter of the Rifa'iya brotherhood. I became friendly with the members of this chapter, which was based in the neighborhood of the *duwwar,* and attended a number of their sessions.

The methodological problem that faced me was how, as a lone anthropologist, to study such a large and complex community in a relatively brief period of time. Since the village was too large for everyone to know everyone else, I was clearly going to have to meet people one by one, and could not assume that after a while everyone in the village would know who I was and what I was doing there. The various surveys I describe below were part of the answer to the problem of how to collect meaningful data in this kind of situation. The use of key informants was another way around the complexity of the situation. Thus, while I could not know everyone in this village of 18,000 people, I could know certain individuals fairly well. Participant observation in such a context has a very particular meaning, for both the observation and the participation have to be somewhat selective.

The language of field work was Arabic. Even though my university graduate assistant was assigned to me because he could speak English, this proved to be an exaggeration. In my case, the reliance on Arabic meant that there were many subtleties and hints in what was said that escaped me. However, here is where the observation came to my assistance. Since my principal topic was work and work relations, clearly in any case observing what people did would have to supplement what people said they did. Unlike, let us say, religious symbolism or mythology, the topic could be observed, and indeed, observation was a necessary corrective to the comments of informants. It was only through observation, for instance, that I saw what regularity there was in the use of the threshing grounds; all my informants denied that there was any.

Surveys can be very useful for generating certain kinds of quantitative data that are true either of the sample or perhaps can be extrapolated to the community (the "universe") as a whole. Certain basic personal data are the most useful and the most reliable within this context. Soliciting the opinions of people through a survey instrument does not strike me as very fruitful in the Egyptian village context. One reason for this is that there are almost always observers to the interview. Even if the interviewer went alone, there are very few contexts in which people are themselves alone in the village, and even then the arrival of the interviewer would be sure to attract some casual passerby or neighbor. This could be avoided, of course, by summoning the respondent to a controlled situation, but then he would sense power and not be at ease. A second reason is that people will often defer to the opinion of someone more powerful or prestigious than themselves. For whatever reason, the few "opinion" type questions I asked generally elicited identical responses from everyone and so were useless for distinguishing between people.

Surveys also do not tell you about relationships. And relationships are critically important for a study like this one. If you want to know about the relationships between patron and client, rich neighbor and poor neighbor, farmer and hired hand, husband and wife, official and farmer, and so on, in the Egyptian context, the only technique is painstaking observation. It means being present when people in these roles come together, and observing the nature of their interaction. It means collecting information through observation of the same individuals over a period of time, checking and cross-checking the information.

The people of Musha almost never refused to answer my questions. I am very grateful to them for that, and for never failing in their hospitality. However, I must observe that they did not always tell the truth. This was sometimes out of fear, sometimes out of a sense of play, sometimes because they did not understand the intent of a question, sometimes because they did not know, sometimes doubtless for other reasons. Trying to sort out the true from the false, and the reasons why the false was given as true, taught me a lot about rural Egyptian society, and so I am also grateful to the people of Musha for that. The unreliability of some of the answers is another reason, of course, why interviews had to be supplemented by observation.

Household Budget Study

This survey is based on a sample drawn from a list of families prepared by the Health authorities for Asyut District. Although this list contains the names of 3,016 family (*usra*) heads, there is reason to believe that it was incomplete. The total Musha population which this list gives is low by 10 percent to 20 percent. Closer inspection and use of the list revealed that at least one sector of the village, the neighborhood inhabited by one of the principal lineages, Bait 'Abdin, was totally absent. Nevertheless, the list, even if only 80 percent complete, was the best available list to use for sampling purposes since it included all levels of the population. The list of landholders was rejected as an alternative since by definition it excludes the landless.

Of the total of 3,016 families, I selected every twenty-fifth name. This produced a list of 120 names. Eventually 107 usable interviews were collected, and they form the basis of the statistical analysis for most purposes. The original total of 120 was also relevant for some purposes. Of the missing thirteen families, twelve had disappeared either through migration or death, and one refused to be interviewed. It is probable that the missing thirteen households were in the bottom half or even quarter of the range. Had they been included some of the figures might have been altered in that direction. No substitutions were sought because it seemed that 107 interviews were sufficient. Furthermore, the number of people covered was larger than the family average might suggest. While interviewing, we dealt with the household connected to the name, whereas the original list was in terms of families.

The survey covered a number of topics. Included was information on each member of the family, such as age, occupation, education, and relationship to the head of the family. It also covered the basic economic situation of the household, such as the amount of land it farmed, how labor was mobilized for that land, whether tractors or pumps were used and under what conditions, the crops grown in the past year, marketing arrangements and the animals and poultry present in the household.

The interviews took place between March and June, 1981. Most of them were carried out in the home of the respondent, and often in the presence of others, family members or neighbors. The interview team consisted of my two assistants in addition to myself. I was present at each interview to add the weight of my presence, to help make tactical decisions in unforeseen circumstances, to ask any follow-up questions the case seemed to require, and to form my own evaluation of the case. The university graduate conducted the formal interview and recorded the answers. The village agent identified the person on our list, and helped us to locate him. He also served as a guarantee to the respondent that the activity was legitimate and had some official sanction. By the same token, of course, he represented officialdom to some people, and this may occasionally have influenced answers. His specialized knowledge of land holdings meant that that data was pretty accurate. The agent also clearly preferred for us to interview people he knew and was on good terms with, and this sometimes tempted him to misread names. However, I am convinced that in the end we always found the right person. He argued that the answers would be more reliable if he knew the respondent well, and doubtless he was right in that, but it seemed more important to retain the logic of the survey.

Women's Time Use Study

This study was designed to discover the basic facts about the economic and social role of women through an analysis of their use of time. The basic instrument was a sheet on which their activities for the 24 hours prior to the interview were listed by the interviewer. This information was supplemented by a range of other questions, relating to women's economic role, to the basic economic facts of their households, and to their relationship with such spheres as health care, religion, and education. The study was designed to visit the same women at three points during the year: September, February, and June, with the intent of seeing what seasonal differences there might be (none were apparent from the interviews).

The interviewers were four graduate students from the American University in Cairo. Each one had a partner in the village, and visited the same twelve women in each of the three research periods. Because of absences at one time or another, we were able to complete 47 sets of three interviews each, and this constitutes the sample for the study.

The names for this study were chosen at the very beginning of the research, before I had access to the family list compiled by the Health authorities. Consequently we used the list of landholders to determine half the sample, choosing the names at random. I wanted the other half to be landless. At the time the only way to reach these people was to ask my friends in Musha to provide a list of landless households for me. Thus this half of the sample lacks randomness, but I feel that all the major variation in the village is nevertheless covered in this sample.

A fully accurate time use study is very difficult. It certainly requires observation rather than recall, and even under the best field conditions there are problems inherent in the recording of the observations. The methodology we used was simple, and the degree of accuracy very approximate. In the end, I use simply citations of the frequency of activities rather than the more problematic figures suggesting time spent on these activities. Yet the effort seemed worth while in order to escape the situation of having a fully male bias in observation, and in order to make some sense out of the data thus generated. This is important because of the central role given to the household in the analysis.

Conclusion

In this first chapter I have given a brief description of the state of the Egyptian countryside in the 1980s and given a preliminary analysis of the problem which I intend to treat: the social organization of agriculture production in a community which is heavily mechanized and totally dependent on irrigation, and in which the role of the state is preponderant. I have summarized the goals I have set for myself in this book, and given an overview of the methodology which I followed in the field in order to tackle this problem. In the next chapter, I expand on the theoretical background of the concepts used here.

2

Agrarian Transformation in Egypt

> In the sphere of agriculture, modern industry has a more revolutionary effect than elsewhere, for this reason, that it annihilates the peasant, that bulwark of the old society, and replaces him by the wage-labourer. Thus the desire for social changes, and the class antagonisms are brought to the same level in the country as in the towns. . . . In agriculture as in manufacture, the transformation of production under the sway of capital, means, at the same time, the martyrdom of the producer; the instrument of labour becomes the means of enslaving, exploiting, and impoverishing the labourer; the social combination and organisation of labour-processes is turned into an organised mode of crushing out of the workman's individual vitality, freedom, and independence. (Marx 1967:I:505–506)

Studies of Egyptian agricultural society are legion, stressing everything from botany to class structure. The argument here is that Egyptian agriculture is now characterized by small-scale commodity production, in which mechanization and wage labor play a key role. The social organization of production takes place within a certain institutional structure, and involves choices about the use of machinery, the mobilization of labor, and the marketing of produce. This petty capitalist social organization of production supports such other institutional features as patron-client relations, deference, and certain religious forms, which in turn provide the context and the rationalization for the organization of production. The argument is not directly one of change, although certainly the picture of agriculture presented here bears little resemblance to the "typical" imagery of the peasantry in Egypt or elsewhere. The focus is on the tendencies towards change *in* the present rather than on the historical background *to* the present. In that sense we can invoke the notion of agrarian transformation.

Two alternative models are available for the understanding of the processes of agrarian transformation in Egypt in the modern period. The "Agrarian Transition" model is derived from those elements in the Marxist tradition that presume that the introduction and growth of the capitalist mode of production imply a differentiation of the population into a privileged few and the impoverished many, as in the passage from *Capital* quoted above. The "Labor Process" model is also derived from the Marxist tradition. It ultimately harks back to Marx's discussion of the social organization of labor in capitalism, and is inductive rather than deductive. I argue in this chapter that the second of these two alternative approaches gives us a better understanding of the situation in rural Egypt (and elsewhere) because its focus is on process rather than status. This model will guide the exposition of data in this book.

The Agrarian Transition Model

The Agrarian Transition model can serve as a starting point for understanding the process of transformation in rural Egypt. In its classic form, this theory derives from the analysis made by Lenin of changes in rural Russia during the second half of the 19th century (Lenin 1960:172–187, 310–318). Lenin in turn borrowed from Marx's analysis of the peasantry. In this passage from *The Eighteenth Brumaire of Louis Bonaparte,* for instance, Marx underlined how the small holdings of the French peasantry in the first half of the 19th century led to the domination of the peasants by capital:

> Two generations have sufficed to produce the inevitable result: progressive deterioration of agriculture, progressive indebtedness of the agriculturist. . . . The small holding of the peasant is now only the pretext that allows the capitalist to draw profits, interest and rent from the soil, while leaving it to the tiller of the soil himself to see how he can extract his wages. (Marx 1963:126–127)

According to this Marxist-Leninist model, there is an internal differentiation among the peasantry under the pressures resulting from the contact with capitalism in other spheres of the society. Gradually economic processes tend to push the rich peasantry into the role of capitalist farmers, while the poor peasants are dispossessed and become the free wage labor employed by these capitalist farmers. For a while, the middle peasantry retains its position as an intermediate group, but gradually most of them are also forced down into the ranks of the poor peasants. Thus a rural economy built around subsistence or self-provisioning among a relatively undifferentiated peasantry is transformed into one based on capitalist agriculture and a bifurcated structure of opposed classes. At the same time, this differentiation of the "peasantry" creates a larger market for the products of the other sectors of the economy, including capital goods for agriculture, fertilizers, and also consumer goods (especially cloth and clothing). In Marx's terms, the town and the country are integrated.

A conflict then erupts between the rich capitalist farmers and the industrial bourgeoisie based in the cities for control of the surplus generated by agriculture. If the industrial bourgeoisie is able to win out in this conflict, the surplus is transferred to the industrial sector and becomes the basis for an industrial development in that country. In the sense that the agricultural sector is subordinated to the industrial one, this could be considered the solution to the agrarian question. At the same time, it leaves workers and peasants (the rural population apart from the capitalist farmers, presumably all subordinated to these farmers) as natural allies against the grouping of the rural and urban bourgeoisie. The urban industrial bourgeoisie is able to win out over the capitalist farmers with their control of the agrarian sector only through its ability to capture the state and to use the power of the state to erect rules conducive to this transfer of surplus.

The Egyptian economist Mahmoud Abdel-Fadil (1975) has explored the ramifications of the model for Egypt during the period 1952–1970. He has assembled a large number of statistics to support his argument that the agrarian transition in this sense occurred in Nasser's Egypt or has been occurring since then. He is concerned to show that there has been class differentiation, essentially on the basis of unequal distribution of the means of production among farmers. Thus even after the various phases of the Agrarian Reform (1952, 1961 and 1969) reduced the ceilings of land allowed to individuals and families, the distribution of land is still highly skewed—less so than prior to 1952, but still such that a small group of fairly large landowners can be detected who use more machinery and are more market oriented. Abdel-Fadil also attempts to show that the domestic market has grown, through the growth in Egyptian production of the various inputs for agriculture, and that the terms of trade are such that a surplus is being transferred from agriculture to industry. However, Byres (1977) in a review of this book, inferred that the agrarian transition had not fully occurred in Egypt, mostly because the rural bourgeoisie still retained sufficient power to prevent the large-scale transfer of rural surplus to the industrial sector.

Many observers of rural Egypt continue to stress the presence of one or more middle groups. Waterbury (1983) tried to steer a middle course between Binder's assertion (1978) that the rural middle class or bourgeoisie has had a dominant influence in Egyptian politics and Harik's contention (1979:43) that the class has declined in recent years. Waterbury argued that the class persists but that its political influence is overrated. To the extent that a rural bourgeoisie or rural middle class persists in Egypt, the argument implicitly would be that the agrarian transition has been "blocked" or has only partially occurred. Glavanis and Glavanis (1983:23) also note the blockage of this process, but on different grounds. They argue that the household remains a significant unit of production, and one that is non-capitalist in its workings (1983:69). If non-capitalist relations of production survive in the household, then the process of differentiation suggested by Marx and Lenin has not run its course. Adams (1986) has also argued for a blockage of Egyptian agriculture, but on quite different grounds: that the state, through its bureaucracy, has been more interested in controlling the countryside through agriculture than in improving production and standards of living. One of the outcomes which he points out is the maintenance of patron-client relations, and hence a rural middle class.

The model itself has recently come under attack on the grounds that it does not particularly well apply to the countries of either Western or Eastern Europe, let alone to Latin America or the Middle East. Goodman and Redclift argue that the simple model of agrarian transition may be too restrictive, and that there is increasing evidence from Europe, Latin America and elsewhere that the process outlined above does not always occur—in fact, never occurs in its pure form.

> The persistence in advanced capitalist economies of family-labor farms, of petty commodity production, considered by Marx to be a "transitional" form, emphasizes the extended and problematic nature of this process. The capitalist farm enterprise does not necessarily emerge as the "typical firm" in agriculture. (Goodman and Redclift 1982:24)

Goodman and Redclift argue that various forces allow a kind of middle peasantry to survive as petty commodity producers. Such farmers retain control over the labor process, generally within the household structure, but produce for and sell on the market. Thus they are integrated into the wider system not through their subordination to capital in the form of wage labor, but through the structures of the market for their products. This situation has given rise to a considerable debate. To the extent that such exploitation or surplus extraction passes through the market process, then exchange or circulation rather than production is involved and we are no longer speaking of a mode of production but of a mode of circulation. Yet the mode of production should not be considered from the point of view of the farmers, but from the point of view of the larger system in which they are encapsulated. Thus de Janvry (1981:104–106), while accepting the reality of the petty commodity category, feels that all these rural people produce for the market and are profit-oriented rather than survival-oriented and so are part (a subordinate part) of the capitalist mode of production:

> The peasant farm retains the formal appearance of autonomy but is, in fact, fully controlled by agribusiness and merchant capital as well as by industrial capital through the policies of the state, particularly cheap food policies. And since peasants are allowed a global return on resources no greater than a

worker's wage, they are, in fact, reduced to the status of workers working at home for capital. (de Janvry 1981:104)

The agrarian transition in Egypt, in something approaching its classic form, has not happened—it has been "blocked" by the continued importance of the household economy of the petty commodity producers—but the capitalist mode of production is nonetheless present in rural Egypt. This is, of course, an ancient phenomenon, since it can be dated at least from the period in the mid-19th century (say at the time of the American Civil War) when Egyptian peasants and large farmers began to grow cotton for the market on a large scale. Here they made their first somewhat bitter contact with the peaks and troughs of the international market. The envelopment of rural Egypt by the capitalist mode of production, oriented towards profit and accumulation, has been lengthy and gradual. The history of this process has often been attacked from various directions, such as land ownership (Baer 1962), the growth of production (of cotton) for the market (Owen 1969) or the history of class differentiation (Hussein 1973). However, what is at issue here is a conceptual problem.

There are various theories for describing the relationship between this human situation of the "blocked agrarian transition" and the capitalist world system. One way is to judge that the capitalist world system in fact occupies the world, and that therefore the world economy is in total a capitalist economy (Wallerstein 1974). This point of view has the practical advantage that it forces us to look at the interrelationships of the system as a whole in order to define the regional or conceptual subsegments of this economy, and their relationship to the whole. However, the distinction is of little use to those who choose to focus on rural areas in Third World countries. If everything is amalgamated under one label, the power of distinction is lost.

Another theory with some currency holds that the encapsulated economy may not be capitalist itself, but instead retains some precapitalist or noncapitalist mode of production, which is then in articulation with the capitalist mode of production (Meillassoux 1964). The articulation theory leads us to look at the variation within a single local community or region (Hopkins 1978). One can argue that there are aspects of a local economy which are noncapitalist, and that therefore the articulation is between different spheres of activity in the same community. Thus one can argue for Egypt, as for elsewhere in Africa (Meillassoux 1975), that the household or the family remains an arena of activity that is not shaped by the capitalist mode of production.

A third theory holds that the periphery of the world capitalist system has different features from the center, but is nonetheless dominated by the laws of motion of capitalism. According to this argument, the center needs to maintain certain areas in a peripheral position in order to draw from them cheap labor, cheap raw materials, and so on. Thus the periphery is not a momentary position, but a structural one from which there is no easy escape. The peripheral areas are part of an international division of labor which assigns subordinate roles to them; they must endure the pressures and the shocks of the capitalist center without themselves having much influence in return.

The model of the agrarian transition is challenging but oversimplified, in particular in its assumption that rural society will be bifurcated into capitalists and proletarians. If the subsistence-oriented, survival-seeking peasant does not persist, the petty commodity producer does, and thus poses a problem of the relationship of this rural sector to the society as a whole, and a problem of the definition of that sector.

The Labor Process Model

We can suggest a way around, if not out of, this dilemma, by turning to another body of theory. This theory is concerned with the social organization of production, the labor process. The analysis of the labor process leads to a focus on the social division of labor, the flow of work, the relationship between labor and capital, the integration of the different tasks, the supply of labor, and the manner of labor control (Braverman 1974).

Marx's *Capital* is an extended analysis of the labor process under the conditions of capitalism as he observed them in mid-19th century Europe. In his initial comments on the labor process, Marx points out (1967:I:178) that "The elementary factors of the labour-process are 1, the personal activity of man, i.e., work itself, 2, the subject of that work, and 3, its instruments," and summarizes (1967:I:183-4), "The labour-process, resolved as above into its simple elementary factors, is human action with a view to the production of use-values, appropriation of natural substances to human requirements. . . . It was, therefore, not necessary to represent our labourer in connexion with other labourers; man and his labour on one side, Nature and its materials on the other, sufficed." However, in his discussion of cooperation and the division of labor under different forms of capitalism, Marx reinstates the nature of cooperation among men as part of the labor process. For Marx the emergence of 'manufacture' is a matter of a change in the social organization of production, i.e., the creation of the factory, while the appearance of 'modern industry' is a matter of new technology such as the steam engine (1967:I:371): "In manufacture, the revolution in the mode of production begins with the labour-power, in modern industry it beings with the instruments of labor." In either case (1967:I:330), "By the co-operation of numerous wage-labourers, the sway of capital develops into a requisite for carrying on the labour-process itself, into a real requisite of production." This is because as the instruments of work change, so the form of cooperation changes (1967:I:364): "The division of labour in manufacture creates a qualitative gradation, and a quantitative proportion in the social process of production; it consequently creates a definite organization of the labour of society, and thereby develops at the same time new productive forces in the society."

The labor process model deals, at least in the first instance, with data on work. In Egypt, this means starting with the household—which either mobilizes its own members or decides to hire additional labor, and in any case acts as a manager of its labor process. Furthermore, we can look first of all at the division of what was formerly (perhaps) a single integrated system of production, as different aspects of the pattern of agricultural production are split off and handled through different agencies—here not necessarily the household, but other forms of production organization. In Egypt there has been a deskilling of agriculture as some of the more specialized tasks (plowing and threshing, machine work in general, marketing) are taken over by specialized individuals or groups of individuals outside the household. Thus the petty commodity producing household is not only linked into the wider system through the market, but also through its involvement in these complex, articulated structures of production.

Friedland, Barton, and Thomas (1981) have suggested the usefulness of labor process theory to the highly capitalized, factory-in-the-field situation of California agriculture. In their discussion of the production of lettuce, they note that in the realm of capitalist agriculture, the labor process is the meeting ground for wage-labor and capital. They observe that:

> The labor process is used to represent the organization of work activities and occupations, *and* the relationship among social categories that are a result of those arrangements. (1981:4)

In rural Egypt, the social categories produced by the meeting of labor and capital are less sharply drawn than in California. The kind of agriculture described in this study often resists centralization under a single management for a large unit, and that is a crucial difference between Egypt and California. Yet it still remains true that the fundamental analysis has to take place at the level of production.

We can follow Friedland, Barton, and Thomas in looking at two aspects of the labor process: labor supply and labor control. In the case of rural Egypt, labor supply for the small farmer is first of all a matter of mobilizing the labor in his own household. Since that almost never suffices throughout the year—almost all small farmers hire people periodically during the year (Commander and Hadhoud 1986:168)—a second aspect of labor supply has to do with access to the pool of laborers who are available for this episodic work. They are drawn from the landless and the near-landless. A land tenure system that denies some people access to land guarantees a labor supply. Many of those willing to work for wages in agriculture are tied up by the larger farmers on a more or less permanent basis, and so are not available to the small farmers. Labor supply is a constant preoccupation, as is attested by all the comments alleging that migration overseas (to Saudi Arabia and elsewhere) has reduced the labor pool. Migration to Egyptian cities and education also play their part in reducing the relative size of the labor pool. The labor situation in rural Egypt has its peculiarities, and these must be part of the investigation.

Labor control is also handled in the first instance through the household. The basic and traditional division of labor in rural Egypt is that based on age and sex, and this is organized through the household. The properly masculine and feminine jobs are understood in terms provided by the culture, and so Egyptian rural culture acts here as a control mechanism. However, apart from such authority as fathers can exercise over sons, there is no outstanding hierarchical control of production.

A large portion of agricultural work involves hired labor, alone or in addition to family labor. Here the principal form of discipline takes the shape of wages and the threat not to hire again. Even large farmers generally deny that their workers are permanently in their employ, and one function of this uncertainty—a worker can always be replaced—is to enhance the degree of control over the worker. Small farmers do not hire regularly enough to use that kind of discipline with any conviction, and so they must rely on inducements such as extra tea or cigarettes to make sure that the work is done. Most work is done on time rates, and so requires supervision. Piece rates, when used for harvesting, winnowing or making bricks, are a form of discipline in themselves and do not require supervision.

The state provides another dimension of labor control, though one that is less immediate than the household or threshing ground organization we have just been discussing. State efforts to control agriculture began with Mohammed Ali's interventions in the early 19th century (Al-Sayyid-Marsot 1984). The chief instrument at present is the village agricultural credit cooperative. The cooperative is intended to be the agent of Egypt's agricultural bureaucracy and as such to specify the areas and zones to be planted in certain key crops and to instruct the farmers on the use of pesticides, fertilizers and new varieties of seed. The cooperative as it was set up in the 1960s at the time of the policy of the unified rotation system was designed to guide and control the choices made by the individual households in their work patterns and organization. The state also contributes to the control of labor through its laws concerning relations between landlord and tenant and between worker and hirer, and it contributes to the supply of labor through its land tenure policies as well as its general development and labor policies, explicit and implicit. However, the policies of the state are only effective if there are people at the local level willing to apply them. In recent years, the agents of the state in rural Egypt have not been very enthusiastic. In other words, not only the formal rules of the state, but the local politics of their application, are important.

It is interesting to note that the prime forms of labor control in Egyptian agriculture are through control of the access to resources (capital). Thus, the land tenure system provides that only certain individuals can have access to the land, and the private ownership of farm machinery is even more limited in scope. Marx, in his discussion of the fetishism of commodities (1967:I:71–83), pointed out that these must be construed as relations between people, not between people and things. Thus it is not the resources that are controlled, but the people and their access to these resources. Nevertheless, the cultural understanding of these matters in Musha is one that stresses the relationship between people and resources. Hence the importance of looking at land tenure rules.

The division of labor in general also enhances labor control. As the degree of specialization of tasks increases, and with it the division of labor in agriculture, the role of the coordinator gains in importance. This role, which in early England became the role of the capitalist (Marglin 1982), derives its importance from the fact that the coordinator is the only one with an overall picture of the labor process. He sees the links between the different tasks, while the laborers engaged to do the work are only supposed to understand the task in front of them, and do not produce a commodity. The coordinator controls the machinery, which only a few know how to operate, and the workers have become deskilled. This is particularly true in Egypt where, because of the size of the farms and the size of the machinery, very few farmers own machinery. Instead, they rent the use of the machinery from their better endowed neighbors. Mechanization in Egypt increases the division of labor, by making the system of a single integrated system of production out of date, and so enhances the need for someone to coordinate all the activities. In agriculture this is particularly complex because of the variety of crops, the constantly changing climatic conditions, the unpredictability of the government, and so on. Hence the role and weight of the large farmer, who by coordinating his own farm sets the pattern (Stauth 1983:88–133). The small farmers (the petty commodity producers) are generally content to follow the lead of the large farmers, whose political clients they are likely to be.

A key variable here is information. Studies in industrial America (Burawoy 1979) show that on the shop floor there is a continual struggle around control of the information and knowledge needed to understand the overall flow of the labor process. Geertz (1979:124–5) stresses the role of information in a Moroccan market. In rural Egypt, the large farmers are likely to have access to a wider and richer variety of information, particularly on the doings of government and on the suitability of new techniques and projects. This gives them a superiority over the small farmers and encourages the latter to follow the lead of the former. This tendency to "follow the leader" is also a form of control of the labor process.

The analysis of the labor process requires some specification of the unit. For Friedland it was the lettuce industry, and he gives his reasons for that, at least partly in terms of the availability of data. Burawoy felt that the labor process could best be observed on the shop floor, while remaining sensitive to the placement of the shop in the wider structures of monopoly capitalism. Here we are concerned with the social organization of agricultural production in rural Egypt, and two units are important. One is the household and the other is the community, the village. By observing the labor process in the fields, on the threshing grounds and elsewhere, we note that these two social units recur. The basic unit for organizing agricultural labor is the household, whether large or small, rich or poor. This is the basic unit for production and for consumption. The household does not stand alone; it is part of a network of other households and individuals rather than self-sufficient. Each household has an extensive pattern of relations with others—it may hire or be hired, it may share work, it may seek technical assistance.

The community provides the arena within which this network of households operates. Values and patterns of social control are lodged in the village community (Stauth 1983:133–146). For a variety of historical reasons, Musha and most other Egyptian villages remain a privileged social arena for the people who live in them. Villagers are more likely to relate to people in their own village than in another, and each village has its peculiarities that help define the social system of that particular village. There is enough similarity between villages that one can talk of "rural Egypt" in general, but it is not a system, merely a category. The next level system above the village community—if we start from that perspective—is the country, Egypt as a whole. This level involves us in urban-rural relations, the role of the state, and so on. My unit of analysis, then, is the labor process in agriculture in the village (here a more appropriate unit than the firm or industry as used in the American studies). The village is, however, not the object of study, but the locale, which analysis reveals also to be a middle-level system.

The fuller analysis of the various aspects of the labor process enables us to circumvent some of the sterile argument about the reality of the agrarian transition, and about the proper terms to use to describe the relationship of peripheral social formations to the center. To some extent, the agrarian transition model assumes that relations of production follow from control of the means of production. The labor process model obliges us to look directly at the relations of production, as they are discernable in the household, on the threshing ground, and beyond. As Eric Wolf

(1981:45–46) stresses, going back to Marx: "The labor process as a whole is a social phenomenon, carried on by human beings linked to one another through social relationships. . . . The technical division of labor and the processes of work operate in crucial conjunction with social relations of production."

Conclusion: Implications of the Models

The classic model of the "agrarian transition" suggests that a former peasant community is polarized into a small group of capitalist entrepreneurs in agriculture and a much larger proletariat. Recent writing has suggested the complexity of this process, and in particular that many cases may be "blocked" in the sense that polarization does not occur completely. The resilience of the household structure means that many peasants survive as petty commodity producers. The process is certainly complex in Egypt, where depeasantization began in some senses 150 years ago, and the dependency of all peasants on the market was complete by the end of the 19th century. Moreover, social hierarchies at the village level have millenia of existence in Egypt.

We can amplify the model of the agrarian transition by examining the labor process in agriculture, even in one village. Broadly speaking this is a situation where (1) some farmers have emerged as capitalist farmers in the last half century, (2) agricultural machinery is increasingly common, (3) a substantial part of the population consists of free wage labor, (4) the continued importance of the household as an organizer of labor for many people represents a "block" to the agrarian transition, (5) the village is largely dominated by outside forces, such as the State and the market, yet retains many autonomous social processes, and (6) in any case, education and migration are allowing many people to escape the system altogether by situating their primary source of income (and hence their work) outside agriculture. The labor process model incorporates the concern with differentiation and relations between classes of the agrarian transformation model, placing them in a dynamic context: it not only asserts that the peasant is replaced by the wage-laborer, but shows how and why.

It is hard to argue here that the stratification is leading to classes aware of their collective interests. Machine rental and wage labor are in a real sense relationships between households and so tend to reinforce the patron-client or vertical ties between people. These ties are also buttressed by traditional relations, even if education and modern religion (here meaning the so-called religious fundamentalism) push in the opposite direction. Many of the off-farm jobs are part of a national division of labor rather than a village or household one. The growth of this sector might gradually integrate the village into a national class organization, with feedback to the agrarian structure. Meanwhile, for our purposes, the dynamics of the labor process take us beyond a static class analysis.

3

A Village in Upper Egypt

The agrarian transformation of Egypt is the general theme of this book. Our concern is with understanding this transformation through an analysis of the labor process rather than the village, which is merely a convenient setting for the detailed analysis that follows. Nevertheless, that analysis requires some furnishing of the stage. The task of this chapter is therefore to situate the village geographically and historically and to give a glimpse of its formal institutional structure.

The process of agrarian transformation is illustrated from the case study of Musha, a single village, which is taken to be not typical but exemplary. Musha is a relatively large village of around 18,000 people located immediately to the south of Asyut city, about halfway between the river and the desert. It is part of Asyut District, a subdivision of Asyut Governorate. It has a land area of around 5,000 feddans, or 20 square kilometers. It is the seat of a village council that serves one other village besides itself. It has a police station, but no *'umda* (village chief). Agriculture is the main source of livelihood, directly through farming or indirectly through wage labor, but many people earn their living from government work, crafts, or trade. The description that follows reflects the situation in 1981, and uses the ethnographic present for that purpose.

The Setting: The Zinnar Basin Region

The broad path of the Nile narrows about half way between Cairo and Luxor. At this narrow pinching of the valley lies the city of Asyut, which has been an important site in Egypt since Pharaonic times. At Asyut, the western escarpment comes to within 2 kilometers of the Nile, its closest point north of Nag' Hammadi. The mound on which the old city of Asyut is built attests to the age of the settlement. To the south of Asyut, the broad flood plain stretches away to Sohag, Girga and beyond. Asyut forms a barrier that marks the northern limit of this distinct ecological zone. Until 1964, the area between Sohag and Asyut, roughly 100 kilometers in length, formed the "great basin lands of north Girga and Assiut" (Lyons 1908:29) that was fed through the Sohagiya canal and its offshoots. The last of these basins, immediately upstream from Asyut, is the largest of them, the Zinnar Basin (Barois 1911:89–98; Butzer 1976:42). The village of Musha lies in the middle of the Zinnar basin, about 15 kilometers by road from Asyut.

Ecological Zones

The Nile valley at this point consists of three parallel ecological zones. Along the banks of the Nile, between the Zinnar basin and the river, is the Sahel. This is a raised levee which was protected from all but the higher floods in the 19th century, and was completely protected after the irrigation improvements such as the construction of the first Aswan dam in 1902. The soil is relatively light, and it is given over today to bananas, palms, and vegetables that are considered to do well in this sandy soil. The Sahel villages also take advantage of their riverfront location to fish. People from these villages trade fish, fruits, dates, and vegetables to the villages in the basin area. The villages supply certain specialized workers, such as palm tree tenders and winnowers, to Musha and the other basin villages.

At the outer edge of the valley there is an ecological zone following the fringe between the desert and the valley. There is a fairly flat area up to 1 kilometer wide between the cultivated flood land and the rise of the western escarpment. The desert fringe and the escarpment are the site of cemeteries and monasteries, and of quarries. Historically, the villages along the edge of the desert just north and south of Asyut were the stopping places of the caravans that came from Kharga oasis and Dar Fur (Meinardus 1969; Walz 1978a). There are some large villages along this edge with noticeable populations of landless who used to exploit the resources of the desert and who nowadays tend to work in the more prosperous basin villages as day laborers.[1]

Between the valley/river edge and the valley/desert edge lie the open fields of the basin itself. This area was flooded annually until 1964, and there are still relatively few trees or permanent installations in the fields. Since the cessation of the flood, the term "basin" has only the significance of a place name; the basin ecology per se is no more. Yet the landscape still shows the effects of the basin ecology. The villages themselves are nucleated, and are raised up above the old level of the flood waters. In some Zinnar basin villages, notably Shutb and Rifa, there is a veritable mound rising 10 to 20 meters above the valley floor. The topsoil here is at its maximum: thick, heavy and dark. The crops are mostly the open field crops of cotton, maize and sorghum in the summer, and wheat, beans, lentils, chickpeas, and berseem in the winter. Apart from onions there are few vegetables. A few gardens protected by walls were established before

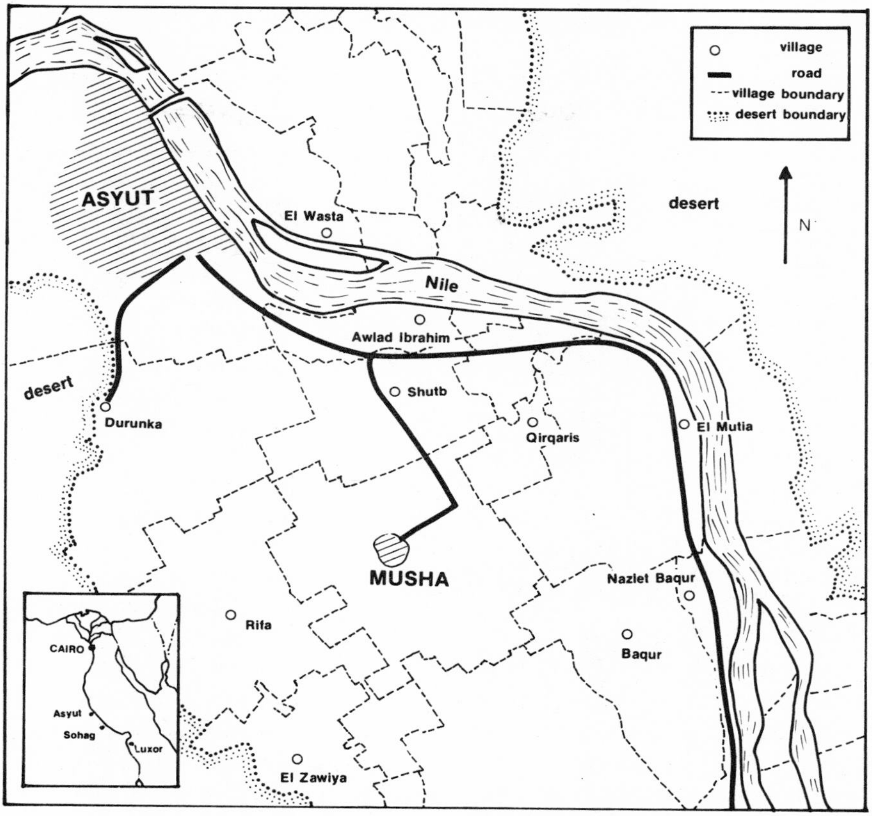

Figure 3.1 The Setting of Musha in the Zinnar Basin

1964, and many more have grown up since. The area planted in grapes and other fruits has increased since then to over 300 feddans, about 6 percent of the village's land area.

The Regional Village System

The villages of the Zinnar basin can be considered as a system (see Table 3.1). Until 1964 they were, of course, all subject to the same irrigation regime based on the annual flooding of the basin land from September 20 until November 1. In the more distant past this may have required some cooperation between the villages, but the modernization of the basin system after 1900 replaced this with a relationship with the Irrigation Service (Brunhes 1902:422). What is more evident today is the pattern of exchanges between villages situated in these three different zones. Among the products exchanged are agricultural produce such as fruits and vegetables, fish, and

TABLE 3.1 Villages of the Zinnar Basin System (1976)

Village Name	Feddans	Population in 1976	People per Feddan	Percent Growth of 1976 over 1927
A. Sahel Villages				
1. Aulad Ibrahim	1,087	4,607	4.24	260
2. Nazlet Baqur	1,146	4,850	4.23	286
3. el-Muti'a	4,611	17,533	3.80	191
4. el-Shaghaba	870	3,124	3.59	176
5. el-Namaysa	310	2,147	6.92	246
Subtotal	8,024	32,261	4.02	211
B. Basin Villages				
1. Baqur	3,162	13,265	4.20	218
2. Qirqaris	738	2,621	3.55	136
3. Shutb	2,533	8,604	3.40	165
4. Musha	4,943	16,442	3.33	181
5. Diweina	4,462	13,547	3.04	199
6. Rifa	4,776	10,265	2.15	205
7. Beni Smei	2,738	10,225	3.73	159
Subtotal	23,352	74,969	3.21	185
C. Desert Fringe Villages				
1. el-Zawya	1,829	15,052	8.23	276
2. Durunka	3,490	19,742	5.66	277
3. Deir Durunka	735	2,090	2.84	175
Subtotal	6,054	36,884	6.09	286
Total	37,430	144,114	3.85	207

Source: Statistical Department, Asyut, Unofficial Figures from the 1976 Census.

labor. Unskilled day labor comes into Musha from the desert fringe village of el-Zawya, and some skilled labor in the form of tractor services and white collar workers goes out to the surrounding villages. There are, however, few marriages or other informal social contacts between Musha and the nearby villages, and generally people from Musha are not knowledgeable about neighboring villages.

The villages in this system are quite large. According to the 1976 census figures, eight of the fifteen villages had more than 10,000 people, and the average is just short of 10,000, compared with around 6,000 per village in Egypt as a whole. The overall density according to the 1976 figures was 3.85 persons per feddan, equivalent to 917 persons per square kilometer. The figures in Table 3.1 show that there is considerable variation between the villages. In particular, one should note that the basin villages have fewer people per feddan of village land than either the Sahel or the fringe villages. They also have slightly lower rates of growth if we compare the census figures for, say, 1927 and 1976. Whereas the population of this group of villages has slightly more than doubled in 51 years, the basin villages have slightly less than doubled.

The Zinnar village system extends from the edge of Asyut city to the edge of Abutig city, a distance by air of around 30 kilometers. Asyut had a population of 214,000 people in 1976, and Abutig of about 40,000. Asyut is a major administrative, commercial, religious, educational, and political center. It is the ninth city in Egypt, and the largest city between Cairo and Khartoum. It is of course the seat of the governorate, and also of a district (*markaz*) that includes Musha with about three-quarters of the Zinnar basin as well as a similar area north of the city. The remainder of the basin is part of Abutig district. Many people from Musha and the other villages travel to Asyut to shop, to study, to work, to visit the doctor, and to transact official business. The villages nearest Asyut, such as Durunka and 'Aulad Ibrahim, are to some extent dormitories for the city's work force. The Coptic shrine of the Virgin Mary at Dair Durunka serves as a pilgrimage center for the Christians of Upper Egypt, and its festival in August is also attended by some Zinnar basin Muslims.

Abutig, being smaller and in the opposite direction, has less influence on Musha. The principal attractions in Abutig are the cotton gin to which Musha's cotton is delivered, located just north of Abutig in Filiw, and the religious shrine of Shaykh Ahmed Ferghal. This shrine has been described by Ayrout who has shown how the village shrines of the entire region, including the Zinnar basin, are symbolically linked to this major shrine through the annual summer festival (Ayrout 1963:104–106).

The Land

The general changes in the irrigation and land tenure systems that modified the social and physical landscape of Egypt beginning in the 19th century also affected the Zinnar basin. A number of events contributed to ecological and political change in the villages. They included the improvement of the basin system of agriculture, the partial regularization of the water supply after the construction of the first Aswan dam in 1902, the cadastral survey of 1905 confirming the private ownership of land, the introduction of steam and diesel pumping engines which made most of the area available for summer cultivation by the 1930s, the construction of the Aswan High Dam in 1964 and thus the switch from basin to perennial irrigation corresponding with the introduction of the mandatory cooperative system in the period around 1964. Power lines carrying electricity from Aswan now hum their way to the north of Egypt across the Zinnar basin, and in 1980 a major drain was built to serve the old basin area. A small airport for cropdusting planes is located just north of Musha. The sixteen Polish-made airplanes stationed there are used only to spray cotton throughout the governorate of Asyut during the summer months (cf. Stauth 1983:104).

Musha's agricultural landscape is highly organized. The land area (*zimam*) of Musha is divided into 70 agricultural sections called *hawds*.[2] The list of these sections is given in Table 4.4. The sections in Musha are usually oblongs. The fields are then laid out in strips, more often in the long direction of the oblong. Both the sections and the strips are oriented either NW-SE or NE-SW. Some fields are as narrow as 15 meters wide and as long as 1000 meters. Thus the knowledgeable observer sees the landscape as a pattern of sections and fields belonging to known individuals and with particular histories. This pattern is overlaid by a second grid, which is formed by the irrigation canals and the network of roads.

The preference for strip fields may reflect the ecological conditions of basin agriculture. Since the land was not completely even, and the flood was not constant from year to year, the most productive sectors were not always in the same place. Long strips best equalize the chances of each farmer getting a fair share of the land for his crop.[3] It might also reflect the preference for not turning the animal-drawn plow around any more often than necessary, as in Europe, although here some of the crops were planted without much tillage anyway.

The Village

The village of Musha[4] is located in the center of the Zinnar basin. It is the only one of the villages whose land does not abut on the dikes supporting the old basin. The land is flat, and to an outsider, featureless. On most days, however, the high western escarpment can be seen 5 kilometers away, and on clear days the more distant and lower eastern escarpment is also visible. The tall buildings of Asyut are also visible from the northern part of the village. The bulk of the population lives in the nucleated central core, built on a slight rise to avoid the flood waters. The 1927 census recorded no one as living outside the village core. Now there is one hamlet, Shahid ad-Dair, clusters of people around each pump, and scattered others living *fil ghayt,* "in the fields." The built-up area itself has expanded recently as people have built houses on land that formerly would have been flooded. The village area is around 75 to 80 feddans by now, resulting in a population density on the order of 50,000 to 60,000 per square kilometer in the inhabited area. The overall density of the village land is 900 persons per square kilometer.

Access

Until 1948 there was no permanent all-weather road linking Musha to the outside world. During the flood the only link was by boat across the flood waters. At that time, the main route to Asyut departed Musha from the northwest corner of the village, near the Coptic Church and the old part of the village. There is a small square here, the old *mawqif*, where departures and arrivals could be organized. In 1948 the government built a causeway (*jisr*) usable even during the flood. This, however, entered the village from the east since it came via the village of Shutb. Consequently, a new village entrance has grown up in the east, and this is where the main taxi stand and bus stop now are. The road on the causeway was paved in 1980, and extended from Musha to Rifa and Durunka. Now the bus makes a complete circuit from Asyut to Shutb, Musha, Rifa, and so back to Asyut, in both directions. Despite this regular bus route the difficulty of transportation to the city is a major source of complaint for the civil servants. Jitney taxis also shuttle back and forth. Some of them appear to be thirty to forty years old, and display a prominent running board, useful for extra passengers. They may carry up to twenty passengers, utilizing the space outside as well as inside. They do not all have proper licensing, and sometimes take unpaved back roads between Shutb and Asyut to avoid the police. Local officials estimate there are fifty taxis, twenty-five trucks, and ten private cars in Musha.

Streets and Houses

The village is divided (conceptually but not visually) into two halves and a large and somewhat indeterminate number of neighborhoods. The Eastern and Western halves of the village to some extent regard each other with suspicion and treat each other as political rivals. The neighborhoods generally bear the names of prominent families. One finds a cluster of large houses belonging to the wealthy and large extended families, and then around this cluster a ring of poorer relatives, clients, workers, and others. Thus neighborhoods, with the exception of one poor area on the southeastern corner of the village, are organized not around wealth or class lines but around patron-client ties. Most of the wealthiest families have their houses on the periphery of the village. Historically, this appears to mean that at some earlier period when the village expanded in size they were able to move to the edge of the village where they had more room for housing, for stabling animals, and for storing crops. The advent of mechanization has added to the advantages of a peripheral location, since tractors cannot easily maneuver in the narrow streets of the village center.

The majority of streets in the village are long and straight, giving the impression of a relatively recent expansion. In the northwestern quadrant of the village, however, the streets are narrow and winding; this appears to be the original core of the village. This presumption is reinforced by the presence in the area of both the major Coptic church, dedicated to Mar Boqtor, and the principal mosque in the village.

Houses in Musha are important for work and storage as well as for domestic life (Lozach and Hug 1930; Berque 1955b, 1957). The typical Musha house with two stories and a roof determines the limits of female space. A fairly typical arrangement is to devote the ground floor to a reception room for the men, to stables for the animals, and perhaps to cooking and other housework. The second floor would then contain bedrooms and other work space for women, and in some houses is also used for cooking and eating. The roof is also useful—not only for hanging out laundry and for keeping poultry and rabbits, and for storing fuel in the form of maize stalks, but also as a recreational and work space for the women and children of the household. Women must work at home, so provision of adequate work space is important.[5] Most houses have a latrine area or toilet (see Table 3.2) and a bathing area.[6] Poor families may subdivide one of these houses, or a recently married couple may divide off an apartment. Other poor families live in former stables and similar circumstantial housing. Except for the very poorest, houses are overwhelmingly built of fired brick. Some include a wind shaft to attract cool breezes in the summer.

Utilities

Musha has had a public water system since 1954 when the first artesian well was dug. Other wells were installed in 1968 and in 1979. They are around 55 meters deep. Currently the water supply system is somewhat erratic. The pressure is low, and often there is no water at all. Many families continue to supply themselves from public fountains, and some water carriers earn their living by delivering water to homes. Electricity was introduced into Musha around 1970. More households have electricity than running water, although in both cases some households formally without these conveniences in fact enjoy them by sharing them with a neighbor. Table 3.2, derived from the women's sample, details the distribution of home conveniences and appliances. Of the fifteen households recording no electricity, ten have radios or other electrical appliances and so presumably get their electricity from neighbors.

Religious Institutions

There are altogether about twenty mosques in the village. At the time of my research, half of these were private (*ahali*) and half were public.[7] Altogether this makes one mosque for each 900 people. The private mosques and some of the government mosques represent the important families of the village and are frequented by members of these families and their neighbors or clients on Fridays and at other prayer times. Most of the major families were associated with one mosque. The principal mosque in the village is named for Shaykh Abdelfettah, who is also sometimes said

TABLE 3.2 Home Conveniences

Convenience	Number	Percentage	
1. Traditional oven	43	91	
2. Radio	37	79	
3. Toilet (latrine)	34	72	
4. Primus stove	33	70	
5. Brazier (qanun)	32	68	
6. Electricity	32	68	*
7. Water	21	45	
8. Television	12	26	
9. Sewing machine	6	13	
10. Washing machine	5	11	
11. Cassette recorder	4	9	
12. Butagas stove	4	9	
13. Refrigerator	1	2	
14. House has 4+ rooms	22	47	**
15. House has 2+ families	11	23	

* Plus ten with a radio or other electrical appliances
** The average number of rooms was 4.2

Source: Women's Survey, 1980 (N=47).

to have founded the village. The imam of this mosque is a young graduate of al-Azhar; the other imams are local people locally trained. Other specialists include Koran-readers and *'ulama* or scholars.

In the fall of 1981, just before the assassination of President Sadat, the government took over all the private mosques in an effort to control the preaching and other activities in them. It is unclear what difference this makes in Musha, where most of the mosques, whether private or public, were essentially the creations of individual wealthy families which served the neighborhoods which these families dominated. The fact that the 'Abdin family mosque was also governmental meant, for instance, that it provided low-paying but regularly salaried jobs for several of the poorer members of the lineage. Government financial support was a positive consideration which outweighed any negative consequences of control over preaching. In any case, the familial structure of the mosques was antithetical to the preaching and activities of the egalitarian Muslim groups opposed to government policy.

The Christian population (11.4 percent in the 1976 census) is not clustered into a wholly Christian area, but there are sections of the village with relatively more Christians than others. Some short side streets, for instance, are largely Christian. Musha's proportion of Christians is less than that of most of the other villages in the Zinnar basin system. In addition to the Coptic church already mentioned, there is a small Protestant (Presbyterian) church serving around 10 percent of the Christian population.

Markets and Shops

There is no system of periodic markets in the Asyut-Sohag area, as there is in many parts of the Delta (Larson 1982). The major weekly markets in the area are primarily livestock markets. These include a Saturday market in Abutig, and a Tuesday market at the eastern end of the Asyut barrage/bridge, that are often visited by people from Musha. A small livestock market in Shutb, also on Saturday, attracts dealers in sheep and goats.

In Musha itself there is a central market place where fruits, vegetables, dry goods, and other products are sold daily. The fish peddlers from the Sahel villages generally set up shop in this market place—as strangers to the village they can do no more. But only a small portion of Musha's shops are located in the market. Fruit and vegetable stands, cloth dealers, and grocery stores are scattered throughout the village, thus accommodating to the fact that most shopping is done by children or women who do not want to move out of their own neighborhood. In addition, there are ambulatory peddlers, who stock up on fruits, vegetables, or dry goods in Asyut and hawk their wares up and down the streets.

The shops are rigorously inspected by the market police based in Asyut, referred to as the *tamwin*, to ensure that the shopkeepers are not overcharging or selling goods illegally, and that the shop license is in order. There is a kind of cat and mouse game played between the market police and the shopkeepers. The shopkeepers tend to keep very irregular hours, and close their shops as soon as they hear that the market police are around. The police try to raid unexpectedly and use out-of-uniform undercover agents. It is tempting to think that the absence of any real concentration of shops in a single marketplace and the irregular hours of the shops are both adaptations to this effort at control. Certainly whenever there is an electricity failure in Musha, someone will guess that the main switch was pulled to hamper the police inspection. When the market police arrive, they generally start with the shops in the market, which makes these shopkeepers very secretive and sensitive about any of their dealings. I had to abandon my attempt to survey the shops in Musha because the shopkeepers were simply afraid to reveal anything to me. They were the only category of people in Musha of whom that was true.

By far the most numerous shopkeepers in Musha were the grocers. According to one official enumeration there were 62 grocers in Musha, or more than one for 300 inhabitants. The grocers were also responsible for retailing some of the goods supervised by the market police, such as soap, sugar, tea, beans, lentils, and so on. Other food stores include greengrocers, butchers, cafes and restaurants. Then there are cloth dealers, tailors, shoe stores, and other retail outlets. Somewhat more specialized are pharmacies, an electrical shop (run by an Egyptian who had lived in Australia and held Australian citizenship), a bakery, and so on. The biggest traders in the village do not have shops. They are grain dealers who tend to work from their homes, which also serve as warehouses, or are found on the threshing grounds on the perimeter of the village. Two mills grind grain into flour for the entire village. The government-sponsored cooperative organizes sales of cheap food and cloth to villagers who possess cards showing that their poverty entitles them to this, and it also occasionally provides meat at cut-rate prices to the same people. This distribution is made outside the normal commercial networks and is organized jointly by the Local Popular Council and the government representatives.

Early History

The earliest references to Musha refer to Christian events and monuments. The Synaxare links the story of the martyrdom of Saint Victor to Musha (Amélineau 1893:266). In the *Khitat* of Maqrizi (early 15th century) there is a reference to a church in Musha dedicated to the martyr Victor, and which is built over a buried treasure (Evetts 1895:344). Musha's Coptic church is still dedicated to Saint Victor, and there are still stories of buried treasure associated with it. Christians in Musha recount stories of efforts by "the Romans" to persecute and kill Saint Victor. They dragged him behind a horse, they threw him into a fire, they put him in boiling water, and so on, but miraculously none of these efforts succeeded.

In a listing of the provinces and villages of Egypt drawn up in 1376, Musha is mentioned as one of 32 locations in the Province of Asyut. At this time it had 3,324 feddans and owed a tax of 10,000 dinars, but had no tax-exempt lands (*rizqas*). This put it in the middle range of the places listed, notable mostly because there was no tax-exempt land (Silvestre de Sacy 1810:700).

Contemporary informants in Musha, both Muslim and Christian, tend to agree that the earliest settlement in the area was a Christian village located where the Muslim hamlet of Shahid ad-Dair is now. After the Muslim conquest of Egypt a group of Muslims came from the north (given as the area of Maghagha or perhaps Bahnasa) and settled on the site of Musha itself, around the area where the mosque of Shaykh Abdelfettah is located. The Shaykh himself is sometimes said to have led this settlement. Some informants say that this occurred "seven hundred years ago." This is not inconsistent with the texts, but the details are lacking. The name "Musha" itself appears to be of Pharaonic origin and might mean "waters of the marsh," which would be consistent with the location of the village in the low-lying center of the Zinnar basin.[8]

One of the villages of the Zinnar Basin system, Shutb, is attested from the Pharaonic period when it was the capital of one of the nomes of Upper Egypt under the name of Shashotep. Asyut was then the capital of a neighboring nome. From the map given in Butzer (1976:78) it appears that the Shashotep nome corresponded roughly to the Zinnar basin, if it existed then. Shutb was also the seat of a bishop in the early Christian period (de la Roncière 1931 I:202).

Recent Political History

At the time of the 1905 cadastral survey there were two *'umda*s in Musha, one from Bait 'Abdin in the West and the other from Bait Shafa' in the East. This dual *'umda* pattern persisted until some time around 1930 when under the premiership of Sidqi Pasha the government combined the two. Either through an election in 1928 or through a physical attack by his henchmen on the other party, the winner was Tammam 'Abdin from the West. Tammam Bey is remembered for his strong personality and dominance of village affairs; although he was said to be illiterate he was also a member of parliament during this period. He held the post for thirty years. When he died, family enemies in Musha and Cairo conspired to prevent his son Mohammed from succeeding to his place. Disgruntled members of the Bait Shafa' from the East supported a rival candidate from Bait 'Abdin, the son of Tammam's predecessor, and there were also opponents in Cairo who had the ear of the authorities there. As a compromise, neither of the sons of previous *'umda*s was chosen. Instead, the grandson of Tammam Bey was named *'umda* at the age of 31 in 1948. Seeing that the post remained in the line of Tammam Bey, the other side petitioned the government to establish a police post and abolish the post of *'umda* altogether. This succeeded around 1957 and since then Musha has had no *'umda*. Tammam's grandson was himself elected to parliament in 1957 and remained in office until 1967 (he ran again on the New Wafd Party ticket in 1984 but was not elected). His prestige and influence in the village are great, and it is noteworthy that he is still universally known as "The Umda" (and not as a former member of parliament), even after his death in 1986.[9]

The Bait 'Abdin, or at least Tammam and his group within that lineage, were linked to the Wafd party in Egypt. Some informants say that the rival family, the Bait Shafa', were linked to the Liberal Constitutional party of Mohammed Mahmoud and such other Asyut province landowners as the Mahfouz family of Hawatka. Others say that they were linked to the "Saadists," a Wafd splinter from the late 1930s on. Both could be true, one following the other. During this period, emotions ran high during election periods, and the leading local politicians tended to have gangs of armed men at their disposal. In 1980 I was told that there was no party organization in Musha because everyone belonged to the same party.

Another prominent member of the Wafd linked to Musha was Albert Khayyat, a member of the prominent Asyut Khayyat family. Wasif Jirjis Khayyat was the founder of the family. He was appointed American consular agent in Asyut by 1861 (Walz 1978b:123). The Khayyat family had bought land in Musha and established a country house and farm there. Albert's father, Jurji, introduced the first steam pump for raising water around 1908, and they also brought a tractor into the village in the 1930s. The political significance of the family is suggested by an anecdote concerning Jurji Khayyat. This "notable of Asyut" was one of several people to sign a telegram sent to the Times of London on behalf of the Wafd, at a time when the Wafd leader Saad Zaghlul was under arrest, requesting the representatives of the British people to make reparations for the injustice to which Egyptians had been subjected (Landau 1953:155). He is also mentioned as a supporter of the Wafdist Fathallah Barakat in 1931 (Al-Sayyid-Marsot 1977:154).

One of the better known sons of Musha is Sayyid Qutb, famous as a leader of the Muslim Brotherhood at the time of Nasser. He was born in Musha in 1906, and left the village in 1921 to continue his education in Cairo. His father had been the representative of the National Party of Mustafa Kamil in Musha. In 1951 he became a member of the Muslim Brothers, and their principal ideologist, and was eventually executed in 1966 (cf. Kepel 1984:40–45). This fact was never mentioned to me in Musha, though it was confirmed when I asked.

Aspects of Musha's socioeconomic history will be discussed in the subsequent chapters dealing with land tenure, irrigation, mechanization, and the role of the state. Nothing we know suggests that Musha's history is at all distinctive in the Egyptian context; only the combination is unique. The broad outlines imply an Upper Egyptian counterpart to the social history of the Delta village of Sirs el-Laiyana (Berque 1957): maintenance of a pattern of dominance by large families, with most showing considerable continuity; involvement in national politics through village notables rather than through mass movements; influence of the irrigation pattern on local social organization.

Public Institutions

The most important governmental institutions at present are the Executive Council, the Local Popular Council, and the Agricultural Cooperative. All three of these institutions are meeting places for some local expression of opinion, and for contact between local opinion and the state. They tend to be dominated by the same relatively small group of village leaders including large farmers and middle level government officials. This section provides a general description of the institutions; political process is treated in chapter ten.

Musha is the seat of a Village Council that includes only one other village, Shutb, but has a population of over 27,500 people, about two-thirds of them in Musha.[10] The Village Council (*majlis al-qarya*) is composed of two branches, the *majlis tanfidhi* ("Executive Council") and the *majlis al-sha'bi al-mahalli* ("Local Popular Council"). The Executive Council and the Village Council are chaired by the *rais majlis al-qarya* ("Chief Village Administrator"), assisted by a secretary. At the time of research, the administrator was a native of the western part of Musha with a degree from al-Azhar University in Cairo. He is an appointed civil servant, and his principal role is to coordinate the other civil servants working in the Village Council unit, and to ensure that proper links between the civil servants and the people of the area are maintained. He also deals with the Governorate officials on behalf of his Village Council.

The present Village Council Head is from the western half of the village. He was named to Musha to replace another man from Musha, but from the eastern half of the village. My informants from the west claimed that they had caused the first man, from the East, to lose his job ("*tayyarnahu*"). He continued to live in the village, and was head of the Village Council in the neighboring village of Baqur.

The Executive Council in Musha has nine members (see Table 3.3), including the Village Council head and the secretary of the Village Council, as well as the chief of the local police post, the Village Bank head, the director of the Office of the Ministry of Social Affairs, and representatives of Agriculture, Education, Health and Housing. These individuals all have either a secondary or a university education. The Village Council head is a graduate of al-Azhar University, and his secretary has a B.Sc. in Commerce from Asyut University. Both are originally from Musha, as is the head of the Social Affairs office, while the Housing representative is from Shutb. The remaining five are all from nearby villages and towns. The council probably does not often act as a body. Most of the services are situated in the *wihda mujamma'a* ("Combined Unit") just to the east of the village on the causeway to Shutb, though the police station is in the middle of the village.

The Local Popular Council (LPC) in office during my field work was elected in the fall of 1979. It included 17 members, including one seat reserved for a woman (see Table 3.4). Twelve of the members were from Musha, and four were from Shutb, with one uncertain in my records. Seven of the 17 had also been members of the previous council, elected in 1975, so there was a substantial turnover. Of the members, seven (41 percent)

TABLE 3.3 Musha Executive Council Members (1981)

Post	Date Appt.	Origin	Education
1. Vil. Coun. President	1976	Musha	al-Azhar
2. Police Lieutenant	1979	Nikheila	Police Academy
3. Social Affairs Head	1979	Musha	B.A. (Soc.)
4. Village Bank Head	1979	al-Zawya	Commerce Diploma
5. Agriculture Head	1977	Asyut	Agriculture Diploma
6. Education Head	--	Nazlet Abdalla	
7. Health Representative	1981	Asyut	B.Sc. Medicine (a woman doctor)
8. Housing Representative	1979	Shutb	Technician Diploma
9. Secretary of the Local Unit	--	Musha	B.Sc. Commerce

Source: Council Records.

TABLE 3.4 Musha-Shutb Local Popular Council Members (1981)

Name	Village	Date elected	Category	Education	Occupation
Jaber	M	1979	Farmer	Reads/Writes	Large Farmer
Rizq	M	1975	Worker	Secondary	Health Clinic Employee
Salah	M	1975	Farmer	Secondary & Law	Large Farmer
Abdelhamid	M	1975	Farmer	Reads/Writes	Farmer
Abdallah	M	1979	Worker	Reads/Writes	Foreman, Asyut Electric
Omar	M	1975	Worker	Primary	Foreman, Musha Vil.Coun.
Mohammed	M	1975	Worker	Secondary	Village Cashier
Yusuf	M	1979	Farmer	Primary	Farmer
Ahmed	M	1979	Others	B.A. Commerce	Sec. Sch. Teacher
Mahmud	M	1975	Others	Teacher's Diploma	Sch. Headmaster
Mukhtar	M	1979	Others	B.Sc. Science	Education Official
Zeinab	M	1979	Woman/ Worker	Teacher's Diploma	Teacher
Zein	S	1979	Worker	Secondary	Petroleum Co. Employee
Sayed	S	1979	Farmer	Reads/Writes	Farmer
Sediq	S	1979	Farmer	Reads/Writes	Farmer
Mahdi	S	1979	Farmer	Reads/Writes	Farmer
Metwalli	M	1975	Farmer	Reads/Writes	Farmer

Source: Council Records.

were farmers, and the remainder all worked for the Egyptian government in one form or another. Depending on the type of employment, they were classified as "workers" or "others." The jobs included (1) employee in the Musha clinic, (2) foreman at the Asyut electrical plant, (3) foreman in the Musha Village Council, (4) Village Cashier, and (5) employee of the Petroleum Company. The others included (1) a teacher in the Asyut Commercial Secondary School, (2) a school headmaster in Musha, (3) a Primary and Preparatory Educational Supervisor, and (4) a landowner who also supervised the weighing of cotton in Shutb. The woman member was also a primary school teacher. The educational level reflected this employment structure—seven could only read and write (a qualification for membership), two had primary education, but three had a secondary education and two more a teacher's diploma, while two had completed university and the chairman of the Council, a farmer, had completed two years in the Cairo University Faculty of Law. The members of the Local Popular Council were essentially drawn from the village elite, whether they were classified as "workers," "farmers" or "others."

The council is headed by one of its members. The LPC president during my field work was a member of the 'Abdin lineage who was also the secretary of the agricultural cooperative, and closely linked to the Umda. Village politics is thus to some extent built around the collaboration between the appointed officials and the elected members of the Local Popular Council. When it is a matter of making sure that the officials in Asyut do not forget Musha, the two work together. When it is a matter of enforcing unpopular rules, there are arguments. The LPC president was the more powerful of the two, by virtue of his economic and social position (a wealthy farmer with a background in the traditional village leadership, but with modern credentials) and by virtue of his personality.

Another key institution in Musha is the cooperative. Socially, the cooperative remains close to village social organization and provides the continuity for some of the institutions and procedures within the villages for handling collective decisions and dispute settlement. The formal role of the cooperative has changed over the years. Currently, the cooperative retains certain functions relating to the organization of agriculture, for instance, the final decisions on the details of crop rotation (the assignment of parts of the village cotton allocation to individual farmers, for instance), the organization of the campaign against the cotton worm, and the supervision of the crop choices made by the farmer and recorded in the farmer's booklet.

The earliest cooperatives in Egypt go back to the early part of the century. The belief that some kind of land reform was needed in Egypt was widespread in the decade before the Revolution (Ayrout 1952; Springborg 1982:134–137; Tignor 1982). Shortly after the Revolution, the first land reform was enacted; this had primarly an anti-feudal character for it simply eliminated the very large estates (Saab 1967). At this time agrarian reform cooperatives were established to link the smallholders on the expropriated estates, but they were conceived as service cooperatives, not production cooperatives (Gadalla 1962:55–61). In this way the Egyptian choice differed from the Tunisian and Algerian options (Treydte 1979). In 1961 the second phase of land reform was introduced (Warriner 1962; A.H. Ibrahim 1982). This reflected a change of policy towards a more doctrinaire socialism. The ceiling of land ownership was reduced to 100 feddans. Mandatory village cooperatives were created, whereas previously there had been voluntary cooperatives in many villages. The registered farmers of each village all had to be members of a single cooperative. These cooperatives were responsible for distributing inputs to the farmers, and for marketing certain crops. The government also established a pattern of unified crop rotation (El-Shagi 1969), in effect imposing a rotational pattern on each village so that the government would have a major voice in deciding how each field would be used. A third wave of land reform in 1969 merely reduced the maximum holding from 100 to 50 feddans, where it remains today.

Although the Egypt of the 1980s has retreated from the doctrinaire socialism of an earlier generation, many of the institutions created at that time still exist. The major change, apart from laxer enforcement of the crop rotation regulations, was the creation of the Village Bank in 1976 (Nadim 1979). At present the village cooperative organization is a multipurpose service cooperative. Its personnel includes both a technical director with a staff of clerks, agricultural engineers, and other workers, and an elected board with a President and a Secretary. The Musha cooperative has 29 employees, including 11 in the office and 18 assigned to work in the fields (drivers and agricultural engineers used as inspectors). The director of the cooperative said with some dudgeon that two men could do all the work. The agricultural engineers are mostly graduates of the specialized agricultural secondary schoool, and the clerks mostly graduates of the "commercial" secondary school. All the employees are natives of Musha. Most of the clerical personnel in the Village Bank is also from Musha, but the director is from a nearby village and lives in Asyut. He is the only significant government official in Musha, apart from the police, not to be from Musha.

The cooperative has an elected board, chosen from and by its members. A new cooperative board of nine members was elected by Musha's cooperative members in the fall of 1981. Previous boards had had ten members. Rules limited the number of large landowners/landholders who could be members of this board. The board is thus supposed to represent the interests of the small farmers. At various times those holding more than five feddans were restricted to one seat out of ten, later to two seats. However, even then they had to win elections. Thus a large landholder had to finish in the top ten in the voting, but if several finished in the top ten, then only one (or two, depending on the exact rule at the time) would be allowed to serve. However, these rules were irrelevant for Musha during my field work, since all cooperative board members were technically smallholders.[11]

The Board members chose two important officers from among their membership, the President and the Secretary. Both were reelected in 1981. In Musha the President was a figurehead title, given to one of the older members. But the Secretary was the most powerful figure in the cooperative, dominating not only the Board but the Director and the other professional members of the cooperative as well. This precedence was reflected in the visits that the president and some of the other cooperative board members made to the secretary's reception room in the period leading up to the 1981 election (for this election, see chapter 10).

In theory the Cooperative and the Village Bank work closely together. The Village Bank took over the financial functions of the cooperative (loans, provision of inputs, marketing of specified crops through the government network). After the cooperative determines how much of the different inputs a farmer should have, based on his landholding and his declaration of intent to plant certain crops, the bank issues them to him. The farmer keeps a booklet in which is recorded his holding and also the uses he has made of the land. The booklet thus contains a record of what the farmer has planted on his land over the preceding years. When a new planting season approaches, the farmer must present this booklet to the cooperative, which verifies it and makes a notation of the farmer's declared intentions for the new season. With this certification, the farmer then addresses himself to the Village Bank for a "planting loan." The Bank makes the appropriate advances of fertilizer, cash or seed, according to the crop and the area.

The Bank is responsible for keeping track of the advances made to the farmer and for collecting its money. At the end of the season, the farmer is paid for his crop through the village bank, which will deduct any money still owed to it. This arrangement is most obvious in the case of the cotton crop, where the government is a monopoly buyer, and where the government involvement in pest control adds to the complexity of the cycle of cultivation. For other crops, once the farmer has purchased his inputs at a fixed price through the Village Bank, there are no further obligations or transactions except in the case of lentils and beans, where he is required to sell the government a certain amount for each feddan planted in that crop. The cooperative retains certain functions relating to the organization of agriculture, such as the final decisions on the details of crop rotation (the assignment of parts of the village cotton allocation to individual farmers, for instance), and the organization of the campaign against the cotton worm.

The Village Bank is an organization of government officials, and represents an effort by the central government to assert more control over the processes of agriculture at the village level. Initially it was hoped that the cooperatives would provide for this channel of government control, but in some respects the evolution of the cooperative has brought it closer to village norms and more responsive to village social pressures. The cooperative remains close to the village social structure and provides the continuity for some of the institutions and procedures within the village for handling collective decisions, dispute settlement, and making sure that the bureaucratic rules do not weigh too heavily on the farmers, large and small.

Conclusion

The geographical setting and the historical background of Musha, and some idea of its major formal institutions are important background for an understanding of the social processes analyzed in this book. The landscape surrounding Musha is ancient, and the village is certainly old, though perhaps not as old as its neighbors. The narrow Nile valley, far from being uniform, presents definite ecological niches; Musha is located in the rich center of one of the principal irrigation basins of the old system. The village shares in the institutional structures of modern rural Egypt, and combines these with traditional methods of conflict resolution and self-government. It is thus an appropriate setting for the analysis of the labor process under the changing circumstances of the agrarian transformation.

Notes

1. In the desert fringe villages in Minya governorate, much of the population is descended from sedentarized Bedouin, but that tradition is less evident here.

2. *Hawd* is the word for "basin," although there is no suggestion that in Musha or anywhere else they were ever basins in the physical sense. Berque translates this term by "quartier" in his book on the Delta village of Sirs el-Laiyana (1957), but here I prefer the term "section." A map in Bösl (1984:253) shows the outline of Musha's sections. *Hawd* is also used to refer to the large irrigation basins such as the Zinnar Basin, and to small bounded areas of the field used to control irrigation water.

3. The most detailed description of the ecological consequences of farming on the land left uncovered by the flood is in Idiart's (1961) analysis of the Lake Faguibine area on the Niger Bend in Mali. He shows how different levels of certainty in the prediction of the land that the flood will make fertile in a given year give rise to widely variant forms of social organization. Lee (1970) describes the situation on the Upper Nile in the Sudan, and Crary (1949) provides the most nearly contemporary account of flood irrigation in Egypt, based on a case near Luxor. Following Raynier, Baer (1969:18) has speculated that the land was redistributed annually in Upper Egypt to make sure that each household head was assigned his rightful share of the village's fertile land once the level of the flood had been determined. An excellent map of field layout in Musha is presented in Bösl (1984:250). It is appropriate here

to mention two classic early anthropological studies laid in Upper Egypt. Both Blackman (1968, but originally published in 1927) and Winkler (1934) stressed folk beliefs and popular religion, and there are some good descriptions of material culture in Winkler (1936).

4. Given the size and complexity of Musha, some comment on the designation of "village" is relevant. I feel that the term is justified here, despite the size, because Musha is the lowest rung on the hierarchy of central places in the Zinnar basin settlement pattern. Possibly a long-term effect of the cessation of the flood will be a change in the settlement pattern, but that has not yet happened. Each of the villages of the Zinnar basin system is independently related to the cities of Asyut and Abutig; there is no hierarchy among them. By other standards, such as size of the degree of the internal division of labor, Musha might well be considered urban even though dominated by agriculture. Yet, since Musha is the lowest rung and is committed to a rural way of life through agriculture, the term of village seems appropriate. It is also the official designation: *qarya.* The most thorough analysis of different village types in Egypt is by Lozach and Hug (1930), now somewhat dated. Berque (1955a, 1955b) developed a comparative analysis of villages in Minufiya. Barclay (1971) reanalyzed the material on Egyptian villages. An analytical survey is in Hopkins and Mehanna (1981). Eigner (1984) provides a more contemporary but more localized account of house type and settlement pattern.

5. Contrary to the pattern in other Arab and Mediterranean countries, the house has no courtyard, perhaps because of the shortage of building space; the roof takes over some of the functions of the courtyard.

6. Musha has no public baths, and the toilets at the mosques are only for the men. For more details, see MetaMetrics (1981).

7. Morroe Berger (1970) discusses the relationship between the State and the mosques in his book on Egyptian Islam.

8. My thanks to Sandra Kelly for suggesting this translation.

9. This story is pieced together from several interviews in Musha. I have not been able to check it against a written record, to help in reconciling conflicting versions. It should also be noted that the Umda told me that the 'Abdin family were originally the *multazims* (quasi-feudal tax farmers) of Musha. The head of the Shafa' family told me that his family originated in a village in what is now Minya governorate and came to Musha after the Muslim conquest, perhaps "700 years ago." A man named Hajj Ahmed Sharuna came south from a village named Sharuna, perhaps near the present-day Maghagha, and had four sons, one of whom became the ancestor of Bait Shafa'. Two others founded other lineages, and the fourth was a *darwish* and lived in Shutb where there is now a shrine in his name.

10. Local government in Egypt at the time of field work was based on the Village Council (Mickelwait et al. 1980:61), since renamed the Local Unit. This is a grouping of two or more villages that share a single set of local government institutions. There are slightly more than 800 Village Councils grouping the approximately 4,000 villages of Egypt. Some of the official statistics referring to villages are based on these Village Council units rather than the "cadastral" villages; care should be taken to avoid confusion. Administrative practice in these villages has varied from time

to time since 1952. Harik (1974:32–100) discusses the changes that occurred until the late 1960s in a village he calls "Shubra el Gedida" in Beheira, and there are other discussions in Baker (1978) and Mayfield (1971).

11. What they were in fact is another matter. At least one, listed as holding 4.5 feddans, farmed ten times that much.

4

People and Land

Any analysis of the relations of production in Egyptian agriculture has to start from some basic facts concerning the productive forces. In this agricultural village, the most fundamental relationship is that between human beings and the land, between man and nature. The active element in the equation is the human population itself, both in absolute numbers and in terms of its level of skill and ability to carry out certain tasks. In this chapter we will discuss the evolution of the population of the village, and also the gradual shift in the mix of skills present. This population largely draws its sustenance from the land, and yet issues of land tenure and access to land channel human activity in agriculture. Here the issue is not the land itself, but the rules that govern the way people use the land.

Population

The most significant productive force in village Egypt is the human population. Yet to determine the size of the village population is not easy. The primary source for the population of Musha is the census record established by the Egyptian government (see Table 4.1). These records suggest certain interpretations, yet one must be cautious for there are inaccuracies and inconsistencies in the published results. For instance, the figures for 1960 and 1980 are anomalous. I assume that the population of Musha at the time of my field work was around 18,000 people. This would clearly put Musha in the most populous 5 percent of Egyptian villages by size. It is the eighth largest of the 236 villages in the governorate of Asyut.

The census figures show a decline in the population from 1907 to 1927, and a consistent steady growth thereafter. The total increase from the low point in 1927 to the 1976 census is 81 percent, or about 1.2 percent compounded annually.[1] This is less than the natural growth rate, with the difference accounted for by out-migration, particularly before 1930. The period of maximum rate of growth comes in the second half of this period, after the increase in the level of the productive forces due to the introduction

TABLE 4.1 The Population of Musha, 1907-1981

Year	Total	Males	Females	Women Per 100 Men	Source
1907	9,510	4,645	4,865	105	Census
1917	9,240	4,274	4,966	116	Census
1927	9,091	4,219	4,872	115	Census
1937	10,596	5,357	5,239	98	Census
1954	11,461				Estimate (1)
1960	16,074	9,088	6,986	77	Census
1966	14,247				Census Estimate
1968	14,702				Estimate (1)
1976	16,442	8,516	7,926	93	Census
1979	17,681				Estimate (2)
1980	16,446				Estimate
1981	18,342				Estimate (3)

Source: Government of Egypt Censuses and Official Estimates:
(1) Water Supply
(2) Health Survey
(3) Based on Number of Women of Child-Bearing Age

of mechanized pumping and plowing, and then later the impact of the Aswan High Dam. The greater intensity of land use that followed these innovations meant a greater demand for labor. As the demand for labor went up, the role of out-migration as a safety valve for surplus population went down, and the rate of population growth increased.

According to the 1907 census, there were 9510 people living in 1,831 houses in Musha, giving an average of 5.2 persons per dwelling unit. No literate females were recorded, but 7.3 percent of the males were so recorded. Overall, males were 48.8 percent of the population. Christians were 10.9 percent, all Copts.

The 1917 census provides some interesting details on Musha life. The population was given as 9,240, and the number of occupied dwellings as 2000. If there were only one household per dwelling, the average family size would have been 4.6 persons. This is not very far from the present average, but it is the lowest figure in the Zinnar basin area, where the average for 18 villages was 5.7 persons per dwelling unit. The low average might be accounted for by an inflated estimate of households, but the fact that there were 1,742 married males for 2,344 married females suggests that a figure of 2000 households would not be far off the mark. There were 2,400 never-married males for 1,935 never-married females, indicating an earlier age of marriage for the latter. Men were 46.8 percent of the population in this wartime year. Overall, 6.9 percent of the population was literate, virtually all men. There were 16 literate women and 621 literate men, the latter being 14.5 percent of all males. The Christians represented 11.8 percent of the population. This was below the figure for Asyut Province

(22 percent), but above that for Egypt as a whole (6.6 percent). Of the 1,088 Christians, 107 were Protestant and 33 were Catholic.

The 1927 census showed a decline in population to a total of 9,091, its lowest 20th century figure, of which 46.4 percent were men. Musha was not the only village to show a decline, but most of the Zinnar basin villages registered an increase for this period. Since there were 2,023 occupied dwellings, the average number per dwelling was 4.5 persons. The entire population lived in the *nahiya,* the village core, because of the flood. There were 7876 Muslims and 1215 Christians, the latter being 13.4 percent of the total. Literates were 10.3 percent of the total population, including 22 percent of the men and 0.2 percent of the women. Of the 4219 men, 2594 (61.5 percent) were listed as active. The majority of these (65.2 percent) were in agriculture, with 11 percent in crafts, 6.6 percent in commerce, and 17.2 percent in "other trades." Only 6 percent of the 4872 women were listed as active, and 77.5 percent of them were in agriculture. The remainder were equally divided between crafts, commerce and other trades.

At the time of the 1937 census, the literacy rate in Musha had increased to 10.9 percent. The proportion of Christians was about the same (12.6 percent). Figures on occupation suggest that 45 percent of the population was active, with 75 percent of those listing agriculture as their principal occupation. Apart from 257 individuals (6 percent of the active population) who listed commerce as their occupation, the other roles are not clear.

The 1960 census figure for Musha is too high compared with the preceding and succeeding figures. The extra people appear to be males, who were 56.5 percent of the population (9,088 men for 6,986 women in a total of 16,074 persons). This proportion holds across age brackets and for both religious groups. This anomaly is increased by the notation that if 13,464 persons in Musha (83.8 percent) were living in families, the remaining 16.2 percent presumably were not. No other village in the area had this many people not living in families except neighboring Shutb, where the figure was 17 percent. The figures thus lack credibility and can not be discussed in detail.

In the 1976 census, the rate of literacy increased to 61.1 percent for men and 22.4 percent for women. The rate for women nearly doubled over the rate for 1960 (11.8 percent). There were 92 people (2 women) with university degrees. While the proportion of married men (age 18 and up) was 69.1 percent, that for married women (age 16 and up) was 65.5 percent. The rate of male activity among those age 6 and up was 58.5 percent, while for women it was 1.2 percent. This figure is lower than some earlier ones, and may reflect the larger numbers of young people staying in school. Males engaged in agriculture were 67.3 percent of the active aged six years and older, while those in services ranked next with 14.8 percent, then those in commerce with 7.3 percent, and those in manufacturing with 3.9 percent.

TABLE 4.2 Summary of Information From Health Department Survey (1979)

Item	
Total People	14,673
Total Families (usra)	3,016
Total Houses (manzil)	2,402
Christians (percent)	11.3
Average Persons per Family	4.87
Average Persons per House	6.11
Average Families per House	1.26

Source: Health Department Survey in Musha, 1979.

The proportion of active women in services was 63.2 percent, a large proportion of a small number. The majority (86.3 percent of the active, non-student population) worked for others for cash wages. Of the remainder, 9.2 percent (all men) did family work without pay, and 3.5 percent were listed as employers. These figures, if taken seriously, suggest a considerable polarization in Musha's population between the few listed as employers and the many who work for wages.

The figures for Musha are given perspective by contrasting them with figures for the village of Shanawan (Minufiya), which has nearly the same overall population (Gadalla 1985). As might be expected, the literacy rate is 10-20 percent higher in Shanawan, but the likelihood of marriage is marginally higher for both sexes. The proportion of economically active is about the same, but the proportion in agriculture is much less (48 percent), while the other sectors are correspondingly higher. The most striking difference is in those recorded as working for others—only 58.3 percent in Shanawan, while the rate of those working independently is three times higher than in Musha.

In Musha I was able to consult a health service population survey carried out in 1979. Unfortunately, the records I consulted are flawed because between 10 and 20 percent of the population was not included in this apparently complete listing. The summary details for those included in the enumeration made available to me are given in Table 4.2. This information was collected in a house-to-house survey carried out by health personnel in the summer of 1979. The working definition of a family (*usra*) appears to have been any married couple or single adult individual and dependents. Thus it corresponds most closely to a nuclear family. This approximates the definition used by the Egyptian census. For our purposes the "house" (*manzil*), which

TABLE 4.3 Demographic Indicators for Musha and Environs (1973-1979)

	Musha Average	All Villages Average
Birth Rate	40.5	40.0
Death Rate	14.3	12.7
Infant Mortality	101.6	101.0
Bilharzia Affected	12.9	14.7

N.B. Birth and death rates per thousand population
Infant mortality is per thousand live births
Bilharzia rate is per hundred

Source: District Health Office, Asyut.

equates in most cases to the household, is the more useful figure as it corresponds to the production and consumption unit.

The household and family size figures given here correspond to those produced by my smaller detailed survey of 107 households in 1981, and to the results of the animal husbandry survey (N=36) in 1979. The 1979 survey produced an average household size of 7.3 persons (Hopkins et al. 1980:33). The 1981 family budget survey produced a figure of 7.6 persons. It is worth noting that Upper Egyptian families and households are consistently shown to be smaller than Lower Egyptian ones.

Some figures on the demographic and public health indicators of Musha and nearby villages are given in Table 4.3. In this table, the figures for "all villages" refer to all villages in the District of Asyut, in other words, the rural areas north and south of the city itself. The range in the birth rate was from 37.6 per thousand (in 1973) to 43.4 per thousand (in 1974), and in the death rate from 11.3 per thousand (in 1978) to 18.8 per thousand (in 1974). The relatively low rate of bilharzia in the area is due to the late introduction of permanent irrigation and therefore to the fact that most of the canals are at some distance from the villages, thus reducing the temptation to enter infected canal water. On these four indicators, Musha is within the regional range.

If the level of health is one indication of the level of ability of the population, the level of education is another one. Musha appears as a relatively educated village, with a fair number of its sons and daughters having reached the university level. In the 1979 survey comparing Musha to two Delta villages, Musha had a strikingly higher rate of education. How this education is related to agricultural production or to village work in general is another matter. Certainly education achievement is highly valued for its role in upward mobility, and that upward mobility is often outward mobility. In the 1976 census, 3289 people were listed as students, 20 percent of the village population. Of these, 31 percent were girls. In 1980-81, there were 2,806 Musha children enrolled in the village's four primary schools and one preparatory school. This represents about 16 percent of the total population of the village. More were enrolled in secondary schools, institutes, and universities outside the village. About 38 percent of the primary school pupils were girls, which is slightly higher than the 34 percent girls found in a Minufiya village a year earlier (Zimmermann 1982a:7). Musha thus has a relatively educated population, and the girls have a relatively greater access to education than in Egypt in general.

Land Tenure System

The second major element in the forces of production at the village level is the land, which is the object of labor, but governed by the rules for access to land. These rules which regulate relationships between people with respect to land are a combination of state rules and local custom. They have the general effect of giving some people direct access to land for farming, whereas others can only have this access by agreeing to work as wage labor.

The basic form of land tenure in rural Egypt is now freehold tenure,[2] though there is enormous complexity in practice. Each bit of land has an owner who retains certain fundamental rights with regard to that land. The owner has sometimes ceded use rights to another, via the mechanism of legal rental; in this case, it is the renter who is recorded at the cooperative as the farmer of that land. The right to cultivate for a winter or summer season is also sometimes rented out, usually at a much higher rate than the legal rental. Owners may trade use rights in land without affecting the underlying ownership, in order to create larger plots for more efficient cultivation. An historical approach is necessary to unravel the complexity of rules and practice. This begins by understanding the three sets of books that govern rights to land.

Land Records and Systems

(1) Cadastral Records. The first set of books derives from the cadastral survey carried out under British auspices throughout Egypt between 1892 and 1907 (Lyons 1908; Berque 1955c). This survey established a land area for each village, and assigned an owner to each parcel of land. As a result, each village has a defined land area, its *zimam,* which consists of a variable number of sections (*hawds*). The survey covered Musha in 1905, and the village and section boundaries have not changed since.

One of the principal goals of the cadastral survey was to provide a basis for taxation. For these purposes, an old system was adopted whereby all the land in a given section was taxed at the same rate. In 1897 the standard criteria for a section were that the area should be from 50 to 100 feddans, in one piece, with a single type of irrigation and one quality of land, with a regular shape if possible, and using natural boundaries (Lyons 1908:65). Many of the sections appear to have been much older units, often with non-Arabic names, but in some cases they had expanded or contracted as land passed in and out of circulation. Each section was assigned a number and a name. In Musha many of the names refer to the families that dominated the sections in 1905. The complete list of the sections in Musha is given in Table 4.4.

The British survey standardized and unified the different land measures, so that henceforth the feddan (area) and the *qasaba* (length) would have the same value everywhere in Egypt. Table 4.5 gives the basic measures and their equivalents. It also established permanent survey lines on the ground in place of the tax-farming social links that had previously existed. The village boundaries are clearly marked on the maps prepared by the British prior to 1919, and the sections of the village were also well-known. At this time, the newer settlements of the 19th century—the estate villages or *'izbas*—were incorporated into formally constituted villages. Before this, the *'izbas* had no recognized place in the rural system, and so often escaped taxation and the corvée (Lozach and Hug 1930).

The cadastral survey established a firm ownership record, recorded in the *daftar al-mesaha*. In some villages, such as Musha, this record survives as the basis for settling land disputes until the present (cf. Berque 1955c:94). Each section is perceived as having a strip pattern, with each strip touching one of the edges, which is the base line. The information needed to determine ownership is the width of the strip along the base line, and the order of the owners. People will say, "Mohammed is west of Abdallah, and Abdallah is west of Mahmoud, and Mahmoud is west of . . ." The list of the owners of the fields in each section, although compiled in 1905, is thus still relevant for settling land disputes: it has never been updated and supplanted. In certain cases, claims to land can be supported or rejected by reference to this 1905 list of owners, although considerable memorized knowledge relating to several generations of descendents and to sales and other exchanges is also necessary to interpret and use this document. At least two copies of the 1905 list were still present in the village, and I have seen both of them used for this purpose.

Table 4.6 summarizes the information for three of Musha's 70 sections, as given in the 1905 register. Of the three sections analyzed here, Abu Mesahil is adjacent to the village on the west, while Shaja'i is on the western edge of the village land and al-Arba'in al-Qibliya is on the eastern edge. The average plot size in these three sections was around 15 qirats while the range was from a single qirat to 7 feddans 4 qirats. Altogether 22

TABLE 4.4 The Sections of Musha

Section (Hawd) Number and Name	Feddan	Qirat	Sahm
1. Ardh Sa'id al-Bahri	79	19	--
2. Ardh Sa'id al-Wustani	77	16	4
3. Ardh Sa'id al-Qibli	77	19	6
4. al-Qama (al-Gomeh)	80	1	4
5. al-'Atut	55	17	4
6. al-Khukh	61	11	4
7. al-Harras al-Gharbi	84	12	--
8. al-Harras al-Wustani	84	17	20
9. al-Harras al-Sharqi	72	17	12
10. al-Zawara al-Bahriya	68	18	20
11. al-Ghafara al-Bahriya	70	12	8
12. al-Qantara	80	16	--
13. al-Ghafara al-Wustaniya	70	5	--
14. al-Ghafara al-Qibliya	69	9	20
15. al-Arba'in al-Bahri	68	18	12
16. al-Zawara al-Qibliya	69	7	--
17. al-Khamsat 'Ashra	87	8	16
18. Dair an-Nahiya	59	23	12
19. Sharq ad-Dair al-Bahri	91	2	8
20. Abu Mesahil	50	2	--
21. Bahri ad-Dair al-Sharqi	52	20	8
22. Bahri ad-Dair al-Wustani	53	--	8
23. Bahri ad-Dair al-Gharbi	95	8	12
24. al-Roka	86	12	20
25. Danifa Sharqiya	86	19	8
26. Danifa Gharbiya	121	20	--
27. al-Shaja'i	66	1	10
28. Rizqet an-Najjar	63	15	20
29. Sharq ad-Dair al-Qibli	84	20	4
30. al-Dhohr al-Bahri	90	6	4
31. al-Dhohr al-Wustani	92	20	20
32. Bajamun al-Bahri	62	13	8
33. Bajamun al-Qibli	68	14	--
34. al-Dhohr al-Qibli	76	17	4
35. Awlad Hassan	77	7	4
36. Awlad Asil	72	18	16
37. al-Bahr al-Gharbi	27	11	4
38. al-Ribeh (al-Raba')	45	23	4
39. al-Mallas	59	16	--
40. al-Bahr al-Qibli	54	18	12
41. al-Bahr al-Bahri	49	20	--
42. al-Bahr al-Sharqi	43	1	20
43. al-Sabil	80	8	16
44. al-Madzub	50	18	20

(Continued)

TABLE 4.4 (Continued)

Section (Hawd) Number and Name	Feddan	Qirat	Sahm
45. al-'Awaija	78	18	16
46. al-Dhohra (al-Zohra)	103	5	4
47. al-Umda	64	21	4
48. al-Bustan	57	16	8
49. Suhail	58	6	4
50. al-Arba'in al-Qibliya	58	20	8
51. al-Settin al-Bahriya	62	16	--
52. al-Rayyan	81	14	20
53. Awlad Mahmud	97	11	4
54. al-Settin al-Wustaniya	81	16	4
55. al-Settin al-Qibliya	82	6	8
56. Awlad 'Issa	79	8	--
57. al-Radaina	69	3	4
58. al-Khairi	59	17	4
59. Makarram (Makram)	68	18	4
60. Rizqet Makarram (Rizqet Makram)	50	17	16
61. al-Shaikh Abdalfattah	62	20	16
62. al-Warq (al-Wareq)	68	22	16
63. al-Bakriya	71	12	--
64. al-Mi'a al-Bahriya	78	19	12
65. al-Mi'a al-Wustaniya	70	3	4
66. al-Mi'a al-Qibliya	65	2	4
67. al-Settat 'Ashra al-Bahariya	70	8	8
68. al-Settat 'Ashra al-Qibliya	46	6	20
69. al-Tayyar al-Bahri	51	14	--
70. al-Tayyar al-Qibli	61	21	20
Total	4,927	1	4

Source: Musha Cooperative Records.

percent of the plots were one feddan and more (cf. Lyons 1908:30). It should be assumed that most of the owners of these plots owned additional plots elsewhere. It does not follow that the actual plots farmed corresponded to those owned. A rough comparison with the present-day pattern in the three sections shows that the average plot size at the time of field work was around 1.5 feddans. This figure is larger than the ownership records of 1905, but may be smaller than the actual figure. Lyons (1908:30) reported that the average plot size for Asyut province was 1.9 feddans, compared with 3.7 feddans in Minya province, and a national average of 3.0 feddans.

(2) Ownership Records. A second set of books concerning land was compiled around 1965, probably to serve as the basis for the records of the new agricultural cooperative. This set of books records land ownership

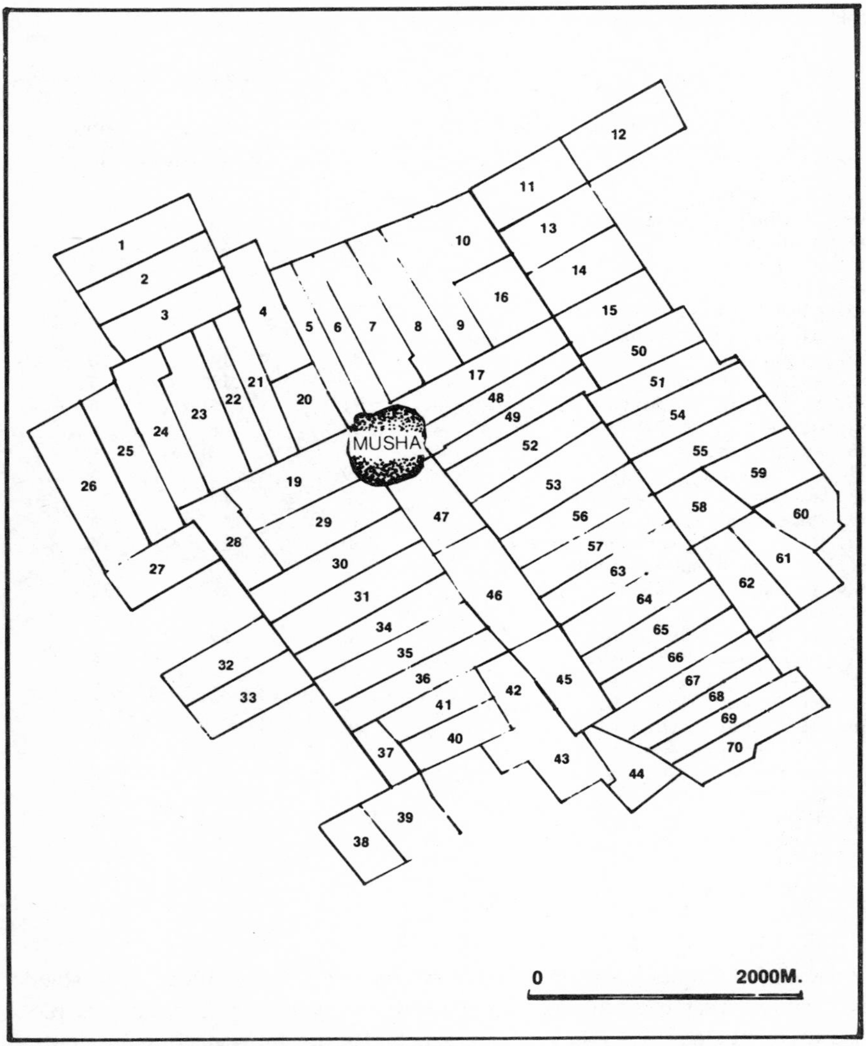

Figure 4.1 The Sections of Musha

(*taklif*) as it was at the moment Musha was given over to perennial irrigation. In principle it serves as the basis for inheritance and taxation. Although the land tax is based on land ownership, in the practice the renter of the land usually pays the tax and subtracts it from the rent due—if the rent is paid at all, for frequently among family members this is overlooked.

In this record each owner is listed separately, together with an itemization of the plots owned and their locations. The information is keyed to the

TABLE 4.5 Basic Land Measures in Rural Egypt and Their Equivalents

Land Measures in Rural Egypt	Equivalents
1 feddan = 24 qirats	4200.834 square meters
1 qirat = 24 sahms	175.035 square meters
1 qasaba	3.55 meters
1 feddan	333 1/3 square qasabas
1 ardeb = 12 kayla	198 liters = 5.62 US bushels

TABLE 4.6 Summary of Data on Three Sections in 1905

Data		Section Number and Name		
		20. Abu Mesahil	27. Shaja'i	50. Al-Arba'in Qibli.
Official Area (1981)	*	50/2	66/1/10	58/20/8
Recorded Area (1905)	*	47/16	61/16	57/12
No. of Names		64	97	101
Average Plot (F.)		.75	.64	.57
Largest Plot (F.)	*	7/4	2/14	3/20

* In feddans/qirats/sahms

Source: Cadastral Survey, 1905.

1905 cadastral survey. There are 4,948 names on this list, some of whom were already dead when the list was compiled. Many of the plots listed here are quite small, less than a qirat,[3] showing the effects of partible inheritance. However, these small owned plots are almost always aggregated into larger ones for farming, so that it is rare today to find an actual plot of less than one feddan. Many of the listed owners are absentees, junior members of families, or deceased, and the property listed in their names is rented or simply farmed by one of their relatives remaining in the village.[4]

(3) Cooperative Records. A third set of books is kept at the agricultural cooperative, and is kept fairly well up to date. This is the register of landholders. Each landholder (*haiz*) has a landholding (*hiyaza*) composed of the land he owns plus the land he legally rents in minus the land he legally rents out. In most cases, the holding includes both land owned (*taklif*) and rented (*ijar*). Contrary to the arguments of Stauth (1983:170–185) or Glavanis and Glavanis (1983:54–63) there is no substantial difference between owning and renting as far as the management and use of the land is concerned. However, the list of holdings makes no effort to localize the land. It is simply recorded that a farmer has a *hiyaza* of 2 feddans; where that is

TABLE 4.7 Distribution of Landholdings in Musha

Size	Number	% N	Area	% Area
.01-.99	201	14.2	118.46	2.5
1-1.99	425	30.1	558.63	11.7
2-2.99	293	20.1	665.92	14.0
3-3.99	164	11.6	513.75	10.8
4-4.99	113	8.0	474.75	10.0
Total .01-4.99	1,196	84.7	2,331.50	48.9
5-5.99	73	5.2		
6-6.99	19	1.3		
7-7.99	11	.8		
8-8.99	17	1.2		
9-9.99	12	.8		
Total 5-9.99	132	9.3	817.79	17.2
10-14.99	32		361.71	7.6
15-19.99	22		367.13	7.7
20-24.99	15		316.17	6.6
25-34.99	5		148.00	3.1
35-50	10		423.00	8.9
Total 10-50	84	5.9	1,616.01	33.9
Total	1,412		4,765.31	

Source: Musha Cooperative Records, 1979.

situated is another matter entirely. It is thus in effect a record of shares held in the common village patrimony, although that is not how people or the government talk about the system.

The holding is registered with the cooperative because this is the basis for determining the responsibility for growing the government required crops such as cotton, lentils, and beans, and for determining the amount of government-subsidized inputs a farmer is entitled to receive. The cooperative issues a booklet to each farmer in which the area of his holding is recorded, and in which the various transactions with the agricultural cooperative and the Village Bank are noted. The *hiyaza* list is a fairly good guide to farm enterprise size, whereas the ownership list is of no use whatsoever in this respect. In Musha there are 1,412 landholders for 4,948 owners, a ratio of 3.5 to 1. This makes it clear that the process of reconstitution of viable holdings occurs in the shift from landowning to landholding.

Musha is a village of large landowners and big farmers. The actual distribution of the holdings for Musha is given in Table 4.7, in which we see that 15.3 percent of the landholders officially farm 51.1 percent of the land in holdings of five feddans or more. The concentration of land in

TABLE 4.8 Distribution of Landholding in Musha and in Egypt

Holding Size	All Egypt 1975	Musha 1979	Ten Villages 1982
.01-.99	39.40 %	14.2%	36.5%
1-2.99	40.67 %	50.2%	50.5%
3-4.99	12.44 %	19.6%	9.1%
5-9.99	5.20 %	9.3%	
10-49.99	2.28 %	5.9%	4.0%
50 and more	.004%	0	

Source: For Musha and Ten Villages the Cooperative Holding Records.
For All Egypt: Harik, 1979.

Musha would be even more obvious if actual farm enterprises could be counted instead of official holdings. One measure of this concentration is that the average holding is 3.37 feddans, compared with an average of 1.28 in the Minufiya village studied by Zimmermann (1982a:36).

Our figures show us that the ten largest *hiyazas* in Musha cover 8.9 percent of the land. Moreover, the tendency to pool holdings into a single enterprise, and to farm land outside the village boundaries, are not reflected in these figures. Both these practices increase as the holding size goes up. According to informal oral information available in the village, there are seven farm enterprises of one hundred feddans and up, occupying more than one-fifth of the land surface (about 1100 feddans). There may be two or three dozen more that farm over twenty-five feddans. These large farm enterprises also dominate the ownership of tractors and irrigation pumps.

Despite this concentration of control over access to land, Musha was relatively unaffected by land reform. Only three families in the village lost land after the second wave of land reform in the early 1960s. They were all families that had acquired their wealth in the previous generation and so had not yet divided the ownership among large numbers of kin. The amount of land that changed hands in Musha was around 150 feddans, some 3 percent of the village farmland. Because the change came after the 1961 laws, no agrarian reform cooperative was ever established in Musha. Some of those who received agrarian reform land were veterans of the 1960s Yemen War. All new landholders simply became members of the new agricultural cooperative.[5]

The Musha data are compared with data from a sample of ten villages collected in 1981, and with a set of national figures from 1975 (Table 4.8).[6] These figures show that the proportion of holdings of five feddans or more is nearly four times higher in Musha than in the sample of ten villages. There are also twice as many holders of five feddans and more in Musha as in the national figures presented by Iliya Harik (1979:39). Furthermore, this disproportion also extends to the holdings of three to five feddans. The proportion of such holdings in Musha is more than twice that of the ten village sample, and half again as much as in the national sample. Correspondingly, the microholdings that are so prominent in the ten village sample, and in the national sample, more than a third of the total, are relatively scarce in Musha, only one-seventh of the total number of holdings.

However, the *hiyaza* does not tell the whole story. In theory the *hiyaza* corresponds to the "farm" in the sense of the basic economic unit, essentially linked to the household. Yet frequently the farm is different from the *hiyaza,* since the arrangements that people devise outstrip the ability of the formal institutions to contain them. There are a number of obvious ways in which the farm is different than the holding.

(a) A farmer may hold land in more than one village. Some of the larger farmers in Musha are in this category, especially those who own land in the villages of Rifa and Diweina to the southwest.

(b) More than one person in a household may have a *hiyaza,* yet all are managed as a single unit. Or a farmer may farm the *hiyaza* of someone in a different household. From 250 to 300 farmers in Musha are in practice responsible for such pooled holdings. Thus the number of farms in Musha would be between 1,100 and 1,200. For the very largest landholders this ensures that no member in the household is registered as holding more than the amount allowed by the 1969 land reform law (50 feddans).[7] For others, it is a way to disguise the true size of their holdings. Others aspire to hold no more than five feddans legally so that they are recorded as small farmers, which gives them certain advantages. The large number of Musha farmers holding exactly five feddans is suggestive of this practice. Finally, in some cases where, for instance, both husband and wife have a holding, it is just a convenience.

(c) The landholder may either rent in or rent out land on the so-called "black market" or "free market." The owner receives five or six times as much rent on the black market, and the renter does not gain permanent tenure as he would if the rental were officially recorded. Many of these deals involve renting land for the season rather than the year in order to avoid giving the renter a legal claim to occupancy.

(d) Finally, there are a few legally landless people who farm without having a holding. Most of them are very poor farmers who rent less than a feddan of land on the black market for winter crops, especially berseem (Egyptian clover) for animal fodder. Such people should be added to the list of actual farmers, but there is no record of them.

Taxation

The sections have always been considered as essentially areas of land with a uniform tax per feddan. After the 1952 land reform, the rental charge for farm land was fixed at seven times the tax. So in effect, by determining the tax on the basis of land quality, the government determines the rental. The range of rentals in Musha is from 45 pounds per year for the least valuable sections ('Awaija, to the south of the village) to 72.80 pounds for the most valuable (Bahri ad-Dair, to the west). The basic land tax is 14 percent of these sums. To this base, three other special taxes are added: (1) *rusum,* 15 percent of the land tax; (2) *aman,* 25 percent of the land tax; and (3) *difa'* (the defense tax), 75 percent of the land tax.[8] Thus the actual tax is 215 percent of the official land tax, or about 30 percent of the rental. The average tax for all of Musha is around 17 pounds per feddan per year. However, those owning (not holding) less than three feddans are exempted from this tax. In the end, about 60 percent of the land in Musha is taxed, yielding a tax revenue on the order of 50,000 pounds. The money is collected bit by bit throughout the year, but especially after the two main harvest seasons in November and in the spring. The tax is collected by three local tax collectors known as *sarrafs*. Tax delinquents are reported first to the local police station, and then to the *niyaba* (court) in Asyut.

According to Muslim law, there should be a tithe on production, the *zaka* tax. This is not collected by the government, but some individuals tithe themselves by giving charity to their less fortunate neighbors. The majority of farmers consider themselves too poor to pay the *zaka,* and of course there is no way of knowing how many people do, since it is of the essence that the charity is given discreetly and without publicity.

Conclusion

Musha, in common with rural Egypt in general, contains a growing population and a stable land base. The rules of access to land appear to operate in such a way that the average size farm has not declined in recent years, and may even have grown. Although inheritance tends to divide the land, there are numerous techniques for reassembling parcels of land to make a larger unit. Onwership of land is commonly taken as the best indicator of class status, and there is indeed considerable concentration of land ownership in the hands of the few. Under such circumstances it is not surprising that there are trends towards non-agricultural employment, and towards migration out of the village, and thus that education is attractive as a step toward either goal. What is less certain is whether the trend towards mechanization constitutes intensification of agriculture. It is clear that the opening up of Musha's land for double-cropping in the 1930s allowed for a surge in population growth, presumably due to more people staying at home. However, the same pattern of extensive field crops continues to characterize Musha's agriculture, and appears to be matched with the strong presence of large, capitalist farmers. In order to grasp the implications of this use of land by people, we must turn to the analysis of the labor process, starting with the household.

Notes

1. These figures can be compared with those for the Minufiya village of Shanawan (Gadalla 1985). The picture is broadly the same. Shanawan rose from a population of 9,013 in 1907 to 16,635 in 1976, for an increase of 85 percent compared with 73 percent for Musha during the same period. On the other hand, counting from Musha's low point in 1927, Musha has grown faster—81 percent instead of 69 percent. Shanawan rose in each census except for a decline from 1937 to 1947, reflecting a different pattern of constraints on population. The national increase from 1937 to 1947 was the largest recorded until then. In both Musha and Shanawan, the rate of increase rose after the 1947 census.

2. The history of land tenure in Egypt is far more complex than can be dealt with here. Baer (1969:62–78) provides a summary of 19th century developments in terms of the gradual emergence of private landownership.

3. Here are three cases at random: A has 18 qirats 22 sahms in seven different parcels, of which several were only one sahm in area, about 7 square meters. B has 2 feddans 22 qirats in ten parcels of which the smallest was 4 sahms. C has 1 feddan 17 qirats 18 sahms in six different parcels, so averaging around 8 qirats.

4. The 1965 list also reveals that around 80 feddans of land in Musha (1.6 percent) is held as *waqf.* An official from the Ministry of Awqaf comes annually to collect the rent.

5. Only one family with land in Musha—the Khayyat family—was affected by the first wave of land reform in 1952, but they elected to give up their land elsewhere and retain the land they owned in Musha, eventually selling it to the Umda in 1981. The head of the family is now a businessman in New York.

6. These villages may not be strictly comparable, since they are in geographically and ecologically different parts of the country: three each in Minya and Gharbiya governorates, and two each in Beheira and Qalyubiya governorates. On the other hand, the contrasts illustrate precisely how Musha stands out from the general run of Egyptian villages.

7. The agrarian reform laws generally stipulate that no one may rent so much land that his holding exceeds his ownership. This is probably the reason why in the village it is holdings (*hiyazas*) that respect the 50 feddan limit, and not ownerships.

8. The Defense tax was instituted in 1956 at 25 percent, and was increased to 75 percent in 1966. Cf. Diraz 1968:149.

5

The Household

The household is the fundamental unit for analyzing the social organization of agricultural production. The household is a relatively small and flexible group that allows its members to carry on several activities at once (for instance, animal care and baking bread at home simultaneously with field labor and visits to government offices) in such a way that the product of these different activities is combined for the mutual benefit of all the members. The role of the household is apparent in its formal structure and composition as well as the range of economic strategies it follows, whether through choice of occupation or through the combination of a number of different strategies by the members of one household. Some of these strategies and activities are the special area of the women, and they will be examined separately in the next chapter. The special interest of the household for the analysis of the labor process is that its internal operations remain largely outside the influence of capitalism, so that it represents a cell with distinctive internal operations even when each of its members participates in the capitalist wage labor economy of the village and of the country. At the same time, the changing nature of the labor process in Musha under capitalism modifies the role of the household.

There are between 2,000 and 2,400 households in Musha. Although the household may formerly have been a self-sufficient unit, providing its own labor and consuming its own produce, this is certainly not the case at present. The farm household has become a petty commodity producing unit, and the landless household is a provider of wage labor. The head of the household plays a key managerial role in the labor process. He must be sure that things are done on time, the inputs purchased, the labor hired, the machinery scheduled, the jobs located, and so forth. The decentralization of the hiring of labor to the household minimizes the need for the hierarchical control of labor. The small size and shifting composition of work groups favor the ability of the household head to make micro-adjustments and decisions. Only the household head follows the crop throughout the cycle even though others do the physical work. In order to understand the role of the household, we must begin by looking at its organization and internal processes.

Household Composition and Organization

The terminology in Arabic is a good place to begin. The word *manzil* is used in some of the official government statistics, and refers to a single dwelling, conceptually with a single door onto the street. The word *maskan* is sometimes also used with the same meaning. In terms of government statistics, a dwelling is normally occupied by an *usra,* a family, here with the connotation usually that it is a nuclear family based on a married couple and their offspring. A more useful term sociologically is *bayt,* literally a house but used in the sense of a household, the people who live together in one place and share their food and living arrangements to some extent. This sense of *bayt* as a production and consumption unit is the basis of the use of "household" as an analytical concept here. The term *'aila* refers to a larger kinship grouping than *bayt,* typically including several households that are fairly closely related to one another and that may cooperate to some extent. The largest unit, however, is the lineage. As a term, its application is limited to the lineages generated around the very wealthy families in the village. It can take in not only all those who are patrilineally related to these wealthy families (Bait 'Abdin, Bait Shafa', Awlad Hassan, Radaina, etc.) but also a certain number of clients and neighbors. To the extent that it includes non-kin, "clan" might be a more appropriate designation. In Musha and in the Asyut area in general, one term that is used for this social grouping is *'asabiyya* (cf. H. Ammar 1966:23–56).[1]

The division of labor by sex and age is actualized within the household. It is where the various streams of income and activity come together and production is transformed into consumption. Households normally consist of adults of both sexes to ensure that the unit combines the outcomes of both male and female tasks. The men work outside the home, as farmers on their own account, government workers, traders, or day laborers, while the women (apart from the few who are government workers) work in the house taking care of household chores, animal care, and some transformation of primary products. Children are called on for household chores, or even for productive activities earning wages in cotton depesting or picking, as soon as they are able. The extent to which the household contains children and old people is a function of the place of the household within the cycle of domestic development.

Households frequently split at the point when the elderly parents die and the next generation succeeds. Each brother then establishes a separate household. If the paternal house is large enough, it may be physically divided into as many sections as needed, and each one will be given its own door.

TABLE 5.1 Household Features by Size of Landholding

Hiyaza	Household Size	Couples	Male Workers	Cows & Buffaloes	Total Crops Grown
0	6.6	1.35	1.92	.15	0
.01-.99	7.5	1.33	1.75	.83	1.42
1-1.99	7.7	1.47	2.20	.53	2.20
2-2.99	6.7	1.09	1.90	.45	2.45
3-4.99	10.7	1.73	2.90	1.82	3.91
5 F. and up	10.6	2.00	3.00	2.63	4.38

Source: Musha Sample of 107 Households, 1981.

One official in the village (the *dallal an-nahiya*) specializes in helping these new households make a fair division of the original house. More anguishing is the split of a son from a father because it runs against expectations. In many cases this is accomplished delicately when the son moves out of the village, establishing himself in an urban area. In some cases, the split occurs even though both father and son remain in the village as farmers. Such a split is only possible if the son controls resources independently of his father—for instance, if he has inherited land from his mother or if he has a government job. The smaller household size among landless families suggests that the reliance on cash wages or trading income tends to encourage each couple to establish a separate household.

Some households continue as extended family households, or as neighboring households linked agnatically or affinally. This is particularly the case for wealthy families, which develop something approaching a lineage structure. Even in these cases, the actual household is usually a nuclear family or a moderately extended family. It seems that wealthy families have fewer children than middle-level or poor families, presumably reflecting a desire to avoid too great a division of family wealth through inheritance. At the same time, the average size of the wealthy households is larger because the household is more likely to be built around an extended family.

Table 5.1 gives information on household size and wealth derived from the household survey I conducted in 1981. This table shows the clear tendency for household size to increase as the household commands more fixed resources such as land. The general tendency is for households with large holdings also to be relatively large and to have more cattle and buffalo. This tendency is also reflected in Table 5.1, which shows not only that large households are more likely to have the organization of an extended family (number of married couples in the household) and have more male workers between the ages of 16 and 60 than small households—which one would expect, after all—but also to have more cattle and buffalo and to grow more different crops on their land. Table 5.1 also indicates that the cut-off point in terms of size comes at the three feddan level. Those with a holding of three feddans and more have an appreciably larger average household size, number of couples, number of male workers, number of cattle and buffalo, and total crops grown than those holding less than three feddans or without a holding at all. The landless have a lower dependency ratio than the holders of less than three feddans by a slight margin.[2]

By far the most common household type is the simple nuclear family based around the presence of a single married couple with their offspring and perhaps other relatives. Households with a single married couple were 56, or 52 percent of the total of 107. In addition, there were 9 households without a married couple, mostly widows with unmarried children, and four cases where the husband had two wives. Assimilating these cases to the basic nuclear family gives the result that 64.5 percent of the households are not extended but simple. Of the remaining 38 households (35.5 percent), 29 had two, 8 had three and one had four married couples. These extended families included both cases where the two husbands were father and son, and where two or more husbands were brothers. About half the households holding three or more feddans were of this type, compared to less than a third of those endowed with less land.

Taking somewhat arbitrarily the number of men aged between 16 and 60 as an indication of the labor force of each household produces much the same result. Overall, 68 percent of households have two or fewer adult male workers. A substantial proportion of these men work outside agriculture, principally for the government, in trades and crafts. Of the 59 landed households, 62.7 percent (N = 37) had only one or two men in this age range. Of the 48 landless households, 69 percent (N = 33) had only one or two men in this age range, and another three had no men at all of this age, so that altogether 73 percent of landless households have two men or less.

Occupation and Source of Income

Table 5.2 classifies households according to their principal source of income. In some cases the assignment of a case to one or another category requires a very fine judgment—for instance, if the father farms two feddans while the son has a government clerical job. Even though the information in this sense is approximate, I believe that the general picture is accurate. About 56 percent of the households derive their income principally from agriculture, and a little less than half of these derive it primarily from their own land. The agricultural specialists include camel drivers and winnowers, people whose livelihood is closely tied to agriculture and are part of the social organization of agricultural production. Overall, around a third of all

TABLE 5.2 Principal Sources of Income by Household, by Size of Holding

Source of Income	Size of Holding					
	Landless	.01-.99	1-2.99	3-4.99	5+	Total
Farms own land	--	--	14	8	7	29
Day labor	18	7	2	--	--	27
Government post	15	2	5	1	1	24
Craft or trade	10	1	3	1	--	15
Agri. specialization	2	1	--	1	--	4
Migration income	--	1	2	--	--	3
Rent or pension	3	--	2	--	--	5
Total	48	12	28	11	8	107

Source: Musha Sample of 107 Households, 1981.

households have a substantial income in the form of a regular salary, mostly from the government. In the case of the landless families and a few others, this salary provides the basis of the household economy. Where the household is also fairly well endowed with land, then the government job and the income from agriculture are usually combined. Thus the phenomenon of the part-time peasant, with one foot in agriculture and the other in the service sector, is well established in Musha. This has also been noted for the Delta, where Commander and Hadhoud (1986:174) note that "Even for the smallest farm units, own-farm work has become a secondary, part-time occupation."

Another indication of occupation can be gained from a list of all the occupations practised by men, both household heads and other household members, as reported in the sample. The principal categories are given in Table 5.3, from which it can be seen that about 20 percent of all reported occupations involved employees (overwhelmingly for the government). Students represented another 20 percent; many are future government employees. However, there is once again a counting problem as many of these men combine farming, trade or a government job in various ways. Even with their imprecisions, these two ways of calculating occupation and sources of income combine to confirm the observation that more and more people are successfully developing a non-agricultural source of income, and are thus escaping the agrarian structure.

Reproduction: Marriage and Family Life

Marriage is generally a matter arranged between families, although the young people have at least a veto. The overwhelming majority of marriages are arranged between Musha families. Marriage exogamous to the village

TABLE 5.3 Individual Occupations Cited

Occupation	Number	Percent
1. Farms own land	84	30
2. Student	56	20
3. Government Employee	45	16
4. Other	28	10
5. Combinations	26	9
6. Not stated	10	4
7. Day labor	8	3
8. Nothing	8	3
9. Trade	6	2
10. Army	6	2
11. Crafts (masons and tailors)	4	1

Source: Musha Sample of 107 Households, 1981.

is rare. In some cases, a marriage is arranged between a partner in Musha and a partner of Musha origin living in one of the cities. I knew of one case where a marriage was arranged between two partners of Musha origin living in different cities.

Arranging and settling into a marriage are not easy. In two of the households I knew best, there was a bride who had returned home shortly after marriage. In one case, she eventually returned to her husband (a Musha man serving in the army in Luxor), but only after considerable delay and renegotiation of the marriage relationship. At least one prominent Musha landowner, known for his ability as a peacemaker, tried to mediate the affair. In the other case, the bride went to live with her groom's mother in Alexandria while he migrated to work in Saudi Arabia. She did not get along with her mother-in-law, and returned home to Musha pregnant. When her husband returned to Alexandria he made no effort to contact her. Perhaps it did not help that the baby was a girl. The bride's father tried to smooth the way for her return, but to no avail, at least in the short run.

In other cases, an eligible bride may wait a long time for the right husband, particularly in cases where there is land involved, or where the girl has been fairly well educated. One schoolteacher did not marry until the age of 30, and then she married her cousin, a clerk in the preparatory school and a grain dealer. One is tempted to suspect that he was galvanized into action by her (brief) engagement to a non-relative. A woman from one of the biggest landowning families in the village did not marry until her mid-30s, and then married a school headmaster twice her age.

Land considerations also probably entered into the case of the two daughters of one of Musha's Christian elders. He was the only one of five brothers left in the village, the other four all working for the government in teaching or banking jobs in Asyut, Cairo, or Alexandria. As such he farmed all the family land, close to 10 feddans. However, of his many children only three daughters survived to adulthood. At the time of field work one was already married to a bank clerk in Asyut, but the other two, in their early 20s, remained at home. In one sense, they were bait for a husband who would be a farmer for the next generation, but at the same time both girls had been to secondary school in Asyut and despite their mastery of traditional home skills it is not clear that their future would really lie in the village.

A successful marriage is a productive one—productive of children, that is. We know generally for rural Egypt that Egyptian women produce close to their biological maximum as far as children are concerned (Gadalla 1977; Kelley, Khalifa, and el-Khorazaty 1982:83–90). There is no reason to think that Musha is any different.

At present, most children attend school. Those who are successful in Musha's primary schools and its preparatory (middle) school must then leave the village to attend secondary school and eventually the university, probably in Asyut. In the recent past, a son who did less well in school was left in care of the family's land, while the others are likely to migrate. Thus as the children mature, some of them are likely to leave Musha for urban occupations, or perhaps go abroad.

It is difficult to generalize about the role of children. They often do small chores around the house, and when boys are older they will help in the fields, or in such ancillary tasks as guiding the donkeys carrying wheat or straw back to the house from the threshing ground. Children are massively recruited each summer to help with depesting in the cotton fields, starting with some as young as six or seven years old and running through adolescents. The adolescents and young adults are also mobilized to pick the mature cotton in October. Virtually every farmer relies on the hired hands of youth for this operation. Most children are available for work only when not in school. However, for the important cotton harvest, the opening of school may be delayed as much as a month beyond the opening date in Cairo (as was the case in 1980) in order to ensure the labor supply.

Production: Household Strategies

As economic units, households select and combine among a variety of resources (the examples given below document the statements made here). First, there is labor, consisting in the ability of the household to fulfil the male and female roles in the sexual division of labor, the ability of the household to carry out the tasks required by its other resources (such as land), and its ability to enter into income-producing activities. The resources of a household are not just the number of people, but the level of skills they have achieved. For those who have only their strength, casual day labor is the response to this requirement. Others, with a bit of capital may learn a skill and attempt to earn an income through a craft (tailoring; masonry; weaving; pottery) or through a trade (dealing in livestock or grains). There are also para-agricultural jobs such as pump guard, camel driver or winnower to attract the worker away from straight day labor. The most obvious investment in future labor productivity is through education. A successful career in education may lead to a government job and thus a regular source of income. The regularity of the income compensates for its small size; and in any case the office hours are not long and people are free to engage in other, more lucrative, activities after hours.

If a household is fortunate enough to include a member endowed with agricultural land, then its strategy will include a way to benefit from this land. Depending on its own labor resources, it may elect to hire workers regularly, or only for the cotton harvest; its choice of crops will reflect the rest of the household economic balance to some extent, though virtually all Musha households choose from the same gamut of crops, with the difference being mainly one of how many crops are grown, and that is a function of "farm" size. A household that has land, for instance, has the option of keeping a buffalo or a cow at home, for then it can grow berseem in the winter and sorghum in the summer as fodder. The buffalo represents a choice for dairy products. The choice of a cow usually reflects a preference for more offspring (calves), and since the calves are sold, more of an involvement in the livestock market. Another option is to invest in machinery. In the 1930s and 1940s many people invested in the pumping engines. Since the 1950s, but especially after about 1975 investing in a tractor and its attachments has been an option. Most of those prepared to make this choice, however, were the farmers with considerable land of their own, and who thus felt that in the first instance they needed the tractor for their own work. Providing custom services for their less fortunate neighbors was only subsequently perceived as an opportunity. Most owners of machinery now receive some income from renting out their tractors.

Thus a household with a full range of resources may have someone (let us say one brother) who looks after the family land, raises livestock, and perhaps has a tractor, while other brothers have jobs in the government, based on some education, and all the offspring of the brothers are pushed to high level of educational attainment to prepare themselves for the new circumstances of the next generation. This division of labor between adult brothers can be seen in genesis in the case of a man with grown sons, some of whom are oriented towards government careers while others help him with the land, the livestock and the machinery. Of course, one possible outcome is that all the brothers prefer the government career and the urban life, so no one is left to mind the farm. Here the larger and wealthier lineages have an advantage, because the larger pool of people makes it easier for them to retain and manage such land within the lineage. In this case we are no longer talking of a single household, but of a network of interrelated households which have chosen different paths and created a division of labor and responsibility between them.

An example shows both upward mobility and family solidarity. A man from Musha became wealthy in the 1930s through acting as a labor recruiter for Musha men to work in the Delta. He eventually acquired substantial land in Musha, and also considerable real estate in Asyut and Tanta. He gradually shifted his headquarters to Tanta, and when he died his sons continued to live there, where they control a fleet of buses and taxis. Only some of his daughters remain in Musha, and the land is managed by their husbands and their husbands' agnates. Even his sisters' sons play a more distant role, as pump guards, petty labor recruiters (since the heyday of labor recruitment is past), and dealers in locally manufactured machinery.

At the other extreme, many households are unable to pull together so many resources, or any resources at all. The extreme cases would be an elderly couple in poor health whose children have migrated, or a widow with small children, or a married man with small children but poor health. In cases such as these, if there is no land and no labor power, the family is thrown on charity, or the remnant must migrate from the village to the city where it seems to be easier to get by. Organized charity takes the form of a pension from the Ministry of Social Affairs. There are a certain number of widows, the elderly, the disabled and so on in Musha who receive this.[3] Another kind of charity is the Islamic alms (*zaka*), which is traditionally given from a wealthier relative or neighbor to a poorer one.

So while some families grow and split and form several households, others migrate from Musha to other parts of Egypt in search of a different range of economic activities. Thus from our sample of 107 households, 9.3 percent claimed a member abroad and 24.3 percent claimed a member elsewhere in Egypt. Still other households disappear completely, through death, poverty, or migration. Thus we found that of our original list of 121 households, six (5 percent) had migrated in the less than two years since the base list was compiled. Five more (3 percent) had died without leaving an identifiable household behind. Still the fact that some households give up or disappear does not mean that the household as an institution is any the less important. In the next section, I present some thumbnail sketches of a range of Musha households, drawn from the sample of 107 cases. They illustrate, better than any generalizations, the nature of household strategies and the concrete results of these strategies.

Examples of Musha Households

The patterns described in the previous sections are illustrated here by a number of case sketches of households. They demonstrate the range of possible strategies present within the village, and give an idea of the role of the household within the labor process as the manager of labor. The emphasis is on the variety of male activities, since women's activities are discussed in the next chapter. The first nine examples are of landless households, and show how seldom they are dependent on agricultural wage labor alone for their livelihood. The second group of eleven households are landholders, and they are presented according to the size of their holding, the smallest first. Here we see how often the household combines agricultural with non-agricultural sources of income.

Landless

1. The head is 60, married, lives with a son of 25, married, one child. They have no *hiyaza* and no animals. The father works as a foreman in a cotton factory in the Delta town of Simballawein, and the son has been working as a government employee in the Musha combined unit for five years. He has a technical secondary education.
2. The head is 38, and the household consists of himself, his wife and six young children. This man used to work in Suez and elsewhere in the North, but a couple of years ago gave that work up and is trying to start a greengrocer shop. It is a small one. He gets fruits and vegetables from Asyut on credit, and pays the supplier after he sells them.
3. The head is 55, and the household has nine members including three couples and four adult male workers. Animals include two goats. The father has been working in the port in Alexandria all his life while keeping the household in Musha. Now the second and third sons (aged 18 and 16) work there with him. The oldest son has been working in the agricultural cooperative in Asyut for four months. Those in Alexandria come home every couple of months.
4. The head is 60, and the household consists of himself and his son, both married, and small children. The father and son work principally as carters, hauling goods from Asyut to Musha. When this work is not available, they work as hired hands in agriculture. The head worked in a cotton gin in Disuq for ten years as a porter/loader. He first began to migrate at the age of 24.
5. The head is 63, and the household has eight people including himself and a son of 24, both married, and small children. They have one buffalo and two donkeys. They combine work as hired hands with

working as ambulant sellers of petty prepared goods such as pickles, lupin, and *bilila;* they have been doing this for 15 or 20 years. They say they would do better as hired hands, but they can not find the work.

6. The head is 48 years old. The household consists of the head and his wife, one son and his wife, one unmarried son, other children. Animals include two sheep. He and his son work regularly for a large farmer, where they are part of a steady crew of three or four men. The younger boy, age 16 does "nothing."
7. The household consists of two married brothers, aged 35 and 30, their wives, and two children. The brothers are day laborers. They go with a labor contractor to Mehalla for four months a year to work as porters/loaders in a cotton gin (from September to December). The rest of the time they work in Musha.
8. The head is 55 years old. He works as the Village Executive Officer (*rais majlis al-qarya*) in the nearby village of Baqur, after having formerly served in the same post in Musha, and having been a teacher. He studied sociology at Cairo University, and became familiar with Ibn Khaldun, Comte and Durkheim. His three sons, aged 21, 17 and 15, are students. The other eight people in the household (there are 13 altogether) are children or of his parents' generation.
9. This household of five members includes an elderly couple, a 17-year-old son, and two others. The husband is 63 years and in poor health. In theory he is a day laborer but because of his health does not work. The son of 17 has heart trouble and does not work. A married son lives in Alexandria but does not help the parents. The husband applied for a "Sadat pension" but is not eligible because he is not quite 65. The wife has applied for a pension through the Social Affairs office, but so far has not received anything.

Landed

10. The head is 39 years old, and the household includes also a wife and a child. The *hiyaza* is 12 qirats; there are two buffalo and a donkey. He sometimes hires additional land to grow berseem for the animals. His principal income is from agricultural day labor. He works his own land himself, but hires a tractor.
11. The head is 47 years old and married. The other adult male is his 20-year-old single son who is studying for the general secondary exam. Their holding is 14 qirats of land rented from a big landowner in the village. He uses only family labor (presumably his own) on his own land. In 1980-81 he grew cotton and sorghum in the summer, and berseem and beans in the winter. His principal income is from

day labor in agriculture, but he does not now work for anyone in particular. He once worked for the landowner from whom he rents land. Then he decided to test his luck in Saudi Arabia. A man from Musha took him to meet a labor contractor from Saudi Arabia in Cairo, and he paid LE300 altogether for the ticket and other expenses. But somehow the wages did not meet his expectations, so he only stayed a year and had been back in Musha for a year at the time of the interview. As a younger man, he worked as a migrant in the north.

12. The head is 45 years old, and has two single sons aged 23 and 18. Then there are his wife and five others, younger and older. He has a holding of 18 qirats rented from three different people, and also rents 6 qirats on the "free" market for berseem. This land is scattered in three sections. Animals include a buffalo and a donkey. He and his sons work their own land themselves. They are also regular workers for a large landowner in the village. They rent a tractor from this landowner and get at least some of their irrigation water from him.
13. The head is 67 years old. His married son of 26 is working in Saudi Arabia. His single son of 17 is still a student. The household also includes the two wives and a child. The holding is 1 feddan 6 qirats, of which most is owned but some is rented from his son and from the land reform. There are two buffalo and a donkey. He grows wheat, berseem, cotton (8 qirats), and sorghum, but only the cotton is sold. The son has been working in Saudi Arabia for three years, and comes home once a year. The head worked in the north in his youth.
14. The head is 62, and lives with his wife, two teenage sons, and one other person. The boys (17 and 15) are students. He has four grown sons working outside Musha, but they don't help him. One has been an employee in the Youth Administration in Asyut for 12 years; there are two in Suez and one in Kafr el-Shaikh. His holding is 2 owned feddans. He also has three sheep, two goats, and a donkey. He hires a tractor and gets water from three different pumps, but does not hire any workers. Farming his own land is his principal source of income.
15. The household consists of two brothers, wives, and children. The older brother (age 37) is a regular worker for the Musha Village Council. The younger one (age 33) is a farmer. Their holding is 2 rented feddans, and they have a buffalo, a cow, and a donkey. The farmer brother hires a tractor, and gets water from two pumps. He only hires workers to pick cotton, and pays them cash. He himself works for others, by the day, for instance in harvesting lentils, and prefers to be paid in cash.

16. The head is 69 years old, and has a household of 20 people. This includes himself and his wife, two married sons, two unmarried sons, 12 children and others. The father has a holding of 2.5 feddans, and one of the sons has a holding of 1 feddan. They have two buffalo. The two single sons work for the government, one in Asyut and the other in Cairo. The two married sons work with the father in the family grain dealing business, which is the chief source of income. The family is much more prosperous than the land holding would imply because of the grain trade.
17. The head is 40 years old, and the household includes his wife and three children. The holding of 3.5 feddans is partly owned and partly rented from his brother who has been in Alexandria for 20 years. There are two buffalo, a cow, and a donkey. He grows wheat, berseem, and sorghum for home use, and beans, chickpeas, and lentils for the government and for sale to merchants. He hires workers through a village labor contractor (here *rais* rather than *muqawil anfar*) for the cotton harvest, and pays after collecting on the harvest. He hires other workers from time to time. He hires a tractor, and gets water from two different pumps because of the location of his land.
18. The household consists of two brothers, aged 45 and 50, and their families. One son of 25 has no stated occupation and may not be present. Two sons of 15 are students. Each brother has a holding of two owned feddans, for a total of four. They have two buffalo, a donkey and two camels. Their principal income is from farming and from transporting with camels. They grow wheat, berseem, sorghum, and beans for home use. Lentils and cotton are sold to the government and to Musha merchants. They hire a tractor and pay for pumping, but engage no workers for their land.
19. The household consists of the head, aged 60, three single sons, and others. The two younger sons (15 and 17) are still in school. The older son (30) is a farmer. The head is "retired"; we interrupted him as he was leading a study group on the Koran in a nearby mosque. The holding is 11.5 feddans, all owned. The only animal is one donkey. They grow wheat and berseem for home use. The beans, lentils, cotton, and grapes are sold. They also grow vegetables. They rent tractor and pumping, and hire workers through a village labor contractor for the cotton harvest.
20. The household consists of the head, aged 73, three married and two single sons plus various offspring and others. The total is 22 people. The holding is 18 feddans (5 owned and 13 rented from one man); they also have one buffalo, four cows, and three donkeys. He owns a share in a pump, but also gets water from two others. He hires a tractor. They have one regular worker. Of the five sons, three are

> government employees (including one working as a teacher in Libya), and two sons and a grandson are still in school. So the family labor power is directed away from agriculture. The wife of the eldest son also works for the government, as a secretary in one of Musha's schools.

Several generalizations can be made from these case studies. Poverty is not simply a matter of land, since some of the landless cases are fairly prosperous while the small holders are hardly better off than the landless. There is usually more to say, however, about the content and structure of a household economy once there is a bit of land. That generally allows for some animals or poultry, and a wider range of activities. For the landless, no matter what kind of a job it is, it is just a job, and afterwards there is relatively little to say. The importance of income in the form of wages for all households is evident. Larger households, with several adult males, have a great deal more flexibility to organize themselves and spread their labor over several possible sources of income.

Household and Labor Process

The household thus appears as the basic unit for the analysis of the labor process in Egyptian villages. Inside the household there is an important and somewhat traditional division of labor, based on the distinction between male and female tasks and on age differences. In this sense, the household is a structure outside capitalism. Outside the household, its members must individually or collectively deal with the labor market, with marketing of commodities and the purchase of consumer goods, and with the implications of government policies on hiring and the introduction of machinery as possible sources of change in the organization of labor in the community.

In this complex natural and social environment, the household represents a coalition of different individuals who can combine fruitfully to take care of the basic tasks, particularly the ones that must be done simultaneously. Yet the evidence shows that the larger households, with more male labor, also diversify into a range of different activities—migration, wage labor, labor on one's own farm, education, enterpreneurial activities, and so on. Farm households with land are in a sense petty commodity producing households, though for certain tasks they employ labor whose product is not a commodity. The laborers are more like the "detail worker" in industry in that they accomplish only one of the series of steps necessary for the final product. The household may perform relatively few of the tasks itself. The role of the household, and particularly of the household head, is essentially a managerial task. He must decide when to seek wage labor, and when to rely on household labor: generally he will rely on family labor when the task is important and supervision of unmotivated hired labor is difficult. Thus the nature of the household has shifted away from a subsistence household (if it was ever there) and towards the basic cog in the system of labor control characteristic of the labor process in contemporary Egyptian agriculture.

Notes

1. This is a term famous in the sociological literature of the Arab world with a somewhat different meaning—"authenticity" or group feeling—derived from Ibn Khaldun. Note that Abou-Zeid (1965) uses the term *badana* to refer to the lineages or feuding groups in the village of Beni Smei', about 10 kilometers south of Musha.

2. The sharp rise in the number of cattle and buffalo once the holding size reaches three feddans may also indicate a situation where the better endowed households are able to continue farming and to explore non-agricultural sources of income, while the less well endowed ones are sometimes forced to choose between these alternatives. One option would be to drop animal husbandry.

3. The local office of the Ministry of Social Affairs estimated they handled 200 cases of the elderly, 70 cases of women living alone without support, 60 cases of ill and physically handicapped people, 60 cases of women living with their dependent children, and 70 cases of refugees from the War of Attrition in Suez (there had once been 500 of these cases in the village). For some general considerations on the role of social security in Egypt, see Tadros (1984).

6

Women and the Household

The household is taking on a new role as the commoditization of the rural economy develops. It is becoming a part of the new quasi-capitalist form of political economy in the village. This process affects the female members of the household as well. As a continuation of the analysis of the household, this chapter looks at women's work in Musha and suggests how that work fits into the overall structure of the organization of work.

Women play a central role in the labor process in rural Egypt, in Musha as elsewhere. Women's activities in an Upper Egyptian village like Musha resemble the general Egyptian picture in some ways, but not in all ways. In contrast to the Delta, women are almost never seen working in the fields, and they are less visibly independent economically. They do not claim to own animals in their own right for instance, and they are seldom active in marketing. Nevertheless, they are still largely responsible for animal care, and derive some income from that. And of course they manage the household itself, thus providing a base for the economic activities of this generation and a nursery for the labor force of the next generation. The changing household, and the changing role of women in the household, suggest the changes in the rural political economy.

The Women's Household Sample

A sample of women from 47 households, with some additional information on four others, was interviewed during the field work (see chapter 1). The information from this sample is the basis for the present chapter. The sample included 388 people, and the average household size was 7.6 persons. Of these households, 32 included one married couple only and another six included none. There were eight households with two married couples, four with three, and one with four, for a total of 13 multiple couple households. Overall, there was an average of 1.25 married couples per household.

A survey of the married women in 47 households produced a total of 76 such women, an average of 1.62 per household (the difference with the preceding figure is accounted for by widows and divorcees). Of these 76 women, 26 were the only married woman in the household (34 percent of the women in 55 percent of the households). The remaining 50 women were in households containing two, three or four married women. If adult but single daughters were added, the proportion of women living in households containing two or more adult women would be even higher.

Of the households on which we have some information (N = 48), 23 or just under half were keeping a buffalo or a cow. The maximum number of such animals in our sample was five, and the average for the households that kept them was 1.9 animals. Another 14 households have other animals (sheep, goats, donkeys, camels). Altogether 37 households have poultry or rabbits. Since these categories do not coincide, only four households have neither animals nor fowl: in two cases the data are incomplete, and in a third the household is centered on a very elderly couple that gets its food from a son's house. So there are virtually no households without some form of animal life.

There are data on landholdings from 46 households. Of these 24 said they were without land. The other 22 households work various amounts to a maximum of 16 feddans. Five of the 22 farm five or more feddans (23 percent), a higher proportion than in the overall population of landholders (ca. 15 percent). Using this rough measure of wealth, the sample is slightly skewed towards the upper end.

Household sources of income, as reported by the women, included 24 of 49 that relied in whole or in part on income from the land. Half of these mentioned another source of income to supplement the land. In five cases, the income from the land was accompanied by income from a salaried job, in three cases by wage labor, in two cases from trade, and in two cases from working as a pump guard. Another 16 (33 percent) relied on day labor alone, while three relied on a salaried government job alone, and one combined the two. The remaining cases included three whose income came from trade, three from pensions, one from services (milking cows for pay), and one from a butcher shop. It is to be noted that those deriving their income from day labor are a much higher percentage here, where the women were answering, than in the earlier figures, where the men were answering, despite the probable absence of the very poor from the sample. The 28 households whose income was entirely from either day labor, the land, or a combination of the two, were 57 percent of the households.

We asked the women to identify their father's occupation. Of the 47 who responded, 27 (57 percent; the same figure as the husbands) reported that their father was a *fallah,* "farmer." Since this term can mean anything from a day laborer to a large landowner, it is not useful as an index of wealth, but the overall figure is of interest because it suggests a relatively low commitment to land even in the previous generation. The other twenty included four workers in Alexandria, three traders, two day laborers (much lower than the number of husbands in this category) and one each: *shaykh 'alim,* driver, Muslim preacher, schoolteacher, butcher, mason, carter, farmer and tailor, camel driver, farmer and clothes merchant, and grocer.

A number of wornen reported absent male relatives. Altogether 22 of 51 (43 percent) households reported a total of 34 absent male relatives. The most common destination of the absentees was Suez (9 mentions), with five in Asyut, and three each in Cairo, Alexandria, "Bahri" ("downstream"), and elsewhere in the Sa'id. Four were in Saudi Arabia, including three sons and a household head.

Women's Work

Women's work in Musha is overwhelmingly a question of work done at home. Only women who are government employees (teachers and clerks, for instance) work outside the home. Adult women never work in the fields, although girls do until the age of about 12 or 13. Men say that it is *'ayb* (shameful) for women to work in the fields in Musha, though they are aware that they do so in other villages. On the other hand, at the peak of the labor shortage during the cotton harvest, I did hear one respected man suggest that women should be recruited to work in the fields. There is no evidence that women aspire to this, and indeed, many find the idea that they might work in the fields ludicrous. About the only reason for a woman to go to the fields is for animal care (collecting weeds for animal fodder). Two women said they had been to the fields in the previous year for the animals (one of them specified that she was originally from the Delta where habits are different). Another pair implied that they might go if they did have animals. The near unanimity of women on this question is supported by observation—I virtually never saw an adult women in or near the fields.

On the other hand 58 percent of the sample said that they used to go to the fields when they were young, but stopped by the age of twelve or thirteen. The activities they went for included cotton pest control, taking animals to the fields, accompanying a father or taking him his lunch, and picking beans. Picking cotton is notably absent—at present this activity also employs young girls. Interestingly enough, the number of women who reported that the daughters in their household went to the fields for agricultural work is much less, 18 percent, and the activities mentioned are cotton pest control and cotton picking. And yet substantial numbers of early adolescent girls do perform some field tasks, in the cotton cycle and also as gleaners, weeders for lentils and chickpeas, and gatherers of weeds for animal fodder. On the whole, apart from cotton pest control and picking, the larger gangs of girls observable in the fields are recruited from other villages.

Women's work in the home includes such activities as cooking and preparing meals, looking after children, washing clothes, cleaning up after meals, cleaning the house, filling water containers either from faucets when the water is running or from water carriers if the house is not part of the village water supply system, heating water for washing and bathing, and so on. All of these activities can be tedious when the water supply is irregular, the dust is blowing, the winter is cold, or the house is crowded. A household without a woman capable of working at these tasks steadily throughout the day is in poor shape. On the other hand, in a household without children or animals a woman may not be fully occupied. Women say they work harder in the winter because the day is shorter. There are differences in the technological tool kit available to the women. A stove was reported by 51 percent of the households; the others use a brazier or open fire. Seven households (14 percent) reported a washing machine, and one of these seven had a refrigerator (see Table 3.2). Interestingly, three of the women in our sample when reporting on their previous day's activities mentioned minor repairs to their house—repairing cracks in the wall or building a chicken coop.

Women generally say that they do not work together with women from other households. Some of them cite a fear that others may conclude they are among those who work for pay in other people's homes. To be known to work for others would cause a loss of status. Thus 60 percent of the women we interviewed (N = 42) said that they did not share their work with neighbors. Another 10 percent said that they only helped family members (where the question of working for pay would not arise). Those who talked about working together with neighbors and friends all singled out baking as the activity that brought them together (29 percent). Baking is one of the most common activities for women in the village: 84 percent of the women mentioned baking on the time sheets we constructed for them. It is therefore also true that most women who bake did not report that they worked together with women from other households. Perhaps baking bread survives as a collective activity because women from several households may find it practical to share the use of the heated oven.

Other domestic activities that are frequently mentioned include washing clothes and preparing meals. In the last generation, Musha families have made use of the mechanical grinding mills to grind their wheat or maize into flour for use in cooking. These mills are run with the same kind of motors that are used to pump water for irrigation: indeed, the motors can be hooked up both to the grindstones and to the irrigation pumps. There were two such mills in the village and a third that had gone out of use. Each mill included from 4 to 8 grindstones—literally stones with grooves chiseled in them to make them more effective—powered by these large motors. Half of the women (49 percent) we interviewed said they made exclusive use of these mills, while most of the remainder said that they still used the hand-powered grindstone only for certain special jobs, such as grinding beans or lentils. Those who said they bought all their flour from the store were 6 percent (3 cases), and another case combined store purchases with the use of the hand-powered grindstone. However, the household's grain must be transported to the mill. This is predominantly a male activity. Only one woman specifically mentioned that she sent her daughter to the mill, and another three said they sent either a son or a daughter. The majority sent husbands, sons, various miscellaneous male relatives and even (in two cases) hired laborers to the mill. The comments of the women we interviewed suggest, however, that a number of stages in the preparation of grain into flour and then into bread continue to be essentially women's work and carried out in the home. Such tasks would include sifting, washing, drying the grain before milling, and sifting the flour again before it is prepared into dough for baking (see Rizqallah and Rizqallah 1978).

In households that keep animals, much of women's time is spent in animal care. In our sample, just under half (23 of 48, or 48 percent) of the households kept either cows or buffaloes, and another fourteen had smaller animals such as sheep and goats. Altogether 37 households of the 51 in the sample kept poultry or rabbits, and only three (including two for which the data were incomplete) had no animals of any kind. As in the wider surveys that we conducted, there was a correlation between household size, landholding size and the number of animals in the household. Women are traditionally responsible for all the work of animal care that takes place in the house. This includes feeding and providing water, milking, and cleaning out the stables from time to time. Women are responsible for transforming the products of the animals. The milk is first boiled and then separated using either a goat skin hung from the ceiling and rocked, or a simple hand-powered machine. The butterfat is boiled again and turns into ghee, while the remaining milk is transformed into white cheese. Altogether 45 percent of women reported that they milked cows from time to time, although smaller percentages mentioned churning and cheese-making as activities (27 percent and 20 percent respectively). They also treat (dry) the dung so that it can be used as fuel (reported by at least 20 percent of the households), while the stable litter will eventually be transported to the field to be applied as manure. Even more than animal care, the raising of poultry and rabbits is a woman's domain. Men generally profess ignorance of the number of such animals in their houses. Spending time raising poultry was also mentioned by 45 percent of the women we interviewed.[1]

Small amounts of milk and cheese are frequently sold to neighbors, and eggs are sold either to neighbors or are collected by dealers for resale in Asyut. In our sample those who reported some income from milk and dairy products were 14 cases or 27 percent (61 percent of those with a cow or buffalo in the house), while those stating that they received some income from the sale of eggs were 12 cases or 24 percent. In both cases, a finer analysis would distinguish between those who sold surpluses occasionally and those who managed regular sales.[2]

We also asked the women if they had any plans for income generating activities. The majority said they had none or gave no answer. Those mentioning some kind of a project were 13/45 or 29 percent. The most common scheme involved developing a business selling eggs or dairy products—7 of the 13 answers. Another four mentioned sewing for money, and the other two answers included one woman who said she would rely on her hand skills without further elaboration and a woman whose scheme involved applying for a government pension. Altogether 15 women, one-third of those who answered, mentioned sewing or embroidery as a skill that they might put to use to earn extra money; far fewer of them actually do it. Four women in our sample reported owning a sewing machine. One woman said she was able to sew on a machine but her husband would not buy her the machine so she could do nothing. Most women in and out of the sample rationalized the purchase of a sewing machine by a combination of the money they would save by sewing for their families and the money they might earn sewing for others. A few women in the village even sewed next to an open doorway as a form of advertising their skills and availability. Actual income generating activities among our sample were fewer in number than schemes, perhaps because women understood the question to refer to an actual job or a full-time activity. The activities mentioned included making cheese, selling poultry, bartering, helping to make bricks, selling vegetables, and a government job.

Women and Food Consumption

Being charged with managing the household, women are also important as consumers, food being the major example. Some foodstuffs consumed in the household are produced by the men working in the fields, and transformed by the women, but an increasing portion are bought, even for full-time farming families. Table 6.1 gives an overview of the diet. For each of the three separate meals, the table includes the top five items mentioned in February and June, with the number of mentions. For the overall figures, the top ten items are included. Products which could be produced in the household include the dairy products (milk and cheese), eggs, and such local grains as wheat and sorghum (in the form of bread), and beans. The *mulukhiya* may also be home grown, but the cucumbers, tomatoes and other vegetables come from neighboring villages or from the Asyut market.

TABLE 6.1 Principal Menu Items

Meal	February		June	
Morning	Tea	(31)	Bread	(29)
	Bread	(20)	Tea	(28)
	Cheese	(16)	Milk	(26)
	Milk	(15)	Cheese	(7)
	Toast	(15)	Beans	(7)
Midday	Cheese	(27)	Cheese	(33)
	Bread	(23)	Bread	(21)
	Tea	(14)	Tomatoes	(14)
	Tomatoes	(9)	Cucumbers	(8)
	Mulukhiya	(8)	Rice	(7)
			Mulukhiya	(7)
Evening	Bread	(25)	Bread	(18)
	Tea	(13)	Beans	(15)
	Cheese	(10)	Meat	(11)
	Mulukhiya	(9)	Cheese	(9)
	Rice	(7)	Mulukhiya	(9)
Overall	Bread	(68)	Bread	(68)
	Tea	(58)	Cheese	(49)
	Cheese	(53)	Tea	(31)
	Mulukhiya	(21)	Milk	(30)
	Beans	(21)	Beans	(23)
	Milk	(19)	Tomatoes	(22)
	Toast	(17)	Meat	(17)
	Tomatoes	(17)	Mulukhiya	(17)
	Rice	(15)	Rice	(14)
	Pickles	(11)	Eggs	(10)

Source: Women's Sample, Musha, 1981.

The information in this table should be compared with the data in the next paragraph on purchase of foods.

In February 1981 we asked women what food they had bought in the previous three days. For 43 households on which we had information there were a total of 220 answers, an average of over 5 items per household. Three additional households bought nothing at all. The most common items (and the number of times mentioned) were tomatoes (35 times), potatoes (23), onions (22), meat (22), fish (16), and oranges (16). Other items included beans (8), cabbage (7), lentils, rice, and cheese (6 times each), radish and *mulukhiya* (5), sugar cane, tea, macaroni, and cauliflower (4), eggs and sugar (3), gas, salted fish, and tangerines (2), and garlic, pickles, oil, soap, candy, sweets, dates, honey, salt, ghee, cumin, chicken, turnips, and okra (once each). Several women mentioned that certain items are bought once a year and stored. They may include *mulukhiya,* lentils, onions, garlic, okra, and green beans. This list of purchases should be compared with the diet table. By comparing the information here with that table it is apparent that bread, while a major item in the diet, is never (or rarely) purchased; hence the importance of home baking.

Generally speaking, although the women manage the household, they do not make the purchases themselves. Each neighborhood has its network of small grocery stores, and the women send their menfolk or their children to make the necessary purchases. About 74 percent of the women said that men or boys made the purchases from the grocer. Fresh fruits and vegetables are sold either from small stands scattered throughout the village, or more frequently by ambulant peddlers. Women are more likely to purchase directly from the peddlers, or perhaps to send their children out into the street. Tomatoes are overwhelmingly purchased from the itinerant peddlers (43 percent), or from a greengrocer (32 percent). Two women reported that they bought tomatoes from a woman vendor. Cooking fuel (kerosene for the primus stove) was overwhelmingly purchased from the grocery store (88 percent); two women reported buying dung cakes (*wagid*) from their neighbors.

Most women (70 percent) reported that they paid cash for all their purchases. Some of them say that credit is only for the civil servants who are paid regularly at the end of the month. Those who buy on credit say they wait from one day to six months to pay, but often attempt to pay at a monthly rate. Yet all grocers keep records of those who buy on credit from them, often on pads of paper hanging from the door frame.

At the time of field work there was concern over high meat prices and over a shortage of government-supplied washing soap at subsidized prices. We attempted to get some idea of how women coped with these problems. Most of the women (70 percent) reported that they continued to buy the same (modest) amount of meat regardless of the increase in prices; the other 30 percent said they either bought less meat or they substituted something else for the meat. Here are some sample answers: (1) "We ate fish for a while but came back to eating meat"; (2) "Instead of buying 3/4 kilo a week, we bought half a kilo a week, but from the same butcher because each butcher has his clients"; (3) "We buy meat once a week, and also buy fish"; (4) "We continue to buy half a kilo a week"; (5) "We continue to buy a kilo every Sunday and a kilo and a half every Thursday"; (6) "If we can find poultry, we buy meat once a week, otherwise twice"; and (7) "We buy meat at least once a week, fish twice a month, and sometimes eat pigeons." In general, people prefer to buy some meat if they can afford it at all, but frequently mix it with fish or poultry, including pigeons. Most of the women we interviewed were also prepared to pay somewhat higher prices for soap to ensure a supply. About half the women interviewed implied they were prepared to buy soap on the open market or even on the black market and thus to pay a higher price for it. Many also mentioned buying the soap from the urban market, where presumably it was available also for a higher price. Only four women said they would substitute local soap for the commercial variety from the store.

Women's Leisure

Women also devote a certain amount of time to recreation in the home. The most common forms mentioned are visits and listening to the radio or watching television. Of the 50 women who gave us information on this topic, eleven mentioned watching television in the 24 hours prior to our interviews, three mentioned the radio, and one mentioned listening to a tape recorder (people sometimes listen to recordings of religious music). Perhaps if we had specifically asked the question the numbers would have been higher. Some women mentioned visiting in the evening with other women, and others mentioned the more formal visiting that accompanies a wedding, a circumcision or a funeral. Recreation outside the home is rarer. Women may attend *dhikr* ceremonies in others' houses, particularly if the families are related, or they may get some recreational value from travelling to Asyut or other cities. If so, this is not mentioned since each visit must have a serious purpose; recreation as a concept does not exist. On balance, then, it is hard to overestimate the important change that television has brought into the lives of village women. The urban stereotype is that it has encouraged women to stay up later at night and so perhaps to rise later in the morning or to take a nap in the afternoon (this is sometimes a subject for complaint by the men).

Women's movements are somewhat more circumscribed than men's. Although the city of Asyut is only 15 kilometers away by road, most women do not go there often. Table 6.2 gives the breakdown for the most distant destinations and the reasons for the trip for 45 women (two others reported no travel at all). It is evident that visits to a doctor are the most common reason cited, followed by family visits (i.e., visits to children or other relatives now living in the cities). The doctor's visits are more likely to be on account of their children than of themselves. Women travel to Asyut to take sons and daughters to visit private doctors and to the city hospitals; they occasionally go themselves. Distant travel for medical reasons used to be more common, but now there are several private doctors available in Musha as well as the government clinic. The attitudes toward medicine in this group of women range from the frequent users to those who say that they do not believe in medicine; children will recover on their own.

TABLE 6.2 Women's Travel

Most Distant Destination	Reason Health	Family	Religion	Shopping	Not Given	Total
Asyut	20	1	--	2	2	25
Alexandria	1	2	--	--	4	7
Cairo	--	2	1	--	2	5
Suez	1	3	--	--	1	5
Tanta	--	--	2	--	--	2
Kafr al-Shaykh	--	1	--	--	--	1
Total	22	9	3	2	9	45

Source: Women's Sample, Musha, 1980-81 (N=45).

Finally, another indication of the activities of women in Musha is their involvement in religious life, specifically in the form of popular Islam known as the *dhikr*. The *dhikr* is a commemorative ceremony of one of the religious Sufi brotherhoods (see chapter 10). In Musha the leaders of the brotherhoods may organize such ceremonies for the internal purposes of the organization—to commemorate the birthday of the Prophet, for instance—but ordinary people often invite one of the brotherhoods to perform a *dhikr* to help celebrate a marriage, a circumcision, or simply because they have vowed to do this once a year. The principal public actors in these ceremonies are men, but the women are also concerned. Their belief in the usefulness of the ceremony may lead them to see it as a strategy to ensure family well-being and so inspire the invitation to the brotherhood in the first place, they prepare the food that always follows the ceremony, and they observe the session from the rooftops. We asked our sample of women if they attended *dhikr* ceremonies in the houses of other people. Of the 44 Muslims in the sample, 21 said they did, usually specifying that they go only if the ceremony is held in the house of a relative. This supports the notion that there is a link between the *dhikr* and the maintenance of family well-being. A few women reported that their husbands opposed their attendance. One woman said her husband argued that now that the ceremonies are all broadcast over loudspeakers, she could stay home and be spared the gossip of other women.

A number of women reported that they prayed at home, often citing that they had learned how to do so from their father or husband. Although we did not ask our group whether they participated, there is a custom in Musha that women visit some of the shrines of the local saints on Friday eve (Thursday night), seeking various favors. They do not, however, make a habit of visting the Musha cemetery, which is 5 kilometers away at the foot of the western escarpment. Like the men, the women are well aware of the major regional shrines of Egypt. One of these is about 30 kilometers away in Abutig. Others are located in Cairo, Tanta and Alexandria, and women are among the pilgrims to these shrines. It is noteworthy in this respect that for two of the women, a pilgrimage to the shrine of Shaikh Ahmed Badawi in Tanta (see Reeves 1981) was the most distant trip.

Education and Marriage

Education is becoming increasingly important for girls and women. Apparently Musha girls did not begin to attend secondary school (i.e., outside Musha) until the early 1960s. Currently about one-third of the primary school pupils are girls. I have no figures, but one would expect the ratio to be lower in the higher grades. Yet there are many Musha young women attending secondary school or university in Asyut and beyond. When they finish there are some jobs in Musha—primary school teacher, secretary in the school system or in the administration, working at the health clinic or in the local office of the Ministry of Social Affairs as a secretary or social worker. Some of these young women may also work outside the village, either in Asyut or elsewhere. One primary school teacher from Musha migrated to Saudi Arabia with her husband to teach school.

We recorded birthplaces for 46 women. Of these 40 were born in Musha, five others in various cities and only one in another village (relatively distant in Sohag governorate rather than a nearby village). These figures suggest the extent to which Musha village remains endogamous, for even some of the cases in which the woman was born outside the village really involve Musha families that have settled in these places. The endogamy also extends to the family. By asking each women in our 51 households, we were able to collect certain demographic information from 76 women. Of these, 62 reported whether their present husbands were relatives: 66 percent reported being married to a relative. In fifteen cases, the type of relative was unspecified. Of the remaining 26 cases, 22 (85 percent) women were married to a patrilateral relative, and ten of these were married to a father's brother's son, the archetypical patrilateral parallel cousin marriage. Thus marriage continues to take place largely within a community and family framework. The values involved in this pattern are reflected in the attitudes concerning the choice of a husband for a daughter. Of the respondents, 57 percent (26 cases) thought that the girl's father or other male relatives should make that decision, while at the other extreme only two thought that the girl herself should decide whom to marry. Another 18 cases (39 percent) suggested in effect that all family members, father, mother, and daughter, should participate in this decision. These answers should be considered to reflect values formally expressed rather than a description of what actually happens.

On the one hand, a girl probably has more involvement in the decision than these answers imply, but on the other hand she has to respect the rules of endogamy and inter-family relations.

Implications of the Sexual Division of Labor

This review of women's activities in Musha shows the extent to which they are responsible for the management of the household. Adult women essentially work only at home. Girls up to early adolescence may work in the fields if the household needs the income earned in this way, or they may glean or collect weeds, again a sign of the relative poverty of the household. Women are involved with such time-consuming activites as baking, washing clothes, child care, seeking medical care for themselves and their children, and looking after animals and poultry. Raising poultry and looking after dairy animals may also yield income, which is generally considered to be the woman's private and personal income. It is not much, but it gives her some leeway. Women's activities in the household complement those of the men in the fields, in the marketplace and dealing with the government. The sexual division of labor in Musha is mostly apparent in the household. This is where the activities of the two sexes are balanced off against one another, and a synthesis is reached. The division of labor in the community is built on this other division of labor, localized within the household.

Throughout this presentation I have stressed the fact that women normally work and live in the house. In other words, there is some degree of "seclusion" of women. What conclusions can we draw from this for the general pattern of social organization in Musha? The emphasis on the seclusion of women creates a standard by which households—and particularly their male heads—can be evaluated. The use (among men) of the concept of "shame" (*'ayb*) conveys the moral dimension of this pattern. A relatively high status household is able to maintain the pattern better than a relatively low status one. Obviously one reason for this is that the higher status household is likely to control more resources. Thus to some extent this is a pattern imposed on the poor by the rich. The outcome of this imposition is to focus attention on the internal organization of the hierarchically organized household rather than (say) on forms of social organization that would be based on similarity of position. Men are expected to be in control of their households; richer households can achieve this better, or at least hide the failure better. If poorer families thus acquire lower moral status, this is reflected in the lower wages and income they receive. Moreover, by making the cash income dependent on male and child labor alone, more pressure is put on the wage earner to cooperate.

At the same time, it is obvious that women's productive activities in the house, or reaching down the street, are an important part of the survival strategies of the poor and very poor. In that sense, the division of labor between the sexes, which is assumed without question as a part of Musha's cultural pattern, serves to create a unit with a differentiated set of activities and resources, and thus ensures the reproduction of the household. In other words, the sexual division of labor within the household can be generated from the overall socio-economic level of the village and its potentialities for productive activity. Under conditions of subsistence agriculture, the sexual division of labor in the household was a viable adaptive strategy. For some households this is also true under conditions of commoditization. The question is to what extent the burden on households to sustain a culturally valued practice contributes to the perpetuation of a certain overall pattern of differentiation of households along status or class lines. To pursue this question means looking at the social organization of agricultural work in Musha.

Notes

1. For more detail on the role of women in raising poultry in village Egypt, see the work of Barbara Larson (1980).

2. In her study of a village in Minufiya, Zimmermann (1982b:13) estimated that a woman might earn LE16 a month (in 1979) from selling butter and cheese, and says that "the dairy products are responsible for about a third of the total cash income of an average farm with 1.3 feddan and one or two cows or buffaloes."

7

Mechanization and the Labor Process

Mechanization in contemporary Egyptian agriculture, involving the use of the internal combustion engine to run tractors, pumps, and some other machines, plays an important part in the agricultural labor process (Saab 1960; ERA 2000:1979; Bremer 1982; Richards 1982). Indeed, the desire to understand the role and place of mechanization in Egyptian agriculture was the initial impulse behind the research which I report on here. Mechanization is prominent in rural Egypt, and makes the situation not at all like the classic Mediterranean peasant situation based on human labor and animal power. At the same time, there remain many unmechanized tasks which require the organization of human labor, and the machines themselves of course require people to make them work.

In this chapter I undertake an analysis of the role of mechanization in the social organization of agriculture. Mechanization plays a role in two major areas, water lifting for irrigation on the one hand and tractors for a variety of field tasks on the other. One general conclusion that emerges is that of the significant increase in the level of capitalization involved in Egyptian agriculture. Although it is important to look at patterns of ownership of these capital goods, it is equally relevant to survey the way in which pumps and tractors fit into the labor process. How do they affect the way in which farmers organize their labor? What new roles in the social division of labor have appeared? What patterns of social differentiation have emerged as a result of the machinery? What have been the processes of diffusion and adoption of these new machines, and how can one account for the choices that have been made?

The introduction of mechanization reinforces the power and position of the larger farmers, and that the choice of technology reflects the perceived interests of these farmers. Although in a strict economic sense mechanization benefits all farmers, it benefits them in different ways. Moreover, it tends to fractionate the labor process in agriculture, so that there is no longer an equation between a farmer or a household and the work that is done on that farmer's land. Increased mechanization tends to lead to increased hiring of labor, and to a radically different labor process in agriculture. Some of these concerns will be treated in the next chapter. Here we are concerned with the presence of machinery and the social organization surrounding it.

The Social Organization of Water Lifting in Musha

In 1889 the French irrigation engineer Barois noted (1889:100) that "on the one hand the Government assumes all authority over irrigation, and on the other the individuals are subjected for the use of the water to no special regulations." This paradox is still true a century later. The state pretends to regulate everything and in fact regulates nothing. The Irrigation Service does not interfere with the way water is used in the village; and the Ministry of Agriculture is concerned with assigned acreages and yields, not with the engineering of water application. Thus this activity largely escapes government supervision and is left to the people to organize. This section describes the local social organization of water distribution in Musha. Five roles are important in this social analysis: pump owner, mechanic, guard, farmer, and the farmer's labor. Sometimes the owner of the pump delegates some authority to a clerk. These roles may each be filled by different people, or one person may occupy more than one of them.

Technical

The historical development of the Musha irrigation system can be summarized in a series of stages.[1] (1) flood only; (2) flood supplemented by wells outfitted with *saqiya*s or Persian water wheels; (3) flood supplemented by wells outfitted with steam-powered pumps; (4) flood supplemented by wells outfitted with diesel pumps; (5) canals utilizing diesel pumping engines for water lifting; (6) a few diesel engines are now being replaced by electric motors. The electric motors are more costly to install and subject to an unreliable current but easier and cheaper to operate.

The Irrigation Service supplies distributory canals with water on a regular basis, with a break in January to allow for cleaning the canals. The distributory canals have no water flowing through them but instead are long pools, filled from one end. The Irrigation Service maintains the water level for a week, and then closes the water off for a week. Usually enough water remains in the canals to irrigate for another couple of days. Musha's land is served by two distributories, one of which is "off" when the other is "on," so that there is always irrigation water in some part of the village's land. Water from the canals is "free" (in theory it is covered by the land tax), and riparians can take as much as they wish. However, they must raise it to the level of the fields. This requirement generates a considerable technology and social organization.

Water lifting in Musha is currently carried out by 70 pumps scattered around the fields. The first such pumps were installed in the early 1930s, and were instrumental in allowing doublecropping in Musha. The pumps were initially installed to draw water from about eight or nine meters below the surface. Each well fed a network of field ditches, and provided irrigation water to a set area, its *zimam*. The system covered essentially all the area of the village by around 1950, but about 15 additional pumps were inserted after the 1952 revolution. After the completion of the High Dam in 1964 abolished the annual flood, and canals were dug to supply water to the fields (Abul-Ata 1977), the pumps were redirected to pumping water from the government irrigation canals into the networks of field ditches (see the maps and discussion in Bösl 1984). The whole Zinnar basin, indeed perhaps the whole former Sohagiya system, shares this water lifting technology and history (cf. Abou-Zeid 1965).

The pumps range in size from 18 to 75 horsepower, with most between 25 and 42 horsepower. Each one supplies a certain zone with irrigation water. These zones vary in size from around 25 feddans for the smallest to as much as 280 feddans for the largest, with an average size of around 70 feddans. Farmers talk about pumps in terms of how many feddans they can irrigate a day (a 12-hour period since there is no night-time irrigation). The daily range of most pumps is from 5 to 30 feddans. It seems that the area commanded by each pump is at most seven times the area that the pump can irrigate in a day.

The task of the pump is lift the water from the canal to the level of the fields. The pumps lift the water 50 to 75 centimeters when the canals are fairly full, and up to 3 meters when the pump is drawing from a nearly empty canal. However, most pumping is done from a full or nearly full canal. The raised water then enters into a network of field ditches, known in Musha as *'abbara*.[2] Each pumping station typically has three or four of these field ditches, usually radiating out in a straight line from the pump itself. The ditches are either parallel to or perpendicular to the field layout. The water is directed down one ditch at a time, although some of the field ditches split once they are away from the pump itself. The maintenance of these ditches is the responsibility of the pump owners, working through the guard.

Social and Economic

The pump sites are very visible nodes in the Musha landscape. Each one consists of a square building to shelter the motor and a semi-circular wall to protect the (old) well. Nowadays there is an underground passage for water from the canals into the well area where the pump can suck it out. Next to these functional buildings are one or several houses for the families that live at the pump in order to serve and guard it. Each of the larger farmers in the village has selected one of his pumps as a kind of field headquarters, and lavished particular attention on a garden surrounding it and added other amenities including in one case a telephone. These centers also can serve as storage areas or as the sites for threshing grounds and other work areas. If a powerful farmer establishes his headquarters at a pump, he may then also receive visitors and clients there, so that the site becomes important from the social point of view as well. This social function reinforces the economic power that comes from controlling a key link in the agricultural system—lifting water from the canals to the fields so that it is available to farmers. The importance of this link is reinforced by the local rule that a farmer is not free to switch from one pump to another—spatial layout of course places strict limits on the extent to which that is feasible, but it was expressed to me as a rule about social and economic relationships and not as one imposed by spatial necessity. This relationship of clientage is somewhat mitigated by the fact that most farmers deal with more than one pump owner/combine because they farm land in different areas.

Each pump is considered to have 24 "shares" (*qirats*), just as a feddan or any other item can have 24 parts. A few pumps have a single owner but shared ownership is the rule. Some pumps are owned by two or three of the large farmers or their heirs, and these pumps tend to be in the areas where these farmers own substantial amounts of land. Other pumps are owned by half a dozen or more people, including medium or small farmers. Again, they mostly own pump shares in areas where they farm land. The division of ownership among many parties reflects the fact that the pumps are old enough and stable enough to have been inherited. The shares can also be bought. The value of a share is said to have increased from LE30 to LE200 in recent years.

Working from a list provided me by the village expert or agent (*dallal*), we can note the following pattern of concentration of ownership. (1) The largest farmer in the village "owns" eleven pumps in Musha, some eight or nine of them outright and the others by being the dominant shareholder. He is a minority shareholder in yet others. (2) The second largest farmer "owns" eight pumps, but one member of the set of brothers involved here told me that they "own" 20 pumps, presumably referring to all the pumps in which they have shares. (3) Another large farmer is listed here as "owning" six pumps; he himself claims five and a half. (4) Four other farmers are listed as "owning" two pumps and one as "owning" three.

At the other extreme, Table 7.1 gives two examples of pumps with divided ownership. In the first case we have nine co-owners, and in the

TABLE 7.1 Shares in Pump Ownership

Name	Number of Shares
A. Fawzi	6
Hilmi	4
Ahmed Mahmud	1 1/2
Demian Sem'an	3 1/2
Hanna	2
Shawqi Yusuf	3 1/2
Labib Yess	2
Haris	1
Ghali Abdelmessih	1/2
Total	24
B. Abdelmon'im	12
Zaghlul	4
Wahib	3
Ishaq	4
Nazir	1
Total	24

Source: Field Notes.

second case five. In both cases some of the co-owners are linked by kinship or marriage with each other. In the first case, Fawzi, Hilmi and Haris are brothers and are linked by marriage at least with Demian Sem'an. Fawzi and his brothers have been building up their shares in recent years: they started with only two. In this case a majority of the shares are owned by a cluster of related Christians. The one Muslim share-owner succeeded the father of Demian as village agent so there is a functional link. In the second case, Wahib, Ishaq and Nazir are all cousins: again, as it happens a cluster of related Christians. In each case a dominant owner keeps track of the records and manages the pump. In the first case cited, it is Fawzi and his brother Hilmi who are the principal owners, living at the pump site, and in the second case it is Abdelmon'im (or more accurately his chief clerk) who manages the pump.

Two other roles are important for the pumps. The first of these is the *usta,* the mechanic who is responsible for keeping the motor running. The second is the *ghafir,* the guard who is responsible for allocating the water among the users and in general for keeping an eye on the land served by his pump. The guard in particular is likely to live at the pump site itself. In some cases, the guard doubles as the mechanic, or the brother of the guard is the mechanic, and then both mechanic and guard will reside at the pump site. Another important role is filled by the few mechanics in the village who specialize in repairing and maintaining the pumps, but they are not linked to any one pump.

The mechanic is paid a small salary by the owners of the pump (I once heard LE100 annually), and probably also receives tips to supplement his salary. On the other hand, it is not a full-time job by itself. The guard is paid a fee, cited to me as LE4 per year per feddan, for his services. This represents an average amount of LE280 per year from the landowners in his pump area. Of course the pump owners will be among those to pay this fee if they also own land in the pump area. The role of the guard as the link between the water supply and the farmers places him in a key position in the labor process. The guards are in constant contact with the farmers and know the state of their crops. But in particular their local knowledge and contacts have enabled many of them to make fruitful use of a tractor. Many guards own part or all of a tractor, in some cases as junior partner to a large landowner, in other cases in partnership with similarly situated men.

The guard knows the theoretical capacity of the pump, in terms of feddans per day, and knows the crops in the field and their irrigation requirements, and so determines which farmers will receive water on any given day. He generally determines the cycle in advance. Once the crops for the season are known, the guard may fix a number of zones according to the pumping capacity of the machine. When the farmer wants water, he asks the pump guard when his next turn will be. In some cases, the guard may only inform the farmer the night before, which can be a problem if the farmer is counting on hiring labor.

Only when the water enters the fields from the irrigation ditches does it become the responsibility of the farmer or his labor. The layout of the field is carefully designed according to the crop. For crops like berseem or wheat, where the water need only be let onto the field, the farmer will simply construct a grid of bunds to control the depth of the water and make sure that all areas of the field receive the correct amount. For other crops, such as cotton or beans, where the base of the plant cannot be submerged, the farmer must construct a network of ridges and furrows. In this case, the water enters into the furrows (*fahl*), and follows them until the field has been fully irrigated. Generally in this case, the furrow network is designed so that the water flows directly without further guidance from the farmer. Irrigating then involves a certain amount of waiting for water to flow while keeping a general eye on the situation, and it is not surprising that many farmers try to combine this task with something else, such as weeding.

For each pump there is an agent in the village who collects the money. The price of a normal watering had been fixed at PT150 per feddan for nearly ten years (since 1972) at the time of my research (but had doubled by 1986). The first watering after a long dry spell could be charged double. The price stability was attributed to the fact that the cost of fuel was constant (and highly subsidized at PT3 per liter). The price in Musha was relatively low compared to other prices in the region. In Kardous, to the south, it was PT8 per qirat or PT192 per feddan, while in Qawata, another village east of the Nile, each field owner paid a set sum per year. The fuel itself is delivered to the pump by one of the two fuel dealers in Musha, who sends out a donkey-powered cart with a fuel tank.

One large farmer who owns five pumps keeps a separate book for each pump. The average number of farmers per pump was around 60, and the range was from 37 to 93. The variation reflects the average size of the plots and the total area served by the pump. In this case, the figures do not include the land of the pump owner himself, so another source of variation is the amount of land he himself holds. His clerk writes down the name of each farmer served by a pump together with the size of their fields, the crop and the number of waterings presumably required. Each watering is then counted at a rate of PT150, and the farmer is asked to pay that amount. In other words, the person collecting the money can calculate how much is owed by knowing the field area (largely constant) and the crop (there are a limited number of standard crops); the number of waterings is largely conventional. Thus there is no need for the operators in the field to keep good records once the crop is known.

In cases where there are multiple owners, as in the cases shown in Table 7.1, the owners also pay for the waterings they receive. Then at the end of the year, the responsible owner works out the balance sheet for the year, and divides any profit among the different owners. Thus at this time the owner of both land and pump will receive some or all of his money back, depending both on the general level of profitability and on the ratio between his land holdings in the pump watering area and his pump shares.

We can calculate the economics of running a pump as follows. The cost of the fuel and the oil represents about PT55 of the PT150 charged to the farmer. There are of course other costs, including a salary paid to the mechanic, the cost of upkeep and repairs, and the cost of maintaining the ditches. The water itself is free. Perhaps we could estimate that PT25 per watering represents profit. If the average feddan is watered twenty times a year, then the net income per feddan to the pump owners would be on the order of LE5. The average pump with 70 feddans would then return

LE350 per year, and the average 1/24 share would be worth LE15 per year. Thus the net income from owning all of a pump would be equivalent to the gross income from one feddan per year. Clearly owning a pump by itself is not enough to make one rich, and owning only a few shares is hardly worth worrying about.

Here are some problems that have arisen in the course of irrigation. (1) Two pumps were so close together that one could not pump without depriving the other of water. A mechanic went to resolve the situation (i.e., it was treated as a technical problem). (2) A large farmer has extended his field ditch network across an agricultural road used by tractors and trucks. For this the government was supposed to fine him LE600 and imprison him for six months. (3) Sometimes the water used to irrigate one crop seeps through into an adjacent field where the water can cause damage to the crop. This is particularly likely when the second crop is lentils or chickpeas that require no irrigation after they are planted. It may also happen when the crop is a new one (like green beans) whose watering requirements are unfamiliar. The solution is to construct tougher barriers between the fields, and to seek coordination between neighbors, but there are still problems. (4) Sometimes the water was not available in the canals at the time the farmer wanted it for his crop. In cases like this, the farmer may contact the Irrigation Service in Abutig or failing that in Asyut. However, only the largest farmers will really have enough weight there to get anything done and because of time lag it is not always possible to do something. (5) The present system of canal irrigation means that the water brings with it all kinds of undesirable weed seeds that were unknown or scarce when the irrigation water came only from wells or from the flood. (6) When the government built a new drain through Musha's land, it divided the western part of the *zimam* of one pump from the pump itself. The government supplied pipes to carry the field ditches across the drain, but it provided only four instead of the six pipes that were needed. The consequence is that not enough water can get across the drain and those with fields to the west are not getting as much water as they need. The solution here was to petition the government irrigation office to supply the additional two pipes. The pump owners appealed to the secretary of the cooperative for help in drafting this letter. (7) One small farmer appealed to the former Umda of the village because he felt that the owner of the pump that supplied him with irrigation water was trying to use his position to force him out of his small plot of five qirats. The Umda sent him to the police.

From this brief listing of certain problems concerned with irrigation we can see that some problems involve fellow villagers disputing with one another and presumably finding local solutions to their problems. The emotion generated by disputes over land does not appear to extend to these quarrels over water. Other problems involve the farmers in a dispute with the government, in most cases as a consequence of the changes in the irrigation system introduced after 1964 which made the government responsible for local irrigation. The drain, the problem with noxious seeds, the problem with the cut road, are all contingent upon the government's decision to construct a network of canals and drains to make use of the potential of the High Dam. If there are any problems with the supply of water in the canals, the farmers must contact the government irrigation officers in Abutig who are responsible for regulating the flow. If this is not adequate, they contact the irrigation district office in Asyut.

The Social Organization of Tractor Use in Musha

In Musha tractors are used for plowing and field preparation, for threshing, and for hauling. Several people in Musha claimed that they (or their fathers) had introduced the first tractors into the village. This appears to have taken place in the 1930s.[3] However, tractors did not become widespread until after World War II, and they probably did not become dominant in field preparation until around 1965 or 1970. This would mean that Musha lagged behind the wave of the spread of tractors into the Delta, which was well underway in the 1930s (Saab 1960). Most of the tractor owners in Musha first owned a second-hand tractor which they bought from a dealer in Egypt for cash. More recently, these old owners plus a few new ones have been buying the Eastern European tractors, mostly from Romania, that were being sold for credit by the Agricultural Credit Bank in Asyut. In June 1981 there were 48 functioning tractors in Musha, with a total of 3,100 horsepower. Thus the average size tractor is 65 horsepower. There is roughly one tractor for each 100 feddans, or one for each 200 feddans of crop area.[4]

Table 7.2 gives the breakdown of tractors by make and horsepower. The scatter of brands and national origins is typical.[5] The first wave of tractors, mostly American tractors imported before 1956, still has a few representatives in Musha, but after 25 or more years of service they are on their way out. The remaining tractors from this period are mostly around 40 horsepower. The usefulness of these tractors in Musha ended when the road was paved in 1981; with their steel spiked wheels they could no longer use or even cross the road, and were sold to villages without a paved road. The second wave of tractors consists of the Nasrs, usually running around 50 or 60 horsepower. These tractors were assembled in Egypt using some parts made in Yugoslavia, and were introduced in the 1960s. They reflect the policy in the 1960s to encourage mechanization of agriculture through newly formed cooperatives, and through a domestic industry as much as possible. The bulk of the tractors in Musha are fairly recently purchased ones, less than three or four years old, among which the Romanian Universals are

TABLE 7.2 Tractor Brands in Musha, June 1981

Brand	HP	Number
1. Universal (Romanian)	65	12
2. Universal (Romanian)	80	13
3. Belarios (USSR)	80	2
4. Massey-Ferguson (Canada/Egypt)	65	3
5. Nasr (Egypt/Yugoslavia)	50	6
6. Nasr (Egypt/Yugoslavia)	60	3
7. IMT (Yugoslavia)	55	2
8. Zetor (Czechoslovakia)	65	1
9. McCormack (US)	45	1
10. Deering (US)	40	2
11. International Harvester (US)	55	1
12. John Deere (US)	45	2
Total		

Source: Field Notes.

the most popular. The Soviet Belarius is similar to the Romanian models. These new tractors represent the third wave of tractors, essentially those imported from Eastern Europe and sold to private farmers, and with a strength of 65 to 80 horsepower.[6] Because of careful maintenance and frequent replacement by new tractors, private tractors are almost always available for work; it is government tractors that suffer "down time" from poor maintenance and delayed repair.

Not surprisingly, the largest farmers tend to own more than their share of both tractors and pumps. Thus the seven largest operations in the village, which farm about 20 percent of the land, own 27 percent of the tractors and have share in 46 percent of the pumps. One family, with one of the two largest operations in the village (about 300 feddans), owned three tractors. Nine others owned two each. Six of these nine represent families farming 50 feddans or more, while the other three are owned by individuals who have chosen to make their living by providing custom tractor services. The cooperative also owned a pair of tractors. Individuals or partnerships holding a total of 5 feddans or more own 91.2 percent of all tractors in Musha.

Several patterns of ownership exist. (1) The tractor belongs to a family owning enough land to make essentially fulltime use of it (ten or eleven cases, including the Umda). (2) The tractor belongs to a family with substantial land but the tractor is still rented out regularly (16 cases, including Khadr and Qenawi discussed below). (3) The tractor belongs to one or more people who operate it as a principal source of income since they have relatively little land, say less than 15 feddans or so (15 cases, including Mirghani and Abdeljalil discussed below).

About one case in six involves a partnership between people of different households. Many others are of course owned by what is in effect a family partnership (pairs of brothers or cousins, for instance), even though one individual may take the lead. Interestingly, many of the owners and partners are from families that have worked as *ghafir* at the irrigation pumps (eight cases). The position of *ghafir* gives them both the capital and the social position in the farmers' network that makes this possible. In several cases, the partnership is between a wealthy landowner who provided the capital for the tractor and a member of a *ghafir* family who runs it.

The equipment accompanying the tractor is fairly standard. While the tractors were generally imported (or assembled in Egypt from imported components, as in the case of the Nasr), the implements are generally manufactured in Egypt. This represents a change from the 1950s and earlier when many of the implements as well were imported (Saab 1960). Except for some of the oldest ones, all the tractors are rubber-wheeled with hydraulic lift. Plowing is done with an adjustable chisel plow (mostly manufactured in Giza), with a variable number of prongs depending on the crop. Most tractor owners, and certainly those who plan to rent out their tractor, have a drum thresher which is powered by a belt from the tractor's take-off wheel. These drum threshers are manufactured in such Delta towns as Sammanud and Mit Ghamr. The drum threshers were developed for wheat, but can also be used for sorghum and beans. The final addition to the tractor is a four-wheeled wagon. This can be used to transport fertilizer and insecticide, and to bring crops in from the field. Most are of Egyptian manufacture, and come from the same Delta towns. Many of the Musha tractor owners said they went to the Delta themselves to order their threshers and wagons, although at least two Musha men had set themselves up as dealers to import the threshers into the Asyut area.

Tractor Management

Most tractors are used by their owners on their own fields and also rented out to clients. There are a few farmers who never rent their tractors out, essentially those farming at least 100 feddans, and a few who have no land, and so rely on machine rentals for their income, but most fall in the middle range. The farmer renting the use of the tractor is responsible for supplying his own labor, and so a complicated pattern of social relationships ensues.

Working with a tractor requires a driver and a manager, who is usually the owner. There is a lot of variation as to just who fills these various roles. In some cases, the owner of the tractor manages it, and hires a relatively young man, sometimes even a teenager, to drive it. In other cases, the driver of the tractor takes on considerable management responsibility and in a sense manages the investment for the actual owners. One arrangement that is made in this case is to make the driver-manager a junior partner, with for instance a one-quarter share, thus recognizing his responsibility and his commitment. Occasionally the driver is a son or younger brother of the owner, and so receives less a salary than a share in the proceeds. There are even a few cases where the owner and manager is also the driver.

The management of the tractor is principally a matter of scheduling the use of the machine. Individual customers approach the manager of the tractor to request its rental for plowing, hauling, or threshing, and the manager must then determine how to schedule these various requests most efficiently. During the busy season in May and June, for instance, many tractors plow in the morning, haul during the middle part of the day, and run threshers in the late afternoon and on into the night. (I have heard threshers working as late as midnight.) It is generally agreed that the threshing has to be done at that time because of the requirement that the crop be absolutely as dry as possible. A humid crop may cause the thresher to jam. There may be some advantage to plowing in the early part of the day, before the sun is too hot. The manager must also take into account the location of the work. For instance, there is an advantage to plowing mostly in one area at one time so as to minimize travel time between jobs. It is also true that in certain areas adjacent fields must be plowed simultaneously. The scheduling of threshing jobs is easiest because in Musha all farmers bring their crops to the threshing grounds at the village periphery. Furthermore, each of the major tractor operators has a known personal threshing ground and so some of the smaller farmers bring their crop directly there. Small farmers generally succeed in threshing, winnowing and removing their crop within a few days, so several may follow one another in the same spot.

Managers must also keep track of payments. Most tractor managers keep a large notebook in which they make notations of the work done, the work to be done, and the amount owed. This system is not perfect. Once I was sitting with a tractor owner when a client came up and said he was prepared to pay what he owed. The tractor owner could not find the appropriate notation in his book. The customer gave him LE20 anyway, and the tractor owner made a notation of that transaction in his book. The customer kept no written record.

About one-third of the farmers (interviewed in the general survey) who gave a specific answer (13 of 41) said they sometimes delayed their payment for tractor work. The proportion may well be higher. Some tractor owners/managers complain about the incidence of credit in Musha, one describing it as "unnatural" (*ghayr tabi'i*). The general practice seems to be, however, that a customer who owes money to a tractor owner is more or less constrained to stick with that tractor the next time they need one. Thus the assertion of customers that they are free to choose whomever they want, whoever is available, each time they need a tractor is linked to the insistence that they do not delay their payment for this service. Despite the fact that debts cause customers to return, owners appear to prefer prompt payment of the money owed to them over any scheme to build up a permanent clientele. They seem to feel that there is plenty of custom work to go around, and so there is no need to compete for customers.[7]

The market in Musha is less monopolized by a few rental tractors than in some other villages,[8] but there is a degree of domination. The 53 farmers who identified the last tractor they used cited 25 different tractors. To this should be added the four who said they owned a tractor themselves and so did not rent one. However, the four most frequent tractors were mentioned from six to nine times, and they totalized 57 percent of all mentions. Very roughly, these four tractor owners correspond to the four points of the compass. Each had more than one tractor and so could be considered definitely committed to the tractor rental market. Broadly speaking, each rental tractor owner draws most of his customers from one segment of the village lands. He will do most of his plowing there, and very likely will do nearly all of his threshing for clients in and around his own threshing ground. Exceptions to this relationship occur when there are kinship (including affinal) relations or other networks that can be explained individually.

The following notes on the economics of running a tractor are estimates intended to convey an order of magnitude, as of 1981. The most important cost to the tractor owner is the purchase price of the machine. For a new machine purchased with credit from the bank, the cost is amortized over a five-year period, and can be estimated at LE1000 per year or slightly more. The cost of a second-hand tractor purchased from a dealer will be much less, but will probably have to be paid at once. Then if we assume that the tractor requires a driver, we can estimate the wages of the driver at LE40 per month or LE480 per year. This figure corresponds to the average of the figures given to me; it may be slightly on the low side. Other out-of-pocket costs include fuel and oil, and repairs. Fuel is heavily subsidized and costs the farmer PT3 a liter, perhaps five percent of the world market price. Oil is also subsidized. Repairs are unpredictable, but are probably not high on new machines in the first years. Let us figure that all these costs together amount to LE1000 annually. Thus prices, wages, fuel, oil and repairs together will amount to something like LE2500 annually.

We can calculate that the average income from tractor rentals is at least LE2 per hour. This has to be an estimate because many of the prices cited are per unit or per task—so much per feddan, or per load—that do not have standardized times. By and large, tractor owners study the market and charge as much as they think customers will pay. New entrants may charge less while they are building up a clientele, but the rate of increase of tractor rental costs is nonetheless quite steep.

Assuming the figure of LE2 an hour, we can estimate that the number of rental hours per year needed to cover the expenses would be on the order of 1,250 or an average of 3.5 hours per day. Most tractors easily work that much. There is, of course, marked seasonality, with high periods in the months from April through July and again in November and December, and low periods the rest of the year. But there is almost always some hauling to be done, and other occasional jobs. During the peak periods, the tractor may be working eight to ten hours a day, and so the annual average would be over four hours per day even if there were no off-season work. For the large landowners, some of this work would be unremunerated work on their own land. But for bookkeeping purposes this could be calculated at the tractor rental value. This method is familiar to the tractor owners of Musha who charge themselves mentally for a rental fee when calculating costs of their operations.

Tractor Owners

The evidence suggests that most tractor owners find it a profitable business. For instance, many tractor owners eventually purchase a second tractor, or an owner may start with a second-hand tractor and then in a few years move up to a new one. However, I did run across a few men who were former tractor owners. Their problems illustrate the process. One middle school teacher had bought a 65 hp Romanian tractor second-hand from a dealer in Mansoura, but sold it again after a year. He complained that repairs cost too much, but added that it did not pay to have a tractor if you did not have a big area of land of your own to work. They only have three feddans, and counted on working for their neighbors, but had a hard time collecting their money. Another man worked as a guard in an irrigation pump. He once bought a second-hand tractor for LE700, and then sold it again for the same price after several years. But he did not have enough land to qualify for a loan from the agricultural bank to buy a new tractor. A fairly large landowner had two first-generation Deering tractors, but he gave them up around 1974 and now hires a tractor whenever he needs one. He claimed that the price was too high, and then quoted unrealistically high prices. Other observers suggested that there may have been a dispute over an inheritance. These three examples suggest some of the problems of village social organization and of government regulations that create difficulties for would-be tractor owners and help to limit the number of people who can successfully own one.

On the other hand, there are many successful tractor owners in Musha. Here are four case studies exemplifying different kinds of tractor owners to illustrate the kind of people who own tractors and what they are able to do with them.

1. Abdeljalil Ahmed. This young man, aged 30, works as an agricultural engineer in the Musha cooperative on the strength of his diploma from the agricultural secondary school in Asyut. His father owns five feddans of land, and he himself rents in another five. His two older brothers live and work outside Musha, one sister is a teacher in Musha, and a younger brother is still at home. His father is a member of the cooperative board. His grandfather had 40 feddans, but also 15 heirs.

Abdeljalil initially bought a tractor as a partner with one of Musha's biggest farmers, Abdelhadi. This was a Yugoslav IMT-558. This arrangement lasted about three years. Then he sold his share in the IMT-558 to his partner, and bought a Massey-Ferguson 62 hp tractor on credit through the Agricultural Credit Bank in Asyut. (Shortly afterwards, Abdelhadi also bought a new Romanian 65 hp tractor from the bank, and henceforth had two tractors.) The total cost to Abdeljalil was around LE6,250, of which he paid LE2,000 down, LE1,135 as the first year's installment, and then four more annual installments of about LE850 each. At the same time, he bought a new drum thresher from the Delta for LE700, and he also acquired a plow and a leveller made in Giza, and a wagon from Mit Ghamr. The total investment was around LE8,000, of which more than half was on credit. The total investment represented approximately the price of one feddan of unencumbered land.

Abdeljalil takes leave from his cooperative job during especially busy seasons. Of course, even that undemanding job leaves him free outside the work hours of 9 A.M. to 2 P.M. He hires a helper anyway for his tractor. In the fall of 1980 he was paying his helper LE60 per month, whether there was work or not, and said that this wage had tripled in recent years. Sometimes the helper will also receive a tip from the customers; but farmers are generally reluctant to give a tip to a tractor operator who is also the owner. The principal operating cost for the tractor is fuel and oil, both heavily subsidized. Abdeljalil relies on mechanics in Asyut for repairs.

Abdeljalil does most of his work on a custom basis for other farmers. He said he had about 50 regular customers, most of whom delay their payments for the work. He considered this number of customers to be about average. He had increased his prices for custom work because his costs were going up and he was discovering what farmers were willing to pay. He charged LE7 to cultivate a feddan of land, a task that takes about one and a half to two hours, and LE6 per feddan for threshing. This last price had doubled in two years. He was energetic in seeking out new areas in which to exploit his tractor. In spring 1981 he was working his tractor outside Musha, threshing in area east of the Nile about 60 kilometers away.

2. Hamed Qenawi. The Qenawi clan is a numerous one residing on the southern edge of the village. Hamed is a man around 40 who lives and farms with his younger brother, Mustafa. They farm 15 feddans in Musha, and perhaps twice as much in the neighboring villages of Rifa and Diweina. They own half an irrigation pump in Musha, and other shares in the adjacent villages. They keep a small herd of about ten cattle, and make a practice of selling milk and dairy products, as well as the increase. Both brothers are married with young children. Hamed is a member of the elected Local Popular Council.

They bought a Nasr 50 hp tractor on credit in 1970, and bought a second tractor, a Romanian Universal 80 hp tractor, in 1980, also on credit from the Agricultural Credit Bank in Asyut. To accompany these tractors, they have two plows, two wagons, two threshing machines, two *nuraj*s, and one land leveller. They hire two drivers, and the younger brother, Mustafa, also works as a tractor driver from time to time, especially for threshing work in the evening. They own some land in the belt of threshing grounds south of the village, and set up their threshing headquarters there. Some smaller farmers bring their crops to the Qenawi *jurn,* while in other cases the Qenawi tractors are taken to the location of the crop. However, virtually all of their customers are on the south side of the village, so none are far away. The drivers said they were paid only LE10 per month, but there were tips in addition and also some payment in kind—such as food and clothing. One of the drum threshers was purchased from Mit Ghamr for LE500 plus another LE50 for transport; it replaced an earlier machine. They began using the tractor and the thresher for wheat about 1975, and for sorghum about 1977. The threshing machine has two speeds, a fast one for wheat and berseem and a slow one for sorghum and beans. They charge LE2 per hour for threshing wheat, and LE6 a feddan for threshing sorghum, but these prices are somewhat negotiable. One time a teenager came to pay for a small sorghum threshing job. Mustafa told him the price was LE1.50. The boy objected that there were only five qirats of sorghum. Mustafa then asked for LE1.30. The boy offered LE1.25, Mustafa accepted it, and the boy withdrew his hand from his pocket with exactly LE1.25 in it. This would be the precise price for five qirats at LE6 per feddan. But were there really five qirats of sorghum? Here is where Mustafa accepted the boy's evaluation.

The Qenawi buy their fuel in Musha, which entails a small surcharge on the price of PT3 per liter, making it PT3.25 per liter. For important repairs, they rely on a specific workshop in Asyut.

One of the regular customers of the Qenawi brothers are the Abdelnur brothers. Jabra and his brother live with their families in a large house on the southern edge of the village, near the Qenawi brothers. They farm about three feddans of land, which is barely sufficient for the fifteen people in the household. They are also active in animal husbandry, buying and selling water buffalo for which they maintain a separate stable area. Jabra also has mechanical skills, which he uses to maintain the irrigation pumps for the Qenawi brothers. Whenever they need tractor work, they call on Hamed or Mustafa, and they irrigate most of their farm land from the Qenawi pump as well. They work on credit, and pay a little at a time as they are able. When I first met Jabra, he invited me to eat a meal at his home, and then sent for Hamed to be present for the conversation as well. Jabra and Hamed were often together on other occasions as well, including at least once when they intervened together to avert a quarrel. Another regular client of Hamed's was his brother-in-law, Ali. (Ali is also a member of the elected Local Popular Council.) His land is west of the village, so this relationship takes the Qenawi tractors further from their home base in the south. He farms around five feddans of land, and has some commercial activities on the side. A third regular client was William Mikhail, who farmed around ten feddans of land, mostly south of the village, and relied on Hamed for some plowing and most threshing.

3. Mohammed Mirghani. This man works as mechanic and guard for the large pump associated with the *khawaja* (the Khayyat family). He has a large family including five sons (one married) and three daughters (two married). Two of his sons work regularly with him, one as pump mechanic and the other as a tractor driver. Mirghani receives LE4 for each feddan irrigated by the Khayyat pump. With 200 feddans, this makes a total of LE800 per year. In addition, he farms about 25 feddans, of which around three are in gardens. Since the Khayyat family has been absent for twenty years or more, his role at the pump is under the nominal supervision of the family's representative in Musha, but in practice he has a fairly free hand.

Mirghani began investing in tractors as early as 1965 when he bought a 40 hp Deering second-hand. Later in 1970 he bought a second-hand John Deere. Both these were steel wheeled tractors manufactured before 1956. Eventually in 1978 he bought a second-hand Nasr 50 hp. All these tractors were purchased on a cash basis. He sold the two older tractors to a dealer from Mansoura after the paving of the road through Musha had made the old steel wheeled tractors a liability. At the same time, he bought his first new tractor, a Romanian Universal 80 hp, with credit from the Agricultural Credit Bank in Asyut. To accompany his tractors, Mirghani bought three identical drum threshers from a manufacturer in Kom Ahmar, near Mansoura in the Delta, and transported them to Musha.

Mirghani's son drives one of the tractors, and the other is generally driven by a hired driver. This driver is paid from LE30 to 50 per month, plus tips from the customers. They perform the usual range of services for their clients, but appear to be less tied to a particular threshing ground than some of the others. They do much of their work on credit, and say they might wait up to a year for payment.

4. Abderrahman Khadr. Abderrahman and his brother Hussein farm about 120 feddans, including a five-feddan garden south of the village. One of the two *'umda*s of Musha came from this family, and Hassan Khadr, the grandfather of this pair of brothers, was responsible for introducing one of the first steam pumps to Musha around 1910, at which time he was the *'umda* of the East. Their current irrigation pump was installed around 1950 and initially drew water from a well. The garden was not created, however, until after the end of the flood in 1964.

They originally purchased a steel-wheeled John Deere sometime between 1954 and 1960, probably buying it second-hand for cash. They then kept this tractor until the time of my research; it was sold when they bought a new Romanian Universal 80 hp. This time they bought the tractor on credit. The price of the tractor was fixed at LE5,850. They paid one-third down (LE1,950), and the balance in five annual installments of LE780 plus five percent interest each year on the outstanding balance. The interest payments thus came out to be a total of LE585, or ten percent of the initial cost, spread over a five-year period. As in the case of Abdeljalil cited above, the cost of the tractor approximates the cost of a feddan of land. When the tractor was delivered, a mechanic came out from the company to spend a day with Hussein to instruct him in the machine's use. One purpose of the new tractor was to be able to haul goods to Asyut and market them there directly. Since the Khadr garden is well off the main road, merchants have a hard time reaching it. However, essentially the tractor will be used only on their own land, and perhaps the land of a few close neighbors and clients. The only farmer I interviewed who rented a tractor from the Khadr brothers was one of their permanent workers, who also irrigates his land from the Khadr pump.

Commentary

We have seen various types of tractor owners. Qenawi and Khadr are among the big landowners, although Khadr is big enough to envision using his tractor only on his own land and Qenawi derives considerable income from the rental of his two tractors. Since the Khadr tractor was new at the time of field work, it is possible that they, too, will discover the income to be earned from this activity. Certainly one large tractor-owning landowner said in the winter that his new tractor was only for use on his own one hundred feddans, but by summer he was devoting considerable time to organizing its rental to smaller farmers. Abdeljalil is an interesting case of the government worker who manages to invest in a tractor. By virtue of his and his father's connections with the cooperative, and by virtue of his own energy, he was able to develop a successful tractor rental operation. Mirghani represents the relatively "poor" farmer who developed a lively business in tractor rentals on the basis of his work as a pump guard. What is interesting in his case is the long period involved and the gradual upgrading of his tractors from outdated second-hand ones to brand new machines bought with government credit.

Conclusion

In this chapter I have presented data and case studies relating to the role of pumps and tractors in the social organization of agriculture in Musha. The emphasis has been on the role of the machine owner and the men hired to work with the machine—mechanics, guards, drivers, and the like. These data underline the growing role of capitalization in Egyptian agriculture, and provide some hints as to the ways in which this process is transforming the labor process. What remains to be seen is the role of machinery in the general labor process, and in particular the relationship between labor and machinery. That is the subject of the following chapter.

Notes

1. The history of the role of Egyptian, French and English engineers in the transformation of the Egyptian irrigation system since the time of Mohammed 'Ali Pasha and Napoleon is broad and merits separate treatment. Some idea of this history can be gained from Barois 1889, 1911; Willcocks 1889, 1935; Ross 1892, 1893; Brunhes 1902; and Sandes 1937.

2. This word comes from the root meaning to carry or to cross; this corresponds to the more common phrase in Egypt, *masqa,* from the root meaning to irrigate. For a comparative studies of local irrigation systems in Egypt, see Mehanna, Huntington and Antonious 1984, and el-Kholy 1985.

3. It is hard to tell the age of a tractor, and harder to guess when it might have entered Musha. The Deering tractor advertized in Egypt in 1928 resembles some of the ones I saw in Musha except for slightly lower horsepower: 30 hp maxmimum. For a general discussion of mechanization in Egypt, see Richards (1980, 1981).

4. Saab 1960:262 assumed that a 30 horsepower tractor was capable of farming about 100 feddans at a time (1957) when there was one tractor per 1,200 feddans of crop area in Egypt as a whole. The ratio of tractors to land in Musha was slightly above average for Egypt in 1981–2.

5. In our Ten Village Survey we found 81 tractors made by 12 different manufacturers, not counting different models of the same make. The most common were

Egyptian-assembled Nasrs, Fords and Fordsons of various origins, and Romanian Universals. See Hopkins, Mehanna and Abdelmaksoud 1982:164.

6. In 1983 in Musha I observed a new Soviet tractor with narrow wheels designed to fit between the furrows and work with a seed drill or weeder.

7. Assuming a relatively long waiting time is an indication of undersupply of tractors, such a feeling would be corroborated by the Ten Village Survey, which found that waiting time for a privately owned tractor can be as long as for a cooperative tractor. Those who cited a "longest" waiting time of a week or more were 46 percent of the cooperative machine users and 21 percent of the private machine users. See Hopkins, Mehanna and Abdelmaksoud 1982:121.

8. In six of the ten villages surveyed in 1982, from 38 to 53 percent of the users questioned cited a single machine owner. See Hopkins, Mehanna and Abdelmaksoud 1982:123.

8

The Labor Process and the Labor Market in Agriculture

The analysis of the social organization generated by the mechanization of water lifting and traction stressed the point of view of the owner or organizer of that machinery. In this chapter a model of the labor process is constructed from an analysis of the social organization of work. The focus is on the flow of work in the community, and on the interrelationships of roles and productive forces. I analyze the role and organization of labor, and stress the integration of labor and capital in the total production process.

The first section summarizes the steps required to produce the two major crops of wheat and cotton. The labor process is typically fragmented in that each step combines labor, machinery, management and other inputs in a unique way. Then I look at the same material from the point of view of the role of hired labor in Musha agriculture. Drawing on this material, I then analyze the relation between capital (machinery) and labor in the agricultural labor process, stressing the transformation of the household into a petty managerial unit. Since one of the issues concerning labor is its relative shortage or surplus, I include here a discussion of labor migration, both internal and external. The historical prevalence of this labor migration indicates the integration of Musha (and rural Egypt in general) into a national or even international (regional) labor market and therefore division of labor. In this sense, the labor process cannot be analyzed solely within the framework of one village, as though the rest did not matter.

The Labor Process for Wheat and Cotton

An examination of the labor process for wheat and cotton demonstrates the complexity of the agricultural cycle from the point of view of the individual farmer. Wheat and cotton are two of the most common crops in Musha (and in Egypt as a whole). Wheat was grown in the winter of 1980-81 by 84 percent of the farmers, and cotton by 79 percent in the summer of 1980. Only berseem was grown by more farmers. Wheat can be taken as representative of the winter crops, and to some degree of such summer cereals as maize and sorghum, while cotton is significant both economically and because the crop rotation system is built around it.

The farmer is the only one who follows a single crop from beginning to end, and he must constantly deal with a wide variety of other people—government officials, machine owners, day laborers, labor contractors for child labor in cotton picking, neighbors, contractors for transport animals, and merchants who are anxious to purchase his crop at a low price while he wants to get the maximum from it. The farmer needs to know enough of the traditional skills of farming to supervise the hand and machine work, but he is also dependent on the owners of the machines and on the government if he is to grow a successful crop. The principal role of the farmer is as manager of a wide range of inputs from outside the household, rather than as the mobilizer and foreman of internal household labor. This conclusion has important implications for control and for the extraction of surplus.

Wheat

Wheat is normally planted in November and harvested in May and June. It can follow cotton in the rotation, but cannot precede it because of the relatively late harvest date. It is an important crop for the farmer both for the grain and for the straw. The value of the straw is about 30–40 percent higher than the value of the wheat harvested from the same area, because of price controls on the wheat. Short-stemmed wheat of the high-yielding "Mexipak" variety is not popular because it produces less straw.

To grow wheat it is necessary to register with the government cooperative, and fit in with the government crop rotation. The village cooperative records the amount of land the farmer holds, and the amount he will plant in wheat. The farmer must then get the Village Bank to authorize his loan—in the form of fertilizer and perhaps seed or insecticide—which he will later pick up from the bank's warehouse.

The next step is to irrigate the land. Each time, the farmer has to deal with the pump mechanic, the pump guard (to determine when water will be available), the owner (to pay his fee), his neighbors (to ensure that there will be no damage to adjoining fields), and perhaps a worker.

Plowing the land involves hiring a tractor and a driver. The owner must be paid and the driver tipped. Someone from the family will generally supervise. Supplementary tasks like harrowing and levelling are rarely done in Musha though they are more common in the Delta. Fertilizer and seed must be hauled from the Village Bank to the home, and then from the home to the field. This can be done by donkey, camel, or tractor, depending in part on the amount involved. If the household does not have these animals or a tractor, they must be hired. Wheat is generally sown by the broadcast method. The worker can be a household member or hired. He may work in conjunction with a tractor so that the seed is covered. Fertilizer is broadcast by hand. Spreading manure (not much used for wheat) requires a great deal of shoveling, loading, and transporting, either family labor or hired labor, before it is plowed under. Farmers do not use insecticide or weeding for wheat.

The wheat is harvested using a small sickle. The very dry plant is cut at its base or simply pulled up by the roots. Most farmers hire labor which is paid piece rates according to the area harvested, though there are some who pay by the hour or day. Family labor is also occasionally used, especially by small farmers. Harvesting machines are available but are not used because they cannot cut low enough to preserve the whole plant. The reaped wheat must be bundled into sheaves. This is a slightly more specialized job than reaping itself, and is done by older men. The worker is paid piece rates.

The sheaves are transported to the threshing ground at the perimeter of the village. The transport is done either by a camel or by a tractor and wagon. Formerly, the camel and driver were paid a share of the load, but now they are usually paid cash. The tractor is paid cash. There is a set amount for any trip regardless of the distance. Camels are easier to load and unload, and can go places tractors cannot, but are slower. After the loading, the field is opened to gleaners.

The grain is threshed using a tractor and a drum thresher. Threshing wheat is a lengthy and tedious job, and the usual gang has five members—one to feed the machine, one to shovel away the threshed crop that has passed through the machine, two or three to hand sheaves to the feeder. The farmer must arrange for the tractor and for the hired labor he needs. The threshed grain is winnowed and sifted. Winnowers are specialists, and because they are working piece rates they require little supervision. The winnowed grain must be measured and sacked. At this critical juncture the owner will be present. The winnower does this job and is paid a share (typically 1/48) of the harvest for the combined operation. The final step in production is to haul the grain and the straw from the threshing ground back to the storeroom in the house. At this stage, animal transport is likely to be used, either donkeys or camels. Farmers estimate the average yield for wheat at around 8 ardebs per feddan, or 2.86 tons per hectare.

The grain is sold to merchants who funnel it into the city. In the immediate past, the government was also a major purchaser of grain. There are also dealers who buy straw to sell to other villages. In either case, the farmer must time the sale right to maximize his profit. Some grain will also be used at home, milled into flour and baked into bread. Farmers may also use their own straw and bran (a byproduct of milling) for animal fodder at home.

Cotton

Cotton is normally planted in Musha in April or May, and harvested in October. Approximately one-third of Musha's land is planted in cotton each summer. The cotton planted in Musha is not the famous Egyptian long-staple cotton, but a more ordinary variety used domestically.

The government issues seed and fertilizer for the cotton crop through the cooperative and the village bank. Plowing for cotton is always by tractor, which is also used to prepare small ridges which raise the cotton plants above the field ditches. After the ridges have been prepared, workers use hoes to prepare low cross bunds which help direct the flow of irrigation water. The labor here is likely to be hired unless the field is very small. Irrigating for cotton follows the same procedure as for wheat, save that it must be done more often. Cotton is planted by hand, usually by a crew of two to five workers. Working as a team they move down one furrow after another. The worker chips a small hole with his hoe and drops several seeds into it. Weeding cotton is carried out by the same kind of work gang, and with the same tool, the short-handled hoe. While weeding the workers repair the pattern of ridges and bunds to prepare for the next irrigation.

Pest control is handled by the cooperative. The cooperative organizes gangs of children and young men to pick the cotton worm eggs off the leaves one by one. The government also organizes aerial spraying of most fields, those that are grouped together, and charges LE22 per feddan.

Picking cotton is carried out by gangs of pickers, mostly adolescents, who are paid per pound picked. They are frequently recruited by a labor contractor with whom the farmer makes an arrangement. The large farmers are likely to deal with a labor contractor from another village who brings in gangs of children from that village. Small farmers deal with a local labor contractor who recruits the children in his street. The labor contractors receive a share in the wages. Farmers estimate their average cotton yield at about 7.5 qantars per feddan, or 2.8 tons per hectare.

The cotton is transported to the house of the farmer, either by camel or wagon. It is then unloaded from the plastic bags the pickers use and packed into large burlap sacks, usually by two men. The sacks are suspended from a strong beam, and one man uses his weight to pack the cotton down while the other man hands more cotton to him. These sacks when full weigh around 180 to 200 kilos.

The burlap sack must then be transported to the government grading and weighing station, again either by camel or wagon. At the weighing station, government cotton graders grade the cotton, and the sacks are weighed. The workers at the station must move the sacks around for these tasks. They are paid both by the government and by the farmers.

The Labor Market

The analysis of the flow of work in the cultivation of wheat and cotton has highlighted the requirements for labor, and in particular for hired labor. Some tasks are done by hand (planting, harvesting), while in others the machine creates a modified labor demand (threshing). In this section, I approach the problem from a slightly different direction, by focusing on the organization of the market for labor power in Musha. Most men and many children perform considerable work outside the household framework. They are part of a labor market that is centered in the village but extends beyond it. The prevalence of commoditization of labor is indicated by the habit farmers have of giving a cash value even to family labor when doing mental accounts of costs.

In Musha there is a labor market. There are men who rely on casual or semi-permanent employment for their living and that of their household, and there are households that rely on the labor market to mobilize the labor they cannot generate from within. The census figures (see chapter 4) suggest that this labor market has been substantial for some time. The commonly accepted wisdom in Musha (as in Egypt) is that labor is much scarcer than it used to be, and that migration abroad is the cause of this scarcity. While there is certainly some truth in that, the situation is complicated and it is well to look at the details before reaching this conclusion.

The analysis of household structure and activities in Musha makes it very clear that households exist in a continual process of exchange with other households. I mean to include under this heading all the various arrangements by which one individual works for another or buys something from another household. The work performed outside the household is essential to the survival and reproduction of the household itself. Apart from work performed for the government, this work outside the household context is mostly carried out for another individual who is in turn a member of a household. There are no firms or impersonal organizations. Hence it is possible to conceptualize work performed outside the household as involving transfers between households, as the basic production and consumption unit, even though the actual exchange may be between individuals.

Most—indeed, probably all—farming households either hire workers or seek income by hiring themselves out as workers from time to time. Very rough figures from Musha suggest that one-third of the agricultural households rely mostly or entirely on hired labor to get the work done, and that another third uses some hired labor (notably for the harvest, for winnowing, for weeding, and for irrigating). Even those who say they rely entirely on family labor (mostly small farmers where one man can look after the land as a part-time occupation) in fact generally hire in tractors, and that always includes a payment for the tractor driver as well. Threshing grains (wheat, beans, lentils, chickpeas, sorghum, seed berseem) is also always done mechanically, and almost always requires hired labor, yet is left out of the very rough figures mentioned above. It is the rare farmer who does not hire labor during the year—perhaps only the smallest farmers who restrict themselves to the fodder crops of berseem in the winter and sorghum in the summer.

One small farmer claimed that he neither hired workers nor sought work himself. Let us look at this case. Ibrahim cultivates 2 feddans of which he owns half a feddan and rents the rest at the illegal black market rate of LE230 a year. The bulk of the labor is supplied by himself and a son; the younger children are still in school. They live on their land next to the new paved road between Musha and Rifa. They keep a water buffalo for its dairy products. He grows a variety of fruits and vegetables. On his own land he grows grapes and a few fruit trees; on the rented land he grows onions for seed, and the usual field crops of berseem, wheat, chickpeas, etc. He also grows small amounts of eggplant, okra, garlic, and onions for his own use. He signals his determination to be independent both by choosing to live on his farm land, a very unusual choice in Musha, and by saying that he would be prepared to sell his top soil for brick manufacture to survive. However, he has to pay for his irrigation water, and rents a tractor for plowing and for threshing his field crops. Furthermore, many of his crops are grown for the market: grapes, onion seed, and chickpeas. Compared to most small farmers, he is relatively market oriented and also has relatively high land costs because of the high rental. He could be taken as the "type" of the small farmer working towards an intensified agriculture using family labor primarily, i.e., for every non-mechanized activity.

When a farmer decides to hire labor within Musha, he will turn first of all to those neighbors, friends and relatives who have worked for him in the past. If he cannot find the labor he needs among neighbors, "in his street," then he will turn to nearby cafes. Would-be workers hang out in the cafes, and sometimes also in the small central market place of the village, the *suwayqa,* waiting for a farmer to hire them for work. The meeting between worker and farmer then takes place the night before the work, and arrangements are generally made for one day at a time. The smaller farmers usually carry out these negotiations themselves, but the larger farmers use younger male relatives or their semi-permanent workers to recruit their casual labor. If the farmer intends to hire a large gang, for instance for the cotton harvest, he may contact one of the men known to work as a village level labor contractor (*rais*) to make the arrangements several days in advance.

In one case, the son of a large farming family learned in the evening that irrigation water would be available for his cotton field the next day, and so he scoured the cafes looking for some men to work with him. Starting late, he was only able to find three instead of the five he wanted, and perhaps for this reason when I visited him in his field the next day this university graduate was working along with them. This was, of course, early summer, a peak period.

People say that in the past, there were so many men looking for work in Musha that one could hire simply by going out to the street, and men came from other villages to Musha to look for work.[1] At present, the paradox in Musha is that would-be employers complain about the shortage of labor, and the lack of enthusiasm of workers for their task, while at the same time there are many seasons of the year when a would-be worker may have a hard time finding work. Insofar as there is a shortage of labor, it is seasonal. At peak periods, the farmer may pay the worker ahead of time to reserve him, and wages are high. At slow times of year (principally in the late winter) those available for work find it very hard to "look for work," and wages are low. If no one contacts them at home ahead of time, their only recourse is to remain available in the cafes in the hope that someone will come around looking for workers.

In addition to the work gangs they hire for special tasks, the larger or capitalist farmers have regular workers. I say "regular" and not "permanent" since both parties agree that they are only hired when needed. They are paid by the day, and are "on call" for their respective employers. At a very rough guess, there is one regular worker for about each 15 to 20 feddans of land held by a single farmer. Put another way, seven of the 107 cases in the household sample earned the bulk of their income as "regular" workers for a certain employer, often carrying out a task involving machinery or the supervision of others. The farms of 40 or 50 feddans thus have a team of workers who may have some degree of specialization among themselves. In one case, one worker specializes in the care of the grape vines, one in the care of the livestock, and two others are all-purpose workers. There may also be tractor drivers, pump guards and mechanics. The largest capitalist farmers also have bookkeepers and foremen, and do not deal with the field workers directly.

The relationship between the large capitalist farmers and the regular workers tends to endure. The workers are competent and trusted to work alone part or all of the time, while workers hired for the day are never left without supervision unless they are working for piece rates. The ability of the regular workers to work on their own is essential in a large operation where several activities may be occurring at once. The workers typically convene at the house of their employer in the evening to report on their activities during the day and to receive their orders for the following day. These sessions involve some give-and-take, but ultimately the decisive role of the capitalist farmer as manager predominates. The workers are part of the *majlis* or "assembly" showing respect for the big farmer and prominent man, and at the same time they are available for errands, carrying messages, receiving instructions, preparing tea, and fetching people. In these large capitalist farm enterprises, the household makes very little use of family labor except to supplement the managerial role of the household head, and instead relies on the loyalties and skills of the regular work staff.

During most of the time that I was in Musha, the going wage for basic agricultural work was LE1.50 for five hours of work, typically from 7 A.M. to noon. This works out to PT30 an hour.[2] The workers were then free to work in the afternoon for additional wages, but both workers and employers generally seemed happy with a situation where the afternoon was left free. Many of the workers had other activities—they grew berseem on a small plot of land, or they were involved in petty trade, or they had some family responsibilities—and the afternoons were available for these activities. At the slowest time of year, in March, wages dipped down to LE1 for the same period of time, and at the busiest time of year, in June, they rose to LE2 for five hours, or even to PT50 an hour for threshing. A worker steadily employed at these wages might earn from LE30 to 40 a month, comparable to the lower rungs of the government service. However, many jobs were not paid on this basis. Harvesting wheat, picking cotton, winnowing grains, transport by camel, loading trucks and trailers were all more likely to be paid by piece rates, and were not limited to the morning hours. For the adult workers, piece rates generally produced a higher rate of pay and longer hours. The labor market for agricultural work extended also to cover other activities, such as brickmaking and construction. Some workers switched back and forth between agricultural labor and construction, while showing some preference for the latter because it was in the village. Because the hours were longer, the income might also be higher.

The Musha labor market also extended to some of the neighboring villages from which workers could be recruited by Musha farmers. The two principal supplying villages were Baqur to the southeast and el-Zawya to the southwest. The larger farmers were better able to tap this source because it required more organization, and a wider range of social relations. Usually workers from other villages appear as large groups recruited by a single labor contractor (*rais*). The contractors are men from other villages who have established a working relationship in Musha, often after working as a pump guard in the field area adjacent to their home village. They then become intermediaries between the two villages. The Musha farmer informs the labor contractor of his needs. The contractor then draws on his knowledge of the home village to assemble the desired number of people. Sometimes the Musha farmer will send his tractor and trailer to fetch the labor, sometimes they are responsible for making their own way. The workers are then paid through the contractor. Workers from outside Musha are prepared to work for 75 or 80 percent of the wages that a Musha worker would demand; this usually takes the form of being willing to work longer hours for the same money.

The contracting system is especially used for the autumn cotton harvest, when the contractor recruits his gang of children mostly from his neighbors and relatives. He is responsible for getting them to the fields early in the morning (the loudspeakers broadcasting a call to morning prayer from the mosques function only at this season as a kind of communal wake up signal), and he is supposed to make sure that they have drinking water. He may also supply cigarettes to the older boys. He maintains some degree of discipline among the children while working. Typically, each picker is assigned an area of the field and works in that area until it is clean. I have seen pickers ask permission of the contractor to move to a new area. On the other hand, there is little the contractor can do about chattering and other minor forms of indiscipline. While the *rais* supervises the work effort, the owner of the field or his representative directs the work in general, to make sure that the work is well done, that boundaries are respected, that no cotton is lost, and so on.

The children are paid according to the weight of cotton picked. The most common rate for the easier first picking was PT100 for 100 *ritl* or pounds, but I heard a range from PT80 to PT150 for the first picking, and rates up to PT200 to 250 per one hundred pounds for the second picking, when the cotton is scarcer and so it takes more time to pick the same amount of cotton. In other words, though these are piece rates, there is an implicit calculation of time. Very roughly, it works out to PT10 an hour. However, the pickers must pay an amount, usually mentioned as PT10 per hundred pounds, to the contractor, who may also receive a similar amount from the owner of the field. Thus if the *rais* mobilizes 20 pickers and each one picks 100 pounds, he receives LE2 from both the pickers and the field owner, for a daily income of LE4.

Some of the smaller farmers prefer to hire their cotton pickers directly. One who did this told me he paid PT150 for the first picking and PT250 for the second picking, so the money earned might be higher in this case. On the other hand 'Amm Mohran added that he generally paid the parents directly for the work of their children, on the grounds that after all it was the parents who had supported the children thus far in life. One boy of 16 to whom I talked also found direct hire advantageous. Nadim felt he would earn more working with a contractor because he would work every day, but on the other hand the *rais* would rouse him early (at 5 A.M.), would not bring clean water to drink, and would take PT10 per hundred from him. He had just finished a day of work for a middle-sized farmer, with a two feddan cotton field, and had been paid at a rate of 120 per hundred for a total pick of 85 pounds, producing a total income of PT102. He planned to return to work for him the following day.

Only once did I hear of cotton pickers who were paid at a time rate. 'Amm Sa'id had hired a group of twelve children from the neighboring village of el-Zawya, and proposed to pay them PT50 a day, and the contractor PT150 a day. He gave as the reason for this difference that the cotton crop was too thin for piece rates to work. Still, making a theoretical calculation into hourly wages, this was a particularly low rate, perhaps half the average.

Hiring children from other villages was fairly common. Those hired from el-Zawya, whether paid time wages or the more common piece rates, returned home every night, a distance by road of about 7 or 8 kilometers. One large farmer had recruited a gang of 20 children from the village of el-Metmar, to the east of the Nile, and they were sleeping in a work area of his house. Another large farmer said he had recruited children from the village of Qaw, east of the Nile and quite a bit to the south. The area around the mosque of Shaykh Abdelfettah (the central religious point in the village, and the only real open square) was also used by a large number of children for sleeping during the month of October. The plastic bag (originally containing Romanian fertilizer) in which they would place the cotton they picked would be folded up and used for a pillow, as if this tool of their trade were their most precious possession.

The agricultural labor market also includes some skilled specialists. Some specialists work or used to work for a share of the crop rather than a cash wage, and their role harks back to the premechanized form of agriculture. Although no figures are available, my general impression is that they are disproportionately Christian.

One such specialist is the winnower, the *muqarqar.* This job consists in using the fork and wind technique to winnow, and then in sifting, measuring and bagging the winnowed grain. The straw and chaff are also sacked and stored, but may be done by other labor. The winnower is paid a share of the final result in grain, which is a stimulus to be as thorough as possible. His share varies from grain to grain, but is typically on the order to 1/48, about 2 percent. People say that it does not take long to learn how to winnow, yet many farmers prefer to rely on the winnower rather than do the job themselves. Of 27 farmers who explained how they organized the labor for winnowing, 19 (70 percent) used the winnower, two hired labor by the hour, and six did the job themselves. The winnower is a respected specialist. Most of these who work as winnower appear to make a good living at it, since they do not seek other casual work in the slack season, though at least one uses his knowledge of grain quality and of where excess grain or straw is stored away to engage in trading in these commodities.

Another specialty is the camel driver. Traditionally, camels were used for most of the heavy transport in the village, though they are now being replaced by tractor trailers and by trucks. Many farmers continue to use camels if they want to transport a load to or from a place that a motor vehicle cannot reach—a narrow street inside the village, or a field without a decent road. Others have simply not made up their mind to switch. Camels are also easier to load and unload than a wagon, since the camel does the lifting (it kneels to be loaded and then rises), whereas men must do a lot of lifting to load a wagon. There are said to be fewer camels in the village than there used to be, but of the 47 farmers who mentioned how they transported their harvest from the field to the threshing ground, 27 (57 percent) used camels all or some of the time, while 30 (64 percent) used tractors all or some of the time. Traditionally, camel drivers were also paid a share of the load (1/30), for any distance travelled within the village *zimam*. However, there is currently a tendency to translate this into a money payment. Certainly a money payment is necessary for cotton, and might spread from there to grains.

There were formerly carpenters who specialized in the manufacture of the traditional tools, especially the wooden plow and water wheel. These tools have been almost totally replaced by the metal tractor-drawn plow and the pumping engine, and so these traditional carpenters have also disappeared. One of the men interviewed in the sample had inherited the skills of traditional carpentry from his father, but was obliged to seek work as an ordinary day laborer since these skills were no longer demanded.

There are also specialists associated with the modern technology, such as the engine mechanic and the pump guard. Guards in particular show a tendency to move into tractor operation and ownership, building on their familiarity with the farmers and the lands in their areas to establish clienteles. An example of how the guard role can build into something more is the family of Mahmoud el-Zennari, particularly his two sons Ahmed and Hussein, who served as combined mechanic and guard for a pump belonging to two of Musha's largest farmers. They were in fact related through the female line to one of these families. The younger brother, Ahmed, looked after the pump, while the older brother had created a "dealership," if one may use the word, in drum threshers centered at the pump. Thus they had moved from pump guard to labor contractor to machine custom rentals to dealers in threshers, spare parts, and used machines.

With the spread of tractors, tractor driving has become another specialization in the agricultural sphere. Most tractor drivers—if they are not themselves the owner of the tractor or a family member of the owner—are paid by the month, regardless of the amount of work. This difference from the regular workers is suggestive of the relative scarcity of good tractor drivers. The monthly wages quoted to me were usually around LE30. This seems low, but the tractor drivers regularly supplement their salary from the owner by receiving tips from the farmers for whom they work. In busy seasons, therefore, their income might be two or three times as much. It is also interesting that many of the tractor drivers, especially those who did extensive custom work, were quite young. I knew several who were around 16 to 18 years old. Their relative youth may also depress their wages.[3]

Since Musha has only been able to grow permanent crops like grapes or other fruit trees since the cessation of the flood in 1964, the skills needed for these tree crops were not initially present. Some large owners imported workers from other villages, east of the Nile, where there was a long tradition of working with trees. There are also seasonal workers who come to Musha from villages in Minya governorate (the Samalut and Matay areas) to prune the grape vines. Most of those who trim and care for the palm trees come from the nearby Sahel village of Aulad Ibrahim, where caring for palms and bananas is one of the major occupations.

The chief non-agricultural use of unskilled labor is in brickmaking and construction, which competes directly with agriculture for the same labor power. Construction is mostly the responsibility of full-time masons or builders who undertake to build or rebuild entire houses, and then hire the necessary labor. The going daily rate for a mason is around LE5 for eight to ten hours of work. Workmen are paid wages comparable to those in agriculture. Minor repairs and changes in the house are done with family labor, sometimes by the women, who may build a granary or a chicken coop or repair a wall.

Brickmaking is carried out by gangs of four or five men. They must have access to earth,[4] to water, and to a work place. Most bricks are made on the edge of the village, because this is where most new houses are built, and because this is where the kilns can be placed. The earth and the water are mixed together, with a bit of straw, and when the mixture has the right consistency it is fitted into molds and the bricks are shaped and laid out in the sun to dry. For this work, men are paid according to the number of bricks produced. LE4 per thousand was the rate quoted to me, and the average production seems to be about a thousand a day for an income, also, of LE4. Again, because it is piece work, self-exploitation and the long day are the rule.

Nowadays most people in Musha prefer fired bricks, and so once the bricks are sun-dried they are built into a stack with a hollow interior. The stacks (*kusha*) are laid by the masons who are paid per thousand bricks laid. Then a fire is built in the interior and kept going for several days until the bricks are fired. The outside layer is generally not usable and is discarded, but the inside bricks are then ready for use in construction. Each *kusha* holds around 30,000 bricks, and it takes several of them to build a good sized house. Usually brickmaking is financed by someone anxious to build a new house, but in some cases the bricks are made on speculation, either for sale in Musha or in Asyut city. The fuel used to fire the bricks is mostly maize or sorghum stalks. Households without enough stalks of their own to use as fuel find others willing to sell theirs.

The Role of Capital

The analysis of the labor process began with the flow of work for two key crops, and then continued with a survey of the key roles in the labor market. We can now analyze the role of capital, particularly in the form of machinery. The labor process involves relations between capital, labor and the state, but centers around the ability of the farmer to coordinate the various tasks. The small farmer manipulates but does not himself control capital. One dimension of the relationship between capital and labor is the practice of hiring labor, while another is the custom of hiring machinery.

The social organization of work around the machines involves a number of different roles. First of all, there is the farmer—the man who has put the crop in the ground, usually in land which he "holds." Then there is the machine owner, who supplies the machine. The machine owner is generally not also the operator of the machine, but hires a mechanic to run the tractor or pump. In the case of the pumps, the owner will also engage someone to perform the role of guard, responsible both for guarding the crops in the fields and the installations and for allocating the water among the different field ditches that radiate from the pump. The farmer may perform the labor himself (especially if it is a task like sowing or irrigating that can be done by one person), or he may hire a work gang (as in weeding or threshing). Thus there are four different roles for tractor use, and five for pump use—the owner of the machine, the owner of the crop, the labor for the machine, and the labor for the crop. Of course in any given situation, two or more of these roles may be combined. Pump mechanics and guards may be members of the same family, or even the same person. The owner of the crop may work himself and mobilize household members rather than hired labor. The owner of the machine may also own the crop. Nonetheless, conceptually there are these four roles, and we have to understand them to grasp the situation.

The role of hired labor by itself may not be indicative of the tendency for work relations to prefigure class relations, for several reasons. (1) All farmers hire labor at some point during the year, and most find no problem in switching from family labor to hired labor as soon as the former is not readily available. (2) Some farmers also work as hired labor occasionally, so the categories are muddied. (3) The large farmers who hire workers regularly have only a small core of permanent workers (and they often deny that they have any "permanent workers" at all). (4) The larger work gangs have a shifting membership and in some cases many are drawn from outside the village. The hirers of labor thus range from the large capitalist farmers to the very smallest, and the category of hired labor includes both the archetypical landless/hired labor combination, and small farmers. Hiring labor appears clearly as a relationship between labor and capital only in the case of the workers for the larger farmers. Here there is a classic relationship between the capitalist farmer and his labor force, but even here the element of confrontation (the "class situation" effect, cf. Weber 1978:47) is limited by the overall organization of the labor process.

Neither the division of labor imposed by machinery nor the wage labor relation are as significant as the relation between the owners and the users of capital. In Musha the 34 or 35 different tractor owners provide tractor services for land preparation and for threshing for the remainder of the population. From one point of view, labor (the farming household) hires capital when it engages the tractor to perform an operation for it. The initiative to hire comes from the side of the household, not from the machine owner. If machine owners are to reap full value from their machines, then they must maintain good relations with their "clients," for a machine owner who loses his clients will not be able to retain his machine (unless his own land is large enough to support it). So from the social point of view, the farmer (who hires the machine) has at least some degree of control over the owner of the machine. Thus we cannot assimilate the farmer to the category of labor working for capital—while that may analytically have some value, it is not true of the social relationships in the labor process itself. We can also observe that Labor (meaning the hired casual labor) and Capital (the machinery) are not in direct relationship with one another, but are mediated by the continuing position of the farmer who in a sense controls neither capital (machinery) nor large amounts of labor (since most farm households fall far short of the labor needed to farm efficiently).[5]

Machinery is now an integral part of the labor process. Renters of machines for the most part no longer really have the option of returning to the old techniques (animal draft for plowing and threshing) in part because they have switched from the working cows to the less suitable buffalo, in part because the wooden tools themselves have been allowed to deteriorate, and in part because few are willing to engage themselves in the lengthy work process needed to carry out these tasks (especially threshing) using animal power.

Both the farmers and the machine owners benefit from the use of machinery. The farmers get the task accomplished quickly; this keeps their labor costs down and also reduces to some degree the work of supervision and management by concentrating it in a few days instead of spreading it out over a month. The machine owners benefit because they turn a tidy profit on their operations. Thus if the payment of rent for machines represents analytically an extraction of surplus, it cannot be taken to imply the immiseration of the farmers, since they benefit from the transaction as well.

On the one hand, the introduction of machines reduces the overall demand for labor. From this point of view, the farmer is paying to the machine owner part of what he previously paid to the workers. (The contrast should not be over-emphasized since about 40 percent of the cost of the crop to the farmer is in labor costs, and only 10 percent in machine costs.) Thus the owner of capital claims part of the share of the increased profit derived from any decline in labor costs.

While the farmer benefits from this shift, the real effect is a change in the distribution of income away from the workers (whether landless or small farmers themselves) and towards the machine owners. We must add to this the idea that the machine owners are increasingly concentrating certain kinds of knowledge and skills concerning the process of work in agriculture—far fewer people know how to drive a tractor or set up a thresher than knew how to drive a yoke of bullocks in plowing or threshing, even though one may not intrinsically be more complex than the other. Thus the introduction of machinery inaugurates a process of redistribution of both money and skills towards a small stratum of people who manage to control the machines (and frequently large areas of land as well).

On the other hand, the introduction of machinery has increased the need for labor at peak moments, such as threshing, without reducing it for such tasks as planting and harvesting. Thus the ability of the household to provide its labor needs has declined, and the reliance on the labor market has increased. This shift means that the labor process has been fractionated. Whereas previously most tasks could be done within the household, now the household is no longer a pool of labor, but a pool of managers, and many people participate in the process of producing such crops as wheat or cotton. The increase in the level of the forces of production through capitalization has modified the role of labor, as it has modified the roles of the household members and the potential pool of hired laborers. The short, episodic nature of the tasks hinders the development of enduring social relationships. More mechanization has led to more hiring of labor (see also Hopkins, Mehanna and Abdelmaksoud 1982:140–143, 236).

The machine owners end up in a position to exercise a certain degree of control over the labor process through their control of significant capital. They make the choices between available technology on behalf of all their clients. They determine the cost of the services. The machinery they introduce guides the organization of labor, for each machine has its own requirements; they are also able to influence the scheduling of work by individual farmers. It is tempting to think that the choice of technology also influences the crop mix which is characteristic of the village—in other words, there may be a preference for open field crops that can be handled by the available machinery rather than vegetables that require a high input of hand labor or a different kind of machinery to which the farmers in Musha do not yet have access.

The household head, acting on behalf of the household, plays a key managerial role in the labor process. The household head mobilizes and supervises the labor, whether this labor is mobilized from within the household, or is hired on the village labor market. He also is responsible for engaging and supervising the use of the machinery. In these twin processes, the household head is effective because he can make the necessary small-scale adjustments. His principal activity, however, is management rather than provision of labor.[6] In earlier days, when the household structures corresponded to the technology—animal traction and hand work—there were many fewer non-agricultural occupations to absorb the household labor force and provide a non-agricultural income. Then and now resources are balanced and distributed within the household, notably as a result of the sexual divsion of labor, and here again a certain managerial role is required.

Although the household appears to be "the same" as it was in earlier days, this is slightly misleading. As the structure in which it is embedded has changed, so has the role of the household. The managerial dimension of its role is more evident, while its role in mobilizing labor is reduced. The new function of the farming household, as the link between labor and capital, requires a different set of skills on the part of the household head. The survival of the independent farming household is based on the advantages of decentralizing control over labor away from the owners of capital (machinery). Thus the labor supervision is carried out in small groups by small farmers who are keenly concerned to get the most out of the labor available to them because their household income directly depends on this. The micro-adjustments necessary here include the various incentives given to labor to produce (supply of tea and cigarettes in the fields) as well as the knowledge necessary to hire labor when needed.

Meanwhile, the kind of landless person or smallholder who would have been a good candidate for casual wage labor in earlier days is more and more finding a way to escape that niche, principally through a combination of education and migration. Thus while machinery slightly reduces the overall demand for labor, and requires larger labor gangs, the labor pool is diminished: parallel processes, but it is hard to say which is the cause of the other. The decline of labor availability in the village, however, is a sign of the progressive integration of the village into a wider labor market. Since migration is the chief mechanism for this, I turn next to that.

Migration

History

Musha's involvement in a wider labor market through permanent and temporary migration has been a fact of life for several generations (Hopkins 1983). Musha workers participated in *tarahil* work as cotton porters (*shayyals*) in Cairo and the Delta very early, and there has long been both permanent and temporary migration to the ports of Suez and Alexandria where the men worked as stevedores. The low rate of growth overall suggests considerable out-migration. The fact that more females than males were counted in the 1907, 1917, and 1927 censuses suggests that the pattern of migration of single males dominated prior to the revolution in Musha agriculture caused by pumping. Since then there has been more of a pattern of family migration. There is still a steady stream of generally very poor Musha families to Suez and Alexandria. Individual men are now more likely to migrate temporarily outside the country.

At the beginning of the British colonial period, Willcocks (1889:247) noted the phenomenon of Upper Egyptian migration, relating it to the ecology of basin irrigation:

> It is owing to the absence of field labour over large tracts in Upper Egypt that the *Saidis* or inhabitants of Upper Egypt are enabled to flock down into Lower Egypt and undertake the contract work, making large profits; in which profits the inhabitants of Lower Egypt, with their superior crops, their plowing and irrigation labours, and perpetual field operations, barely participate. This all goes to swell the profits on the lands irrigated by basin irrigation.

The work done by the Saidis in Lower Egypt generally did not involve actual work in the fields. It was more likely to involve contract labor on the maintenance of the irrigation system and work in the cotton gins, particularly loading and hauling sacks and bales of cotton.

Some people from Upper Egypt also migrated to the cities after the 1880s and 1890s when the free market in labor emerged and there was no longer such a shortage of labor as earlier in the century (Baer 1982:76). Baer (ibid., following Ali Pasha Mubarek) notes that in 1907 some 30,000 people from Asyut province lived in Cairo, and that "Many of Cairo's porters were from Musha village (Asyut)."

Internal Migration

In the past, and to some extent in the present, there have been two different patterns of migration. There was a seasonal migration to the cotton gins, organized by labor contractors from Musha who knew the labor market in the Delta, and there was a temporary migration of individuals to the port cities of Suez and Alexandria. The "temporary" migration was usually for a period of years, sometimes as many as ten or twenty, and was not organized through labor contractors. It would frequently fade into a third pattern of migration, permanent migration, since the worker would in many cases bring his family with him. Permanent migrants from Musha have created sizeable Musha colonies in both these port towns. Links are sustained between Musha and these colonies through visits, trade, and marriage. It is not uncommon to find women from Musha families who were raised in Alexandria or Suez but who married back home and have spent their married lives there.

Many men from Musha have participated in both types of labor migration to the north. In interviewing men in their 50s and 60s, I found that only those with considerable landed wealth or another source of income had not had some experience as a young man working in the cotton gins of the Delta, or in the port towns of Suez or Alexandria. Approximately half the landless households in the household budget sample had some involvement with this pattern, about equally divided between the gins and the ports.

Here are some examples. (1) 'Amm Mokhtar, born in 1919, worked for the British army in Suez and elsewhere from 1939 to 1949, when he returned to Musha to raise his family and farm 3 feddans. (2) His matrilateral relative, 'Amm Sherif, also worked in Suez and elsewhere starting around 1939 and continued until after the 1952 Revolution. He married while still a migrant, but always kept his household in Musha, returning home every three or four months for a brief stay, but his family now provides the guard and mechanic for a pump, and so he found it possible to settle permanently at home. (3) The chief miller in the main flour mill worked in Suez and Alexandria for nine years after the Revolution. (4) Abu Hassan worked for many years as a longshoreman in Alexandria, and probably for that reason married late. He also once tried a year in Libya, but did not last. (5) One grocer in Musha learned the business working for a Cypriot in Suez and Ismailia. (6) 'Amm Farid has been working all his adult life in Alexandria while keeping his family in Musha; now two of his sons are old enough to work there with him. They return home every couple of months for a visit.

Many of the families surveyed report one or more brothers working in Cairo, Suez, Alexandria, or elsewhere. In some cases, these men have split off from the village household, while in other cases they continue to visit and send money, perhaps initially to ensure that they can use the network when the time comes to seek a wife. A new marriage reinforces the network, and provides another link between the internal migrant and the home village.

Sometimes entire families leave Musha to settle in Suez or other northern towns. Of the 121 names of my original sample list, six (five percent) had moved out of Musha with their families between the summer of 1979 and the spring of 1981, less than two years. Four of these went to Suez. Available information on these families suggests that they were landless and with minimal labor power; two of the six were headed by women, presumably widows.

Seasonal migration was and is organized by labor contractors. The pattern is distinct from the *tarahil* pattern reported from the delta (El-Messiri 1983; Stauth 1983:185–196). In the Delta, labor contractors engage workers for a period of forty days to work in the New Lands of Tahrir Province or on Cairo construction sites, and the workers then spend a period at home before starting off again. In the Musha case, perhaps because the distances are greater, the engagement tends to be for an entire season, and the destination is frequently the cotton gins of the north.

The organizers of the seasonal migration to the cotton gins in the north were the labor contractors (sing. *muqawil anfar*). Several men from Musha made fortunes in this way. Hamid started as a pump guard, then worked as a labor contractor before investing his money in land in Musha and in urban real estate in Asyut and Tanta. Abu Abderrahman began as a labor contractor, then became involved in the operation of cotton gins in Beni Suef and Kafr el-Zayyat. Abdelkhalek made enough money contracting labor to build up an estate of 100 feddans in Musha.

The successful labor contractor needed to have good relations in his home village, which served as a pool of labor. Men would generally only agree to work for a labor contractor whom they knew and felt they could trust because he was from the same village community and could be influenced through traditional village mechanisms. The labor contractor also had to have good relations at the receiving end, usually the cotton gins of Middle and Lower Egypt, and he had to know the market. In general, the labor contractor was responsible not only for recruiting and providing the labor to the gins, but also for labor discipline. The gin operators would provide the technical direction, but it was up to the labor contractors to make sure that the workers worked, that the labor power contracted for was actually realized in the form of labor. In many cases, this meant that the chief labor contractor would designate a younger man, often a relative, to remain with the gang in the cotton gin to ensure good labor relations. The contractor had to satisfy both the bosses and the workers to be able to bring together the same deal another time. The contractor knew and maintained relations at both ends of the system.

Labor contracting continues in Musha, but on a much reduced scale. The introduction of extensive doublecropping in Musha after the 1930s created a larger labor demand in Musha, and probably encouraged the labor contractors to attempt to use the labor on their own newly purchased land to grow cotton. But there are still cases such as the two brothers who work in Mehalla with a labor contractor from September to December each year, or the man in his 60s who works as a foreman in a cotton gin in Simballawein. One Musha labor contractor, Abu Ahmed, got his start working for a relative, probably as a foreman, and has since gone into business for himself. In the fall of 1980 Abu Ahmed said he had about eighty men working for him in the Delta, loading and carrying sacks of cotton. The base of operations was the town of Sammanud, and his brother was there supervising them when he was in Musha. The workers are paid a set fee per sack of cotton, and the labor contractors are paid part of this fee and an equivalent amount from the cotton gin operators. The workers probably pay the contractor between 5 and 10 percent of their income, and they in return receive about PT15 per sack. Thus the labor contractor receives around PT3 to 5 per sack, half from the worker and half from the hirer (the capitalist). Because the workers are paid piece rates, both they and the contractor earn more for working longer hours. Abu Ahmed said that the previous year had been a good one for his work, for he had cleared LE4,000 to 5,000. He also supplemented his work as a labor contractor by importing threshing machines from Sammanud to Musha.

Migration Abroad

Currently the pattern of migration outside Egypt has engaged the attention of many people. Migration abroad for professionals (mainly schoolteachers) began in the 1960s or earlier, and involved a wide range of Arab countries such as Algeria, Libya, Yemen, Saudi Arabia and the Emirates (Dessouki 1982). Recently a number of agricultural personnel have gone to Iraq. Since Musha has always produced a good number of schoolteachers and agricultural engineers, it has long been part of this movement. This migration is organized by the Egyptian government and the host government, and is considered to be temporary, i.e., for a period of four or five years. This rotation became a way to ensure that all teachers had equal access to a lucrative assignment. In more recent years, however, skilled, semi-skilled and unskilled laborers have begun to migrate abroad. The numbers involved for all Egypt are the subject of a heated debate, but they are high and rapidly increased following the sudden upsurge in oil wealth in the 1970s (S.E. Ibrahim 1982:63).

The household budget sample turned up a number of cases of migration abroad. All in all, over ten percent of the households in my sample have a history of migration abroad. This appears marginally higher than the result of 7–10 percent obtained by Commander and Hadhoud (1986:172) in three Delta villages. Extrapolated to the population of Musha as a whole, my results suggest that there were between 250 and 300 Musha people working abroad in early 1981. This figure coincides with the guesses of knowledgeable informants. The details of the cases from my sample are given below.

1. The household head, age 40, has been working in Saudi Arabia for a year. He is divorced, but his children are living with his mother. The household is landless, and he worked as a day laborer before migrating.
2. The household head, age 48, has been working as a hospital clerk in Saudi Arabia for a year. His wife, mother, and eight children remain at home. The holding of 2 feddans 16 qirats is cared for by a male relative. He was recruited in a group of fifteen, including seven from Musha, by a man who came from Saudi Arabia and found them through intermediaries.
3. The household head, age 50, is in Saudi Arabia. The son has a diploma but is unemployed. They own 20 qirats, which are rented out.
4. The household head, age 47, returned to Musha from Saudi Arabia in 1981 and now works primarily as a day laborer. Before leaving he had a regular job, now he works around. He is 47 years old.
5. The household head, age 41, returned to Musha from Lebanon in 1981 for a visit, but his return was delayed by the war. He worked in a bakery in the Christian sector of Lebanon. He had previously worked in Saudi Arabia. He has a holding of 12 qirats, and a household of eight persons including wife and children.
6. The household head, age 50, has been working in Saudi Arabia for two years. The household of nine includes his wife and children. There is a holding of 1 feddan 8 qirats. He was a small farmer before migrating.
7. The son, age 26, of the household head has been working in Saudi Arabia for three years, and comes home once a year. The head has a holding of 1 feddan 6 qirats, and there are six persons in the household, including the son's wife.
8. The household head, age 50, has been working in Saudi Arabia for four years. His son of 25 is in the army. The household includes eight people: head's wife, son's wife, and children. The holding is 1 feddan. Before leaving for Saudi Arabia, the son was a laborer.
9. The brother of the household head, age 27 and single, disappeared to Saudi Arabia and perhaps elsewhere; they rarely hear from him. The head is a single young man of 30 who teaches in the Musha preparatory school. The holding is 2 feddans 10 qirats, which they farm with hired labor.
10. The household head, age 40, is working in Saudi Arabia as a builder. The household included his father, now 70, also a builder, and also the wives and children of both men, nine in all. The father owns 4 feddans.

11. One of the sons in this household of 22 people is a teacher in Libya. Other sons have government jobs in Egypt. The holding amounts to 18 feddans, and the household also owns shares in pumps.
12. The household head, age 41, is a secondary school teacher working in the Emirates. Another brother is a teacher in Egypt. The household includes 12 people; the holding is 5 feddans; they own a tractor.

It is readily apparent that it is not the very poor who migrate abroad. They cannot afford the cost of doing so. The cost may include both the cost of the ticket and the passport, and in most cases the migrant feels obliged to leave a sum of money with his family to tide them over until he can begin sending remittances. In Musha the cost of departure was estimated at LE400 or more, roughly a year's income for the poor majority. Some people sold land to finance the trip. The data also show that the migrants were not unattached young men, but were mature men in their 30s and 40s, with a wife and children at home. The average age of the twelve men was 42, and ten of them were married while one was single and one divorced. This picture is confirmed by a comparison between emigrants and non-emigrants carried out in an east-bank Giza village (Khafagi 1983:140–2). She notes that migrants "own more land and come from higher income households than do the non-emigrants."

Saad Eddin Ibrahim (1982:11–16) has described some aspects of the network that passes Egyptian migrants to Saudi Arabia. There has to be a sponsor in Saudi Arabia to legitimate the migrant's presence there. Since the Saudi sponsor, unlike the labor contractor taking workers to the Delta cotton gins, cannot know both ends of the migration route, there are also Egyptian recruiters. The migrants I talked to in Musha had mostly been recruited, or had made their contacts, through a Musha man who in turn was connected to the Saudi system. Several of these Musha men were identified to me; they include some of the big landowners and other knowledgeable and powerful people in the village. Only one man reported that people had come to Musha to seek recruits, and that was for a white collar job.

In theory, the sponsor provides work for the men himself, but in practice he often hires them out to other people, retaining a substantial portion of their salary. Thus in many cases unskilled migrants to Saudi Arabia are sponsored by entrepreneurs who do not necessarily have a precise job for them. They are then used as casual labor in construction. They may find themselves fully employed, but apparently not always. For this reason, some (like #4 above) conclude that they cannot make enough money in Saudi Arabia to make it worthwhile, and so return home.

Migrants are more likely to bring money with them on their annual visits home than to send it back. When they do send it back, they prefer to use intermediaries, at least for the final stages to ensure that it reaches the right person in Musha. There is also no desire to publicize how much money is flowing in. One migrant told me that he sent the money via a bank to his sister, who is married to a Protestant minister in Cairo (this minister was responsible for arranging his first trip to Saudi Arabia). His sister then forwarded it to his wife through the post office. When migrants return they are likely to supply their families with such luxuries as televsion sets, electric fans and the like, and to build or rebuild their homes. One migrant in Saudi Arabia was financing his brother's project of opening a tractor repair shop, and another had invested some of his income in a new tractor. (This was the only example of a tractor bought with migration income that I came across.)

Returned migrants are commonly blamed in Musha for bidding up the price of land, but with farm land at LE7,000 a feddan, there is not yet much evidence for sales. There has been increasing pressure on the prices of potential building sites at the village perimeter, which run to LE2,500 a qirat. The interest in building sites reflects the temporary nature of the migration: people find it feasible to base themselves in Musha while earning an income at a distance, a return to the old seasonal migration pattern. Families remain, and so houses are needed.

Migration abroad is also commonly cited in Musha as a reason for the shortage of agricultural labor. In my list of migrants, seven out of twelve (58 percent) had worked in agricultural labor before leaving. (Of those absent at the time of the survey, only five of ten were in this position.) Extrapolating, the total draw-down on the agricultural labor force would be from 150 to 200 individuals. However, most of these would not be young men, but men perhaps looking for an alternative to strenuous field labor in their mature years. The young men who leave Musha are more likely to do so after receiving their education, and are more likely to remain within Egypt either as civil servants or as workers in the urban areas. For instance, more than one hundred officials from Musha are said to be working in the New Valley (Kharga and Dakhla), but I have no systematic information on the size of this phenomenon.

Migration Strategies and Labor Markets

Migration abroad sociologically resembles the old migration to the port towns to work as stevedores and porters in that the migrant goes alone, and expects eventually to return enriched to his home community, where his wife and children remain as hostages. They are gambling that a few years of effort and privation will raise them to a higher standard of living, to some kind of "take-off point." Yet the process is not old enough to be sure that this will be the outcome. The old migration to the port towns was one of single young men; it is now one of families fleeing the poverty of Musha's lowest stratum. The current migration abroad is one of somewhat older men concerned about their families' well-being; it seems unlikely at the moment that it will generate family migration abroad. Migration by men alone assures the receiving country that most will eventually return home, and it ensures that most money will be sent home to care for the family.

In sum, migration abroad for the individual is one of a series of alternative strategies. Other alternatives include internal migration, local business enterprises such as shops, continued wage labor, and above all making sure that the next generation is educated enough to have a wider range of opportunities. For the local community such as Musha, migration is also a form of insertion into a national and international or regional labor market and hence division of labor. In that respect it is coupled with education.

Migration to Egypt's cities or the Delta reflects the growth of a labor market corresponding to that country; this dates well back into the 19th century at least. Migration abroad is a far more recent phenomenon, which began in the 1970s, apart from a few individuals who were seconded abroad by the Egyptian government to work in professional and teaching jobs. At the time of my field work in Musha, people were aware of the importance of this new trend, but there had not yet been any significant economic consequences for the community, such as occurred due to the enrichment of the labor contractors of the period before 1935. For the labor process in Musha, migration of all kinds is significant mainly for removing a large part of the labor force. This has several probable consequences. By reducing the size of the labor force, it contributes to increasing the cost of labor. But at the same time, the most militant are likely to migrate, and so are the very poor who would otherwise be a drain on the collectivity. Any revolutionary effects on the social organization of production are still in the future.

Conclusion: Labor Process and Labor Market

The Musha labor market appears highly segmented. Only a relatively small number of people are actually available on the free labor market, since many men have found other ways to earn a living, either outside agriculture or in jobs connected to agriculture but outside the free labor market. Women do not participate in agricultural work at all, and adolescents or children are not interchangeable with men since each task has its own specification. Most farming households compete for at least a small share of this labor pool. The capitalist farmers dominate the scene, hiring many of the workers and setting the wage that everyone must pay. In this respect it is noteworthy that they are the ones who hire the large gangs from other villages.

There is a complex wage structure. The "basic" wage is the day rate quoted for agricultural labor that is fairly unskilled. Yet there are some jobs that are paid piece rates, and others that require special skills to do with machinery, that result in higher daily incomes. The fact that workers are hired only for a day at a time means that bargaining and renegotiation can be continual. Wages show a tendency to rise and fall according to principles of supply and demand. The big hirers have the power to force wages down, and yet the small farmers benefit from this as well since their profit margins are smaller. It is clear that the willingness of men from el-Zawya and Baqur to work for lower wages than the Musha men acts to depress the general level of wages in the villages. The lower wages paid to adolescents and children are probably less of a depressant because there is so little competition for jobs between them and the men.

Control of labor is diffuse. It rarely comes through direct confrontation between boss and worker. Instead it comes from the need of the worker to be hired and rehired many times a year. He consequently needs to maintain a good reputation as a worker. Furthermore, the division of labor and of tasks means that the management of the household farming activity is quite separate from any individual task. The household head (the manager) must mobilize different kinds of labor for different jobs—a tractor to plow, a gang of kids to pick cotton, a few men to plant or weed cotton, a camel for transport—and each of these kinds of labor sticks to its speciality and is not concerned with the overall outcome. However, in case all these organization factors fail to have their effect, the hirer is always out in the fields with his workers, "standing behind them" to make sure that they do a good job, and that they work for the agreed-upon period. The only exception to the constant supervision are the regular workers, usually tied to their bosses by years of common work and personal relations. On the other hand, many of the men of Musha prefer not to work in circumstances where they feel too closely supervised in an impersonal setting. They prefer to work for the smaller farmers who are only occasional hirers because they feel the relations are warmer, and the treatment is likely to be better. This means they are apt to receive cigarettes and tea. Others will seek to escape the hierarchical control of labor altogether by seeking employment outside agriculture, in government work, trade, or migration.

Mechanization has altered the labor process. In the last two chapters I have analyzed the complex, articulated structures of production characteristic of Musha agriculture. Agricultural machinery has now become a mainstay of the labor process, although many hand tasks remain. Mechanization has had the effect of creating a labor market by breaking up the household-based labor process, by making it difficult or impossible for a household to supply its labor needs without recourse to hired labor. At present the labor process is broken up into many discrete tasks, each of which is handled by a different combination of labor and capital. Only the farmer is a commodity producer; he achieves this by hiring in labor and machinery. Neither the labor nor the capital is thus directly concerned with the quality or the quantity of the output, but is concerned to be paid for the effort. This very complex division of labor and labor process relies on the skills of the farmers, small and large, who must combine the elements and attain the right result.

Notes

1. Before 1964, in the days of the flood, the cotton harvest had to be completed by September 20 each year. The importation of labor from other villages reached a crescendo in the final weeks and days before the water was let into the Zinnar basin. Some of the social links that allow this recruitment from distant villages hark back to these days.

2. Radwan (1977:31) has argued that while cash wages tripled, real wages in rural Egypt remained stable from 1948 to 1974. However, there is considerable evidence that they have risen since then. This is a highly controversial subject throughout Egypt due to the unreliability of reporting of actual wages (oral reporting after the fact) and disagreement on what is being counted (variation in the length of the day, the nature of the task, etc.). For some of the debate, see *Mechanization, Migration, and Agricultural Labor Markets in Egypt* (Richards and Martin 1983), especially the articles by Richards, Martin and Nagaar (1983) and by de Janvry and Subbarao (1983). See also Adams (1985) and Commander and Hadhoud (1986).

3. Most of these young tractor drivers said they had learned their skills from the tractor driver for the village cooperative society. This suggests another way in which the cooperative may be furthering agricultural mechanization in the village.

4. During my field work in Musha, all the earth used to make bricks was in theory taken from the earth excavated when the government built a new drain across Musha's land in 1980. Thus in theory no top soil was being removed, though I did find one example of it.

5. From another point of view, even the smallest farmer possesses a substantial amount of capital, especially if he owns his land—the price of a feddan of land is only a little less than the price of the commonly available tractors.

6. Roumasset and Smith (1981) make a similar comment concerning the situation in the Philippines. They start out to "investigate how intensification of production, induced by population pressure, leads to further division of labor and the transition to labor markets" (p. 403), and then go on to argue that "As hired labor is increasingly relied on to perform these arduous tasks (e.g., transplanting rice, harvesting, weeding . . .), the farm operator specializes in management and supervision and performs himself mainly those farm operations where shirking is difficult to control" (p. 405). They refer to the situation wherein "unskilled labor is provided primarily by landless workers and skilled labor is provided primarily by the farm family" (p. 406) as "hierarchical specialization" (p. 405).

9

Marketing

Throughout this study, I have stressed the degree of monetization in Musha agriculture, and the extent to which agricultural products have become commodities. In the last chapter I showed how labor has become a commodity, and stressed the importance of the rental market for machinery. This chapter analyzes the organization of agricultural marketing in Musha. Trade in agricultural products, as much as migration, shows the articulation of the village into the wider economy of Egypt and the world. Here we are less concerned with the balance of trade between rural and urban and more concerned to show how the process works. This brings us to consider the role of the merchant in the capitalist development of rural Egypt. A full analysis of the labor process includes the role of the merchant and marketing since production is largely oriented to the market. Moreover, capital influences the social organization of agriculture through marketing as much as through mechanization.

The presence of a market is a dominant fact of life for the people of Musha. They sell a good deal of what they grow, and they buy a good deal of what they use. The few remnants of the old subsistence economy are in wheat, still used to bake local bread, and dairy products, poultry and small amounts of vegetables, where only the surplus is sold. Prices are a never-ending source of speculation in conversation. In its less useful form, this involves endless and learned disquisitions on how high prices are nowadays compared with what they once were. In its more poignant form, this involves constant alertness for changes in price, visiting markets to ascertain the going price for livestock, or asking travellers the prices of familiar items in other villages and towns.

The Organization of Marketing

The marketing situation is complex. In the first place, there is considerable government intervention. This principally takes the form of "forced deliveries" for some of the basic field crops. The system began in the 1960s and changed from time to time. At its peak, this system affected cotton, wheat, beans and lentils in Musha. Around 1979 wheat was removed from the list. The government is a monopoly purchaser of cotton. For the other crops, each farmer registered as growing more than a certain minimum of that crop (say one feddan) is required to sell to the government a given amount of the crop per feddan. For example, a farmer growing three feddans of lentils would be required to supply two ardebs for each feddan, or six ardebs, whereas the normal yield is around 3.5 to 4 ardebs. A farmer is required to sell 2.5 ardebs of beans per feddan; the yield is around 8 or 10 ardebs. The government price of both these crops had been raised 30–40 percent the year I was in Musha.[1] The farmer is then free to make whatever use he wishes of the remainder of the crop.[2]

In addition to government purchasing agents (through the Village Bank), one also finds merchants in Musha who deal in the basic cereal grains, i.e., wheat, beans, lentils, chickpeas, maize, sorghum, and barley. For the most part these grains are sold out of the village and end up in urban markets. Here the market, like the government purchases, fulfills a centralizing function. For other items, however, the merchants are arbitraging—speculating on price variations between rural areas. This is true for straw, livestock, and some fruits and vegetables.

Government Purchasing: Cotton

The government has been the only legal purchaser of cotton since the early 1960s when the network of private cotton brokers was eliminated by government fiat.

When the farmer has sacked his cotton, he must transport it to the cotton weighing station in each village. Here the farmer's name is written on the sacks in black paint. A cotton grader (*farraz*) comes twice a week to grade the quality of each farmer's cotton. Once this is done, the sacks are weighed and the result—quality and weight—is recorded by two or three people keeping separate records. The sacks are then kept until the company sends a truck from the cotton gin at Filiw near Abutig. The farmer is paid LE27 for each qantar of cotton immediately by the Village Bank. Once the full calculations have been made, he should receive an additional amount. These calculations reflect the information on quality and also any deductions to which the farmer is subject. The deductions include the cost of seed and fertilizer as advanced by the Village Bank, and the cost of pest control as administered by the cooperative.

The farmer must pay for the transport as far as the cotton weighing station in the village, and he must pay the station staff for their services. In 1980 the farmer paid PT10 per sack for weighing and grading. The staff also received PT2/3 from the company for their effort. One way to avoid this stage is to transport the cotton directly to the Filiw gin. This solution was taken by one of the larger farmers in Musha, who was then paid an extra 15 percent, which more than covered his costs of loading and transport. Loading, at PT15 per sack, is a big expense, but was the same whether the farmer transported the cotton one kilometer to the cotton weighing lot or 30 kilometers to the gin. He produced around 600 sacks of cotton that year, equal to over 100,000 kilos (50 tons). By delivering the sacks to Filiw, he received around LE2 extra for each sack, of which perhaps PT30 represented the cost of loading, unloading and weighing. This option was only open to the largest farmers, and in fact the second largest farmer in the village simply delivered his cotton in the village.

The weighing station in the village was a bit of a bottleneck. The secretary of the cooperative reflected the unhappiness of the village farmers when he complained about this to the Village Bank representative one day in the guest house. The problem first of all was that the lot was too small, and so some farmers had to wait their turn before delivering their cotton there. These delays to the farmers interfered with their preparations for the winter crop cycle. This was then exacerbated by a dispute between the ginning company and the truckers over trucking rates, so that there were further delays in hauling out the weighed and graded cotton. Thus the cooperative secretary asked the Village Bank director to make sure that the weighed and graded cotton was removed from the village weighing station as quickly as possible. These delays on the government side also caused delays in paying the farmer. Since the sale of the cotton crop is probably the biggest single cash inflow for most farmers, they postpone paying their own debts and their purchases until this moment and are anxious to be paid as quickly as possible.

The price is fixed by the government each year. It is considerably less than the world market price. This is a sore point with farmers who are well aware of this disparity. The price appears to be fixed for essentially political reasons—that is, the government fixes the price that it thinks will provide sufficient incentive to farmers to grow their cotton carefully and that it justifies in terms of providing a decent if modest income to the farmers. It thus includes certain assumptions about an appropriate income for farmers. At the same time, the government tries to maximize the gap between the purchase price and the resale price on the world market; this is intended to be a major way in which rural surplus is extracted for the benefit of the government's modernization and industrialization plans. One of the consequences of holding the price to the farmer down is that there is a certain risk of fixing a price too low to provide him with a real incentive. The farmer is also driven to put the squeeze on his labor and pay them as little as possible. Cotton is labor-intensive and so the effort to keep costs down produces a reliance on child labor and, in general, an effort to argue workers into lower wages. Thus the surplus is extracted not only from the farmers, but also indirectly from the workers.

Centralizing Merchants

There are around 100 to 150 men in Musha who trade in grains. This includes some large and some small, and some who specialize in certain grains while others will deal in any of them. In general, their role is to purchase grains from the individual farmers and transmit them to the consumers in the urban areas; hence they are "centralizing merchants." They must have some capital to enter the market (the more the capital the higher the level of the entry point), and they must have accumulated a reputation for trustworthiness. They must also know how to judge the quality of grains and how to judge measures, and they must keep abreast of price fluctuations.

The marketing system involves many links. The farmer sells to the village merchant, who sells to the Asyut-based middleman, who in turn sells to the big city merchant. The traders in Musha are likely to buy the grain directly on the threshing ground. They buy it by the kayla (a measure of volume; see Table 4.5), the twelfth part of an ardeb, and store it until they are approached by a merchant from outside the village. The village dealers generally sell to an Asyut-based middleman. The middlemen can not afford to deal with each individual farmer. They prefer to deal only with merchants in the village with whom they are familiar, or with farmers large enough to have a respectable amount by themselves.

Such a middleman buys from the Musha merchants by volume and sells to the big-city merchants by weight (kilo). The middleman must thus be aware of the different value of the volume measures from village to village. The weight of the kayla varies about five percent from one village to another, and so in order to avoid cumbersome and costly reweighing (costly because of the labor needed to lift the sacks), the middleman has to know how to make the equivalence between the two systems. He also has to know which village traders he can trust to give an honest measure.

In Musha even the biggest farmers do not take their goods to market themselves, but wait for merchants to come in from outside. Since they are cutting out the role of the village merchant (and perhaps in extreme cases the regional middleman as well) their profit will be greater. One time I noticed a group of merchants from outside Musha trying to make a purchase from one of the largest farmers in the village; they had a Musha merchant with them as a guarantor.

Another reason for the extended chain of links needed for this commercial connection is that marketing depends to a great extent on trust. This is particularly true when payment is delayed as it often is. Trust thus substitutes to some extent for capital. The buyer must also trust the seller to provide honest measure. In rural Egypt it is difficult to trust someone you do not know. Hence the role of the middleman in the example just given: the out-of-town merchants trust him, and so does the Musha farmer, because he is known to both sides and can guarantee each to the other.

One of the largest grain merchants in Musha is Saad Abdelmon'im, 69 years old and a trader for the last 20 years. He deals in grain not just in Musha but throughout this portion of the valley. He is registered with the cooperative as a holder of 2.5 feddans, clearly an insignificant part of his portfolio. He works with some of his sons (he has three living at home) and together they buy up grain from the farmers on the threshing ground and store it until they can resell it to a bigger trader based in Cairo or another city.

Mahmoud Hussein, another trader, deals in grains but also specializes in collecting eggs for sale in Cairo and other cities, sending them out in pickup trucks. Smaller traders may combine trading with another activity. Thus Rifa'i works as a clerk in the local middle school, and also trades in beans and lentils (these are the crops still subject to the government delivery system, so that smaller amounts of them may be available than of other crops). He and his father also farm a small holding. There are some petty traders—the only ones actually to work out of shops in Musha—that specialize in making petty purchases and equally petty sales. I once observed one of these, a man of 71, haggling over the price of maize with a ten-year-old girl for what eventually turned out to be a purchase by him from her worth PT85. Thus they buy in small amounts from people who are using their store of grain like a bank account, drawing from it as they need it (meanwhile waiting for a price rise, cf. Reeves 1983). These petty traders are prepared to sell equally small amounts to customers looking for small amounts of grain, perhaps because they also have small amounts of cash.

I once talked to an Asyut-based middleman, originally from the village of Shutb but living in Asyut. He is associated with two other men, both from Asyut. They have a truck to haul for them. Their job is to collect the grain from the villages, bulk it, and then sell it to the merchants who come down from Cairo. The merchants from Cairo can not do this directly because they do not have time to learn all the villages, measures, and people, and because the amounts involved are too small. The middlemen are prepared to wait for a delayed payment from their Cairo merchant partners provided something is paid down, but then of course they themselves must delay their payment to the village merchants, who may have to delay their payment to the farmers.

Another possible arrangement is suggested by the activities of a dealer in chickpeas from Tanta. This merchant established a lot near one of Musha's threshing grounds where his staff would buy and stock chickpeas.

This lot also served as a storehouse for chickpeas from some neighboring villages. For Musha operations, however, the Tanta dealer was in partnership with Saad Abdelmon'im, and their lot was located adjacent to Saad's house. Thus the presence of Saad served as a guarantee to local sellers that they would not be cheated. The merchants had engaged a staff of four or five men from the neighboring village of Aulad Ibrahim. As the chickpeas were bought, these men would spread them out to dry, then rake them over, resack them, and prepare them for the trip to Cairo by truck. The men working here counted on being employed for three or four months. In this year (1981), the farmers were all counting on the price to rise from around LE90 to LE100 or more, and so they were slow to sell their crop.

Timing is important in setting the price, and the ability or willingness of the farmer to wait for the best market price is an important element in determining that farmer's income for the year. Conversely, merchants are interested in buying right away, from the farmers who need money badly enough to sell straight from the threshing ground. Or they may wait until just before the new crop is harvested, to attempt to drive the price down in anticipation that the new crop will cause it to drop shortly anyway. A merchant with a stock may also be anxious to sell at this point to raise the capital with which he can do business in the next harvest season. Thus one group of merchants from Nag' Hammadi bought a truckload of beans from a Musha merchant less than a month before the new harvest: the timing was clearly an important factor in setting the price.

Some farmers also speculate on the market prices. Thus for instance some farmers were constrained by the crop rotation system to grow lentils. They collected the government-supplied inputs for lentils, then planted chickpeas instead. Chickpeas are very similar to lentils, require the same amount of work, and have roughly the same yield per feddan. But the price is about 25 percent higher. Now the farmers were still liable to make their forced delivery to the government for their lentils allotment. So they would buy lentils from the local grain dealers in order to resell (at a loss) to the government. Even though they would take a loss on the lentils, this loss would be covered by the extra profit earned by growing chickpeas, and so they would come out ahead—provided the prices of lentils and chickpeas remained stable. Of course, the grain dealers raised their selling price for lentils because they knew that these farmers had to buy in order to meet their commitment to the government. This in itself reduced the gap between the two prices.

Arbitraging Trade

Certain products are characteristically traded locally, within the region, counting on local price variation, or simply differences in availability. They include straw, livestock, and vegetables. Each one has its own specialists and its own organization. Straw dealers are also not the same as grain dealers.

Musha is a major supplier of straw to the villages to the south. The straw is used for animal fodder, particularly during the months from April through November when berseem is not available. Although it is not particularly nutritious, it does fill the animals' stomachs. Under Egyptian market conditions, the value of the straw per feddan is about 30 to 50 percent higher than the value of the wheat itself—one of the reasons why the short-stalked MexiPak wheat is not favored and why hand harvesting is still preferred.

Three men of my acquaintance—let us call them Mahmoud, Damian, and Fawzi—were preoccupied from mid-February through early May, 1981, by this trade. None of them had systematically been involved in straw trading before. Fawzi was a professional winnower, Mahmoud the village *dallal,* and Damian was a prominent farmer who had a good sense of organization. They began by making an arrangement with a man they knew in the village of el-Atamna, about 60 kilometers to the south in Sohag governorate. This man was the son of a Shaykh in a religious order in el-Atamna who had been a frequent visitor to the related religious orders in Musha. This religious connection meant that people knew and felt they could trust each other. The religious link thus provided a key bit of support for economic activity. Although Damian and Fawzi were members of Musha's small Protestant community, Damian at any rate had known the Shaykh for fifteen years, and each had stayed at the house of the other on various occasions. According to the arrangement, Mahmoud, Fawzi, and Haidar, the son of the Shaykh, would be partners (Damian was merely an observer at this point). Mahmoud and Fawzi would buy up straw in Musha, and arrange for it to be sacked and transported to el-Atamna. There Haidar would sell it to his neighbors. Each link in the chain was built on trust—the Musha sellers trusted Mahmoud and Fawzi (at least up to a point); these two knew Haidar; and Haidar knew and trusted his el-Atamna customers. This trust was necessary because the traders had no capital and so they had to wait for the ultimate customers in el-Atamna to pay before the money could be passed back to the original sellers in Musha. The element of trust did not preclude the need to keep individual copies of the financial records (on scraps of paper, for no one thought to buy a notebook).

This trust was not taken for granted but was continually reinforced. Thus at a weekly *dhikr* meeting (see chapter 10) in Musha shortly after the first truck load had been sent to el-Atamna, two members of this *tariqa* chapter attacked Mahmoud, also a member, because they had not been paid as soon as they expected. The disputants directed their comments to the senior member of the order present (third in the hierarchy, and also a relative of Mahmoud's), so that he was brought into the dispute as a circumstantial mediator. The *dhikr* that evening never generated much religious activity because everyone became so embroiled in this economic dispute. The quarrel was presumably ended when the "mediator" led a joint recitation of the *fatiha,* the opening passage from the Koran.

On another occasion, some farmers who felt that the straw dealers were delaying their payment too long banged on the door of Fawzi's house to demand their money. This was very effective as a tactic, because the three were highly embarrassed at this public display. Mahmoud said that the one thing he did not like was to have people banging on his door asking for money (even if it was Fawzi's door). They spent considerable time that day calling in debts and borrowing money to collect the LE100 or so that they needed to pay the people who had sold them the straw on credit. On yet a third occasion, one of the senior farmers in the village chided Mahmoud for asking too much profit on his dealing in straw. Mahmoud denied that the profit margin was as wide as this farmer implied, and said that their expenses (loading, transport) ate up much of the difference in the prices between Musha and the villages to the south. It was hard to say whether the farmer was joking or serious, but in either case the element of social control was clearly present.

At the time of the first trip to el-Atamna, the price of the straw was LE22 for a *haml* (a "load," equal to 250 kilos or 550 pounds) in Musha, and LE27.50 in el-Atamna. The costs—sacking, loading, and transport—amounted to about LE3 per load. At one point they were paying PT70 per load for sacking, weighing and loading, and were renting a truck for LE15 per trip, which works out to around PT150 per load. In addition there were toll stations along the road that had to be dealt with one way or another. According to their calculations, they ought to be making a profit of LE2.50 to LE3.50 per load, or a rate of profit of about 15 percent. At another time, they claimed to have made a profit of LE111 for four trips and 28 loads. This would make a profit of LE4 per load, or a rate of about 18 percent. If we assume the higher profit margin, this means that the three persons involved each made a profit of LE9 per trip. On the other hand, each trip meant one or two days of work for each man—not physical work, but arranging, supervising, arguing, and travelling. At this rate they were not earning much more than an ordinary laborer making bricks who might clear LE5 a day. At most, counting only days worked, and figuring the minimum of one day of work per trip, each one was making LE8 per day. And sometimes it hardly seemed that they were coming out ahead at all. In fact, whenever I heard them settle their accounts, it seemed to come out closer to LE1 per load, a rate of profit of around 4 percent. I do not know how to account for this rather significant difference. Later on, when Damian became a partner, the same profit had to be split four ways.

The same group of men became involved in other deals. A man called Abderrahim came to Musha from the village of Meshta, just north of el-Atamna, seeking to buy straw. He addressed himself to one of Musha's larger farmers, Mohammed Ahmed, because in the past he had hired camels and adolescents for cotton picking from Meshta and so he was known there. Mohammed referred them to the Mahmoud-Fawzi-Damian group. They agreed to sell him straw at LE22 or 23, in addition to which Abderrahim would pay for the labor and the transport. But although he paid for it, the Musha trio had to organize and to some extent supervise it. Furthermore, Abderrahim was not in a position to pay the Musha men until he had sold the straw in Meshta. The Musha men had to make several trips to Meshta to collect their money. Once, when the three made a trip to Meshta, he was reluctant to pay, or at any rate to pay fully. He alleged that there was chickpea straw mixed in with the wheat straw. Fawzi, as a winnower the team's expert on quality, indignantly denied this and insisted that even if true it didn't matter. On another occasion he tried to pay only a portion of the amount due, but when the Musha men refused to leave without the full amount, he managed to produce the balance. Once when we were approaching Meshta, the three men said they did not want to accept a meal from Abderrahim (they had already agreed to eat with their friends in el-Atamna). But when Abderrahim served a meal, they ate from it, and then afterwards in the car complained that it was only pigeon, not the meat sauce their friends in el-Atamna served them. The tensions involved in this relationship reflect the fact that the business partners did not know each other previously. The deal worked anyway—they sent four truckloads of straw to Meshta—but not without a lot of anxiety and worry. (The Musha men were even "unable" to remember the somewhat unusual name of the Meshta man.) Again, the profit was less than overwhelming, especially considering that it had to be split four ways. The Musha three were making a pound or two of profit on the sale to Abderrahim. That would have netted them a little over LE20 each for a minimum of four days of work. I never heard the straw dealers calculate their income in terms of the number of days it took to earn it; that part of the calculation is mine.

On another occasion, the three loaded a truck of straw for Shattura, south of el-Atamna. This time they bought the straw for LE20 and sold it for LE25, but had to cover the expenses of loading and transport themselves. On the other hand, the Shattura people paid right away. They were dealing with a man they knew slightly, since he had had dealings in Musha before. They estimated their profit at LE10 for the three of them, representing the wages for one fairly long day of work.

Sometimes they (but particularly Damian) tried to expand the business by bringing back products from these other villages for use or sale in Musha. Thus Damian first came along on the trip because he was interested in buying pepper seedlings to plant in his own fields in Musha. Once, they brought back dates. On another occasion, they took part of their price in garlic. Then Damian tried to sell this garlic to the people of Musha. He opened the door to his storeroom, where the garlic was kept, and trusted to word of mouth to bring in customers. Since garlic is the kind of product that people may buy in large lots to store for the year, some customers did make fairly large purchases.

During this period, the three friends were not the only ones to be trading in straw. Several of the big farmers in Musha either loaded and dispatched trucks to southern villages themselves, or allowed dealers from these villages to load up on straw from their stocks. The easiest deal is to let others load up from one's stocks, and the profits are probably highest if one is selling one's own straw. Smaller-scale merchants sent camels loaded with straw to some nearby villages.

I saw another dimension to this trade at the time of the wheat harvest several months later. At this time, certain dealers from Musha had established themselves on the threshing grounds with scales, and were purchasing straw directly from the small farmers. By buying at this time, they got the lowest price (the increase from harvest to late winter might be from LE15 to 22) and so could eventually reap the largest profits, probably without committing nearly as much time and energy as the three petty dealers I have been describing. Mahmoud and Fawzi were bitter at this show of economic power, recognizing that they did not have the capital to invest in stock themselves. They knew that the following year they might be in a position of buying this same straw from these capital-rich dealers for a higher price. Part of Mahmoud's reaction, however, was to clean out part of the lower floor of his house so that it could be used to store straw while speculating on a price rise.

Livestock

People from Musha frequent several livestock markets. For sheep and goats there is the small Saturday market in nearby Shutb, and a number of petty traders work this market. For cattle, water buffalo, camels, and donkeys, people go either to the Saturday market in Abutig or to the Monday market in Ma'asara, at the eastern end of the barrage across from Asyut city. There are additional markets to the south, at Tema, about 30 kilometers beyond Abutig, and to the north, at Manqabad, about 20 kilometers north of Asyut. Thus there are livestock markets about every 25 or 30 kilometers in the valley. Individual farmers are likely to deal at these markets through intermediaries who are familiar with the other individuals and with the ways of these markets. Thus a farmer wanting to sell a buffalo may commission one of these brokers to sell it for him. Or, if the dealer has a little capital, he may buy the animal himself and try to sell it in the market. Similarly, someone interested in buying an animal may commission a broker. The prices for animals that are bought and sold in the village reflect the prices current in these livestock markets. Someone intending to buy or sell an animal will inform himself of the going prices, perhaps by attending the market himself at first to sample the prices. Nothing is so individual, of course, as the price of an animal, especially when the buyer must judge by eye and experience the weight, health, and quality of the beast. Again, the reluctance to deal with strangers encourages this system of professional brokers who know their customers in the village and each other.

The animals are transported to the market by truck, and so the cost of transport (perhaps one pound per animal) must be added in as well. However, such an amount is small compared to the price of the animal. In February 1981 a fullgrown cow sold for around LE500 to 600, and a buffalo cow for around LE700 to 800. Prices were slightly lower in the markets to the south. As far as I am aware, however, there was little arbitraging between markets—although perhaps there was a tendency to buy at Abutig and sell at Ma'asara. Instead, the speculation consisted in buying animals to fatten at home and then to resell them hoping for a profit. Most animals were bought at least once in their lives. Households would sell off their young animals and then buy the mature ones they wanted. It seems that the establishments that actually raised the animals were those of the large farmers which had a large enough volume to take the risk of losing an occasional growing animal.

Fruits and Vegetables

The two principal fruits grown in Musha are pomegranates and grapes. There are several hundred feddans of the latter, and around 40 feddans of the former, mostly belonging to the Umda. These fruits are bought by merchants from the towns to the south of Musha, from Abutig to Sohag and Nag' Hammadi. These merchants bring their trucks right into the fields, and the fruit is loaded there. If the merchant organizes the labor to pick the fruit, then the price to the owner is somewhat lower than if the farmer picks his own grapes. In theory, farmers could try to market them themselves, but I came across no case of it. Even the biggest producers, such as the *'umda,* prefer to wait for merchants to seek them out. In the fall of 1980, grapes were sold for LE170 to 200 per ton. Since a feddan produces around ten to twelve tons, the income is around LE2000 per feddan per year. Offsetting this are relatively high labor costs, because of irrigation, cultivation, and the struggle against field rats, and the fact that the land produces no income at all for four or five years while the vines are maturing.

Musha farmers do not grow many vegetables. Farmers who grow onions feel they are able to sell their crop directly from the field, either in bulk to a merchant who seeks them out, or in small amounts to other Musha people who also seek them out. One farmer took some onions home with him and tried to sell them from his house. Customers came, but his (marriageable) daughters disapproved, saying it was shameful. That criticism did not prevent him from shortly engaging in an even larger-scale effort to sell garlic brought back from the south. Nevertheless, the point remains that the network for selling fruits and vegetables within Musha is underdeveloped, and this probably discourages people from any ambitions they might have to start growing vegetables. Musha's greengrocers mostly supply themselves from wholesalers in Asyut, rather than directly from Musha producers. The peddlers on the street selling cauliflower, tomatoes, and other vegetables are from neighboring villages and to some extent confirm the pattern of small-scale retailing directly from the producer to the consumer.

Eggs

Most eggs are produced in small quantities by individual households. There are merchants in Musha who collect these eggs house to house and then sell them in bulk in cities from Asyut to Alexandria. In order to carry out this trade legally, they have to have a license from the government. This license requires them to sell one quarter of their eggs to the government for PT3, about half the price they pay for them in the village. However, one large and fairly well-capitalized enterprise was able to sell its eggs for twice as much (PT14) to a man in Asyut who would hatch them and sell the chicks. The higher price reflects the different goal, and also the fact that these chickens were of a known breed, not just "baladi." Thus the structure of the marketing of eggs resembles wheat and other cereal grains: it is a centralizing structure (cf. Zimmermann 1982a, b).

Capital and Trade

The important role of the traders in the productive process of agriculture in Musha should be clear. Trading is an activity at the village level which is carried out by men or by families, occasionally by partnerships. Trust is an essential ingredient in marketing, as many operations involve delayed payments or other problematic features. Thus the networks of traders and customers are built up largely on the basis of personal acquaintance.

There is also considerable specialization in trade. There are grain dealers, those who trade only in certain grains, some kind of a division between petty traders who buy and sell from the village population, and larger traders who begin the bulking process which exports grain to the cities. There are straw traders and livestock dealers, not to mention those responsible for bringing agricultural machinery into the village. There used to be cotton dealers/brokers,[3] though these were abolished when the cotton market was nationalized after 1961.

The most successful traders are those with adequate capital. With capital, they can buy when the price is low, and hold on to the grain, livestock, or straw, until the price has risen sufficiently to give them a profit. They are thus less concerned with arbitraging between rural zones with different prices, and more concerned with speculating on the annual fluctuation and cycle of prices. They are tied into a price structure that reflects urban rates, and for many crops the prices are affected by the forced deliveries to the government or by imports under the U.S. commodity imports program. Nevertheless, with luck, skill and capital, the traders are able to maintain or expand their position from year to year. They are part of the population that lives indirectly from agriculture, and at least in the analytical sense absorb some of the surplus value produced in agriculture. They further the commercialization of agriculture, and thus the process of political and social differentiation of the village population.

Notes

1. The price of lentils was raised from 35 to 50 pounds per ardeb, and the price of beans was raised from 27 to 35 pounds per ardeb.

2. The village cooperative sometimes bargains with the government over the size of the forced delivery. In 1981 the cooperative on behalf of the farmers claimed that the cold weather had damaged the lentil crops and that since yields would be low the government should slacken its demands as well. The government did reduce the amount per feddan required as a forced delivery, though in the event it was hard to see afterwards that the yield had declined appreciably.

3. According to El-Shagi (1969), when the private cotton traders came to the village in search of cotton, they generally dealt with the large farmers first, for they had large enough harvests to make it worthwhile, and bargained until they agreed on a price with them. The small farmers were then generally forced to associate themselves with the large farmers, because no one could expect the dealers to make a special trip to the village for a small amount. This circumstance led the dealers to favor the large landowners at the expense of the small ones—for instance, by giving them a higher evaluation of the quality of their cotton crop. The large farmers benefited more from the system of private traders than the small farmers did. However, the small farmers also appreciated the private dealers because they would pay in advance, and would sometimes give credit for consumption expenses, which the government purchasers will not do. By the same token, of course, the small farmers were often in debt to the cotton dealers. In a survey taken in Abu Ziyada/ Abu Siada (Kafr el-Shaikh governorate) in 1965, four years after the elimination of

the private cotton dealers, 74 percent said they were satisfied with the new system—85 percent of those farming less than ten feddans, and 24 percent of those farming ten and more feddans (El-Shagi 1969:102). The special consideration that the large farmers had enjoyed from the private cotton traders had given way to an equalized system where all cotton of the same quality received the same price (El-Shagi 1969:101–2). Similarly, Harik (1974:40–41) tells how one of the big landowners in a Beheira village, before the 1952 revolution, used to borrow money to buy the cotton crop before the harvest at a depressed price.

10

Politics in Musha

The state and the political process in general play a role in the labor process. We have noted the role of the state in fostering mechanization, influencing marketing, and encouraging certain kinds of migration. Politics serves as a control function for the social organization of agricultural production; its significance is therefore to sustain the ideology that justifies and rationalizes the village social organization, and in particular the village stratification system, and to resolve the disputes that emerge between individuals with conflicting interests within the context of the labor process. All the examples of conflict that came to my attention were at least on the surface cases of conflict between individuals. The social-political processes described here create, support and reinforce the economic structures of Musha. They serve as additional bases for the understanding of the relationship between the social organization of agriculture and the class system.[1]

Political Process

Formal Politics

In Musha, three formally constituted bodies are important for village governance. These are the Village Council (VC), the Local Popular Council (LPC) and the Cooperative Board. (The first two combine Musha and Shutb, but the cooperative concerns only Musha.) In chapter three we examined the formal aspects of these institutions to provide background to the analysis of the labor process, by suggesting the role of the state. Here we look at another dimension of the political structure. These collective bodies are superimposed on the structures and processes of traditional village politics centered around large and wealthy families, and their functioning suggests a great deal about the political economy of the village.

The Local Popular Council scheduled a meeting every Monday, and it managed to meet most weeks. The principal topics of discussion had to do with the physical upkeep of the two villages. Thus the LPC together with the appropriate figures in the Executive Council were responsible for the water supply (from several artesian wells), for street cleaning and maintenance, for matters of public health and education, and so on. Bus transport between Musha and Asyut was a perennial issue. This matter concerned particularly the civil servants, and since they were a majority of the LPC it was bound to arise. Also representative of the kind of issue that comes up was a suggestion that the age for entering school be reduced from 6 to 5 1/2 years, to match the situation prevailing in the cities. This issue was introduced into the LPC meeting as one that had been discussed in the Education Committee, composed of nine members of the LPC, and chaired by its senior teacher-member. Another issue, which I will discuss at greater length below, was the problem of laying out new streets in the areas into which the village built-up area was expanding.

The LPC thus played the role of a sounding board where certain kinds of issues could be raised and called to the attention of the authorities. It was not a place where actual decisions could be made, and it did not play the role of a forum where competing interests in the village could thrash out certain issues and reach a decision binding on all. Any issue that really (and perhaps adversely) affected the interests of the more powerful villagers had to be worked out in another arena. Again, to anticipate, we shall see this illustrated by the debate over street layout.

The President of the LPC talked of a contrast at the local level between *sulta sha'biyya* and *sulta tanfidhiyya* (popular power and executive power). This is summed up in the relations between the President of the LPC (popular power) and the President of the VC (executive power). Because the "executive power" has the staff and the continuity, and are the ones actually able to do something, the representative of "popular power" (i.e., himself) must persuade, cajole, and oblige the executive power into doing what it should do. On the other hand, the secretary of the VC worried whether the executive had the power to enforce a rule against the objections of important men in the community. This uncertainty and sense of weakness on either side was perhaps induced by the fact that many of the decisions would ultimately be made in Asyut or Cairo—for instance, a decision to lower the age of entrance into school or to expand bus service. In these cases, the LPC relied on the ability of the President of the LPC and on the President of the VC to lobby the relevant authorities in Asyut or Cairo.

If the local level is not responsive, one can try to evade it by moving up the ladder. The next level above the Village Council is the District Council, not considered in Musha to be of much use, perhaps because the District is headquartered in the same town as the Governorate. Sometimes one can circumvent the District Council by working through the Governorate Council, but the problem is that this Council is dominated by the personality of the

Governor, who was not regarded in Musha as a sympathetic figure. On the other hand, the President of the LPC, together with the President and the secretary of the VC, make frequent trips to Asyut to call on various government officials there to seek approval or action on projects that are important to the village. Thus more important than the meetings of the LPC is the fact that the position of the President of the LPC gives a certain clout with authorities in Asyut. This clout is increased if he works with the President and/or the secretary of the VC. After all, these individuals are natives of Musha and so can have the interests of the village at heart.

The VC also works together with villagers on specific improvements. For instance, in one area, the inhabitants wanted a new water main to replace an old rusty one and to make it possible for all the families in this area to be hooked up to the system. Each one contributed around LE35 to 40, and so they collected LE700 to pay the VC workers to get the job done. (There was also a quarrel between two of the men over the requirement to pay, so the collaboration did not come easy.) In this same neighborhood they later contributed about LE1,500 to buy an electric pump and a tank-wagon which will be used to empty out the latrines in the neighborhood mosque.

The election of the board of the village cooperative also illustrates the interaction of the village and the formal institutional structure. The most recent cooperative election was scheduled to be held in 1980, but it was delayed for a year because of uncertainty and maneuvering at the national level concerning the future role for the cooperatives. Eventually in May 1981, the list of candidates was opened. For this occasion, the secretary and the director of the cooperative received written statements of candidacy at the cooperative office. These statements were often dictated to the candidate by the secretary. Each statement specified the land holdings of the candidate, his wife and children. Eventually, eight of the ten outgoing members presented themselves for reelection (*yanzal fi al-intikhabat*); of the other two, one was working in Saudi Arabia and the tenth had died. Altogether, there were fifteen candidates, all technically small holders, for nine seats. Some were from large landholding families. The major political cleavage in the village is between the eastern half and the western half. Of the fifteen candidates, five were from the West, seven from the East, one was from the South, one was not identified, and one was a Christian living in the center of the village.

The elections were originally scheduled for August but were actually held in November 1981. The results are given in Table 10.1. Six of the incumbents were reelected, two were voted out, and three new names were added. On the whole, the candidates representing the West did better than those from the East, which is consistent with the political pattern of recent years in Musha. The one Christian candidate lost, although he is a member of the

TABLE 10.1 Election Results, Musha Cooperative, November 1981

Names	Votes	
A. Winners		
Salem	831	West, Incumbent
Salah	822	West, Secretary
Fadhel	779	West, President
Fadl	735	West, New Member
Abdessalam	728	East, Incumbent
Abdelmon'im	708	New Member
Mohammed	690	West, Incumbent
Abdelzaher	657	East, Incumbent
Ali	611	East, New Member
B. Losers		
Ahmed	588	East, Incumbent
Rizq	574	Christian
Sayyid	569	South
Omar	548	East, Incumbent
Ibrahim	426	East
Fuad	--	East, Withdrew

Source: Field Notes.

LPC and is generally a respected figure in the village. The total number of votes suggests that a maximum of 73 percent of the eligible voters cast ballots. This is probably close to the theoretical maximum, if we assume that women, migrants, the very old and infirm, etc., do not vote. The biggest vote getter won the votes of 59 percent of the total membership, and the lowest won 30 percent.

The election was part of the on-going political process in the village, in this case confirming the dominant position of the group of men who had run the cooperative board in recent years and who were also involved in the LPC. In contrast to this council, the cooperative board included few or no civil servants; it was more properly a farmers' board.[2] More precisely it was a small farmers' board. The Secretary and perhaps others, although officially small farmers, were in fact large farmers. However, they were fairly vigilant in looking after the interests of the small farmers. This showed up in their interest in farm machinery, in their suspicion of the role of the Village Bank, and in their willingness to receive supplicants out of office hours and outside the office setting. It was also important that they were willing to work with small farmers on the basis of personal relations rather than respect for bureaucratic procedure.

Informal Politics

The real power hierarchy in the village was poorly reflected in the formal institutions. At the apex stood the Umda, by virtue of his family background, personal history, wealth and personality. He was known as "the Umda" even though the post had been abolished years before. His grandfather had been the powerful *'umda* of Musha for many years prior to 1947; he himself was relatively well educated for a man of his generation (secondary school; he liked to quote the few phrases of Shakespeare he remembered); he had been a member of parliament after the revolution; and he farmed close to 300 feddans. A generation earlier, the *'umda* had been an extremely important figure in the village. In a large village like Musha with many wealthy families, there was some devolution of power to these other large families, but on the whole the *'umda*'s prestige was not challenged. A certain number of the heads of large families were named as *shaykh al-balad*. This role remained, and in 1980, there were six in the village, including one Christian. But the *'umda*'s power was not otherwise curtailed until the creation of a police post in the 1950s led to the elimination of the post altogether—leaving a still very powerful individual, whose wishes, even expressed second or third hand, often had the force of law.

The Umda was clearly dominant in the Western part of the village, where he was supported by other powerful (in wealth and personality) members of his own lineage and by similar individuals from other families, and his position was respected in the East as well. This precedence was reflected in the visiting pattern at his house. In the Eastern part of the village the key position was held by a cluster of related families centered around the family of the former Eastern *'umda*. On both sides of the village there were recently wealthy families whose social status, not yet consecrated by time, was reflected in the aspersions sometimes cast on their honesty.

The LPC president (The Hajj) was another very powerful individual in the village. He clearly had more personal power than the VC president. He was an active large farmer in the village; he was the secretary of the Cooperative Board; and he was closely associated with the Umda. He had attended Cairo University Law School for two years, and was familiar with the ways of the law and the administration. He was commonly praised in Musha for being "polite" in the sense of well-educated and respectful of others. He was always available in the village (the VC president, although a native of Musha, lived in Asyut and came out to his office daily). This was particularly evident since people came to seek out the Hajj at all hours of the day and night at his home or at the other places where he was known to be found. The fact that men could do business with him at night was a considerable convenience for busy farmers and traders, especially when compared to the relatively short hours of the government offices (essentially from 9 A.M. to 2 P.M.).

Men would bring papers and other business relating both to the LPC and to the Cooperative to the Hajj in his reception room, where he would hold court in the evening. Everyone who came would be offered a glass of tea and a cigarette, and could join in the general conversation, sharing a few jokes along with the concerns. Needless to say, no one's business was truly private in this context, even if from time to time, someone might attempt to seek privacy by whispering or in extreme cases even by drawing the Hajj aside. But at least it could be conducted at a convenient time, in a congenial atmosphere, and among peers.

One February evening, the Hajj was in his reception room with a gathering including members of both the Cooperative Board and the LPC. As is usually the case on such evenings, the host, who is presumably the person there of highest status, dominates and leads the conversation. This evening the Hajj was discussing the advantages of having a refrigerator. This pleasant conversation was interrupted when someone mentioned that a public fountain in another part of the village was leaking water to the point that the road was covered. The Hajj then sent one of his workers (who normally sit in the background at such soirees) to fetch the Village Council employee in charge of water pipe maintenance. About 15 minutes later, Omar came from his nearby house, apologizing that he was tired because he had just arrived from a job in Shutb. The leaky fountain was discussed, and it was agreed that the next day Ali would shut off one of the faucets to stanch the overflow. Formally the Hajj is not in a position to instruct an employee of the VC. He was, however, able to influence his behavior and expedite the solution of the water spill problem.

On another occasion, the Hajj helped a pump owner draft a petition to the Irrigation Service concerning a problem resulting from the new drain. He was able to make sure that the petitioner got the names and technical terms right.

The evening gatherings, such as those at the house of the Hajj, are essential to the socio-political process in Musha. A group of men will gather in the reception room of one of the wealthy farmers. These men will include the men who work regularly for this farmer, as well as other smaller farmers who may be neighbors either in the village or in the fields. To some extent, these evenings are a form of recreation—men gossiping, smoking, and drinking tea together. They resemble in some ways the evening gatherings of the religious brotherhoods. But they are clearly an arena in which values are reasserted, social control is exercised, and political support is solicited and sustained (cf. the comments of Gilsenan 1983 on a North Lebanese village). They are hierarchical in the sense that the host dominates conversation and sets the tone of the evening, and in the sense that it is always assumed that the host has some claim to precedence over his guests. This precedence is least when the gathering is essentially a gathering of patrilineally related men, in other words, a lineage, and it is most in the case of someone like the Hajj who is in a position to do favors to many people and accepts the role. This emphasis on precedence makes it hard for the wealthy farmers to visit each other: who would accept the role of lower-ranking guest?

This discussion of informal politics suggests the strength of a hierarchy of persons. The Umda was at the peak of the social pyramid. Those entitled to spend the evening with the Umda were his own top employees and other big farmers. The Hajj would regularly spend time in the evening with the Umda, sometimes leaving his own reception room after a certain period of time in order to visit him. The Hajj, in fact, made it quite clear that his relationship with the Umda took precedence over most of his other activities.[3] He was in a sense a junior associate of the Umda, and for instance accompanied him to Asyut on business. The Hajj defended the Umda's interests in the village councils.

A hierarchy is established in this system because there are some who receive guests at times, and visit at other times. The case of the Hajj is one example. The village expert agent is another. He would receive evening visits from simple men looking for help and favors. While he did not make a practice of sitting with the Hajj, he was frequently called there because of his specialized knowledge. When he was there, he was extremely deferential, on occasion remaining standing while his expertise was being delivered and discussed. He was, however, most uncomfortable at the idea of approaching the Umda and avoided that whenever he could.

Once when the Hajj had to leave his own reception room to attend a mourning reception (*janaza*), he left his half-brother in charge. Now Sayyid was normally a nearly silent member of the group in the Hajj's sitting room, but having been left in charge, he delivered himself of what amounted to a virtual monologue on various technical aspects of agriculture for about an hour until the Hajj returned. At this point he retreated into his usual silence. Sometimes a lineage will have its own guest house, or *duwwar,* as a public place in which members of that lineage can gather on neutral territory, so to speak, and receive their guests. The *duwwar* is less elaborated in Musha than in some other Asyut villages I have seen, perhaps because of the importance of the big farmers and their evening sittings. These evening gatherings are an extremely important locus of communication in a society like Musha, where all communication is face-to-face and there are no public gatherings in which information can be transmitted and opinions aired. The gatherings I have been discussing here also resemble the evening sessions of the religious brotherhoods, and the formal mechanism for settling disputes.

A Dispute

Planning new streets gave rise to a dispute which illustrates the relationship between formal and informal politics in Musha. People concluded that, since the annual flood had ceased, low-lying areas adjacent to the village could now be built on, and the increased population and increased prosperity made opening up new areas for housing desirable. The issue came before the LPC when some people requested permission to build in these areas. The question was problematic because of different opinions on the width of the streets. The owners of the land argued for relatively narrow streets—from one *qasaba* (3.55 meters) to 5 meters wide was sufficient, they thought. The Village Council felt some obligation to implement government standards stipulating that the streets should be 8 to 10 meters wide. The wider streets would be advantageous for the probable future use of trucks and tractor-drawn trailers, and for the future installation of water and sewage pipes. However, the owners of the land were concerned to protect the value of their land. The price of building land had risen so high (LE2,000 per qirat) that they were unwilling to lose any of it to the government for roads.

A month after the question was raised in the LPC, there was a meeting (*jalsa*) in the office of the VC president. The VC president was there, as well as his secretary and the father of his secretary, a retired teacher who was one of the village experts on land ownership and measurement. The Hajj was supposed to be there, but he arrived late and left early. This left his client, the village agent, to defend his interests and those of his patron, the Umda. Also present were some of those who owned land in one of the areas in question, in particular two Christians, uncle and nephew, who were among the most prominent Christians in Musha (the nephew as actually a lawyer in Asyut as well as a landowner in Musha, and the uncle was the Christian *shaykh al-balad*). One of the questions that arose in this meeting was to determine the status of the meeting. The VC secretary contended that *"as-sulta tanfidhiyya mawjuda"*—arguing that this was a legitimate meeting empowered to make authoritative decisions. The point here was to apply the law to all equally, not according to the personality of the individual. Later in private, the secretary was not so confident that the executive power really had the ability to enforce its own rules with regard to street width. The purpose of this meeting had been to create some facts before the matter was further discussed in the LPC meeting the following Monday.

However, one perhaps unpredicted outcome of this meeting is that it became apparent that the exact property boundaries in the area in question needed to be redrawn and confirmed. In particular, the boundary between the property of the two Christians needed to be reaffirmed. So a few days later, the village expert agent together with the retired teacher, Hajj Mahmoud, went out to the disputed area with their measuring rods (a rod is also called a *qasaba*) and a team of men and set to work to define the boundaries. All those with land in the vicinity were there to keep an eye on things. And a few days later, one of the landowners in the area called on the President of the LPC to check out his position, and then the following day went to visit the Umda. Doubtless other visits and representations were being made. At any rate, the issue was then shelved for the time being. What is interesting about the process involved is the shift from what looked like a direct confrontation in a formal setting to a more diffuse and informal process in which more and more people were involved, thus making it increasingly difficult for anyone to take a decisive action. From this point of view, even the very ostentatious measurement of the plot boundaries could be seen both as a delaying and as a publicizing tactic.

Dispute Settlement

The resolution of disputes in Musha illustrates one key aspect of the political process (cf. Ammar 1966:57–60 for Silwa). An examination of disputes both gives an idea of the significant issues in the community, and suggests how the social system comes into play to resolve conflict between individuals. The most common technique for dispute settlement is mediation by someone of higher status in a dispute involving those of lesser position. Thus it relies on patterns of social inequality. Generally the outcome does not involve determining who was right or wrong, but involves reaching a solution that gives each party some of the disputed property, or something of equivalent value.

The most common form of dispute in Musha concerns property, particularly farm land but also including houses.[4] A fairly typical land case is the one involving Suliman and Abdelaziz. Suliman had been buying up small parcels of land in an area east of the village, and the assumption of various conflicting rights had led him into a dispute with Abdelaziz over a small parcel of this land (about five qirats or .2 of an acre). Suliman is a quietly energetic farmer aged about 40 years; he farms about five feddans but owns no mechanical equipment. Abdelaziz is an assertive man of about 50 years; he owns some shares in a pump and a tractor or two, and altogether farms about 25 feddans. Suliman is a Christian, Abdelaziz a Muslim.

The dispute came to public notice when Suliman went to the police to accuse Abdelaziz of plowing land belonging to Suliman. The police then sent Suliman to the cooperative's land expert (*dallal*) to determine the land rights involved, and Suliman recruited another Christian, Jabra, who was older and more skilled at these matters, to accompany him. Working out the land rights was intricate, for it required working with the 1905 cadastral record and a handful of old deeds that Suliman had in his possession.

Furthermore, the arithmetic necessary to manipulate the figures is considerable, inasmuch as the feddan is divided into 24 qirats and the *qasaba* is divided into 24 parts (*qubda* or *habba*). Field dimensions are commonly given in the records in terms of the measurements of their borders; this has then to be translated into measures of surface. Since the feddan is equal to 333 1/3 square *qasaba*s, which is not a multiple of anything, the arithmetical difficulties have to be seen to be appreciated. During this process, the land expert let Suliman and Jabra do all the work, occasionally asking additional questions to make them aware of a new dimension. The land expert also produced the necessary registers. Presumably Abdelaziz was going through the same process on his side, although I was not a witness to that. At any rate, there were several evening meetings of the various participants.

Several nights later, all the parties concerned met in the house of one of the largest landowners in the village for a *sulh* (reconciliation meeting). Those present included Suliman and his associate Jabra, representing one side, and Abdelaziz and his associate Badr (a member of the village cooperative board), representing the other. The peacemakers included the large landowner, Ahmed Bahnasawi; a respected retired schoolteacher, Hajj Abdelhamid, who reminded them that he had taught everyone arithmetic; and Mahmoud, the land expert. Bahnasawi had used his prestige to ensure the presence of Abdelaziz; getting Suliman to attend was no problem since he was in effect the plaintiff. In fact, Abdelaziz arrived half an hour after Suliman did, and his "second" came even later.

Shortly the assembled group agreed on the facts of the case. Then it became a question of what to do about it. The peacemakers, Bahnasawi and Hajj Abdelhamid, suggested in effect a compromise in which the land would be split, and Abdelaziz would pay Suliman LE100 as compensation for any rights he might have lost in the process. (This sum was based on the cost of the land at the time it was purchased, which was before a sharp rise in the price of land.) Abdelaziz was not eager to agree to this, and it took a lot of persuasion by Bahnasawi in particular, with the help of others in this special atmosphere. Hajj Abdelhamid tried to appeal to Abdelaziz's sense of status by saying that as the better-off disputant he could afford to agree to this compromise, then stressed the trouble that he himself had gone to, by saying that he had skipped his supper to come to this meeting, and finally argued that it behooved everyone to show how Egyptians could settle their quarrels peacefully in the presence of the foreign observer. Whether any of these arguments had much effect on Abdelaziz's stubbornness is unclear.

Eventually, after much shouting and waving of arms, Abdelaziz agreed to the terms. Then Hajj Abdelhamid sat down to write out a document specifying the agreement. Beginning with the invocation, "In the name of

God, the merciful, the compassionate," the paper stated the names of the two disputants and the location of the land. Hajj Abdelhamid made sure that everyone present agreed on the figures to be included. Then he wrote down the names of all those present who were in effect witnesses to the agreement. Finally he wrote down the nature of the agreement itself. This paper was then signed by Suliman and by Abdelaziz (using his thumb print) and by four others as witnesses. The chief peacemaker, Bahnasawi, acted as the guardian of the agreement, and kept the two copies of the agreement. By this time, Abdelaziz had left, and Suliman's only remaining concern was to get the land expert, in the presence of witnesses, to mark out the actual boundaries on the ground. It was agreed that this would be done shortly, but in fact it was not done for more than two months, when the crop in the field had been harvested.

This example is fairly typical of the methods that people in Musha have for settling their own disputes without reference to government institutions. In fact, they were quite self-conscious of this aspect of the *sulh,* and many pointed out to me how good it was that in Musha people had a way of sitting down to thresh out their problems so that they did not degenerate into violence; they used words instead of fighting. One key ingredient was the willingness of respected men such as Ahmed Bahnasawi to act as a mediator and a guarantor. As in the case of the dispute over street layout, the circle of those involved tended to broaden out until a large enough group of people was assembled. These people were more interested in encouraging an agreement than in the details of the agreement itself, and the disputants had to compromise in order to retain the respect of their fellow villagers and also if they were to retrieve some benefit from the confusion. The dispute itself is more likely to have had its roots in the extremely complicated land tenure provisions, exacerbated by the bullying assertiveness of Abdelaziz and the quiet persistance of Suliman. There was probably an extra incentive to bring community pressures to bear on this quarrel. The two disputants were of different religions, and people are aware that a dispute that takes on a configuration of Muslim versus Christian could be damaging for everyone in the village.

A similar process was called into play in a dispute over a house in the village. In this case, a Christian man was living in the house of a Muslim from Musha who preferred to live near a pump in the fields. But when the owner died, his children wanted to reclaim the house. Unable for reasons of law and custom simply to expel the occupant of the house, they tried to get him to accept a certain sum of money as an indemnity in exchange for leaving. The man was landless and worked in Musha as a winnower, and seasonally in the Alexandria port. The occupant was holding out for as large an indemnity as possible, while the heirs tried to mobilize support among their prestigious neighbors for their position, hoping to get the occupant to agree to move out. The principal discussions were being carried out in the house of a third party who was also trying to bring the two parties to agreement. Eventually a member of this "neutral" family (a member of the LPC) took the occupant of the house aside, and they agreed on a compromise indemnity of LE400 which would be paid to the occupant if he left within six months. This money was to be paid to the person who had arranged the compromise and held in escrow, as it were, until the house was vacated. Interestingly enough, when they came to write up the *waraqa* ("paper"), it was stipulated that if anyone reneged on the agreement there would be a fine of LE1,000. This was clearly aimed at the occupant of the house, who was also the only one to sign the paper. (An unusual feature is that it was specified that there would be no date and no signature of witnesses on the paper.)

Although in some respects this process resembled the early settlement of a land dispute, there were some differences. One is that the facts of the case were not at issue, and the rights of each party were known. More important, however, is the rather lowly status of the occupant of the house. He had no actual supporters among the men who were gathered to settle the problem, and who were all property owners, so his only tactic was to hold out as long as he could. There was indeed some concern for his fate—and that of his family of six children. The group expressed the idea that he would use his indemnity to buy a small plot of land on the edge of the village so he could build his own house there—though the construction money would have to come from somewhere else. The indemnity he received would cover about 70 square meters at the going rate for building sites, a reasonable area under the circumstances. I am not sure anyone actually expected him to do this, but the size of the indemnity was calculated with this in mind to make it a fair compensation.

Unlike the land dispute analyzed above, this one was seen as very much a dispute involving Christian and Muslim. The various participants in the *sulh* frequently referred to this aspect. After the agreement was reached, the owner of the house made a speech stating that some of those involved were Muslims, and so *qurayb* ("close ones," meaning those with the same religion), while others were Christians and so *jiran* ("neighbors"), and he did not want to see any trouble between them. Later on, one of the Christian elders involved told me that he was glad this dispute had been resolved before it turned into a serious quarrel that "left people dead."

The mechanisms that operate within Musha to encourage a peaceful solution of a dispute through negotiation and mediation are less effective when the dispute involves people from more than one village. In one case, a dispute erupted involving some land (about 3 feddans) in a neighboring village. The land in question was in the *zimam* of Rifa, and was owned by a man from Rifa. However, it was legally rented out to some people from

Musha, who were thus the holders. These people in turn had rented the land on the black market to some farmers from yet another village, Diweina. The dispute broke out when the Musha holders tried to eject the Diweina farmers from effective possession of the land. The latter argued that their use of the land for a period of time gave them permanent rights. At this point, a crowd of people from Diweina were on the land, and a crowd of people from Musha went to expel them by force. The Musha people had their guns, and they shot and wounded five of the men from Diweina. One of the Musha leaders said that the purpose of this operation was to intimidate the Diweina people so they would not assert whatever rights they had. Afterwards the police from Asyut were able to intervene, and they arrested three of the Musha men, charging them with responsibility for the shooting. No one expected them to be held for long. In the event, a couple of weeks later a *sulh* was held in Asyut city under official police auspices at which the problem was resolved by dividing the rights in the land between the two claimants. The Musha people continued to be disdainful of the Diweina people, saying that they were less "civilized" ("had less *hadara*") than people from Musha or Shutb.

In this case, too, the quarrel which erupted was eventually contained by a wider circle of people with differential prestige—and in this case in addition the possibility of the use of force—but it was settled through mediation and compromise rather than by a strict application of legal principles. Those involved in the quarrel from the Musha side included the mediator in the second example, and cousins of the mediator in the first example. When the quarrel involved people from different villages, the option of violence was much easier to contemplate, and all the values favoring compromise and mediation were at least temporarily forgotten.[5]

Religious Brotherhoods and Social Organization

The role of Islam or of religion in general is beyond the scope of this book. One aspect of Islam, however, is of significance for the discussion, for it shows how the hierarchy evident in social and economic life is reflected in the social organization based on religion, and how the religious structures act to reinforce that hierarchy. I refer here to the continued existence of the Islamic "brotherhoods" (*tariqas*) which function in some ways as a metaphor for the social organization of Musha.

I assume there is a certain relationship between the mode of production and its symbolic expression. Musha has a differentiated network of mosques and religious specialists, and a pattern of brotherhood activity linked to household life-crisis celebrations and the major Islamic feasts. The brotherhoods are also useful in creating intervillage networks, as we saw in our discussion of marketing. Islam informs the sacred geography of Musha and helps symbolize the integrity of the community before the outside world. Mosque, shrine, cemetery, and the pattern of the "patron saint" support this symbolism. Within the community, the practice of Islam reflects and reinforces the pattern of social status, and contributes to the reproduction of the socio-economic system. Thus Islam plays the role of an ideology supporting the boundaries and organization of the community, while the different currents of Islam mirror changing world views.

Musha follows the Islamic calendar of festivals. The fast of Ramadhan is apparently universally followed. The pilgrimage is an important institution and returned pilgrims enjoy special prestige and status. *Zaka* (alms) is practiced in the form of individual charity, and men regularly gather in the mosques for prayer and study. In addition, the people follow the cycle of festivals associated with the major saints of Egypt, notably Shaykh Ahmed Badawi of Tanta, Shaykh Ahmed Ferghal in nearby Abutig, the principal Cairo saints such as Sayyidna Hussein, Sayyida Zeinab, and others, from Alexandria to Qena.

We have already seen that the name of Shaykh Abdelfettah is associated with Musha's principal mosque. There are also legends stressing his miraculous interventions, mostly at the time of the founding of the village. Near the mosque is a separate shrine dedicated to the Shaykh; this separation allows the women of Musha to visit the shrine every Thursday night. A shrine dedicated to Abdelfettah's father, Shaykh Abdillah, is nearby. Shaykh Abdelfettah left descendents (*awlad ash-shaykh*). These descendents are particularly responsible for the upkeep of the Musha cemetery, located just inside the desert about 5 kilometers from the village. The cemetery also contains a second shrine to Shaykh Abdelfettah, just as it contains duplicates of all the saints' shrines in Musha. There are also family burial plots, some with a shrine or cupola. The principal festival is the *mawlid* of the Shaykh, held normally in November of each year, just after the cotton harvest has put some money in farmers' pockets. This festival involves performances of the *dhikr*s of the principal brotherhoods in Musha, held on the large square just outside the mosque, and some secular dancing in which Christians also participate. The high point of the festival is known as *laylat al-fuqara* ("night of the poor"). Prior to this evening, the head guard of the village (*shaykh al-ghafar*) and the head of the descendents of Shaykh Abdelfettah circulate in the village soliciting donations which will be used to buy meat and otherwise support the festival. The large landowners, and in particular the Umda, are major contributors. The Umda normally contributes a water buffalo by himself. The meat from these animals is then distributed to all the "poor" of the village. Some in the village see this very clearly as a symbolic redistribution of wealth from the rich to the poor that reinforces economic hierarchy.

The religious brotherhoods are active in Musha. The principal ones are the Rifa'iya, the Shadhliya, and the Mirghaniya. Each of these has several chapters in Musha, and there are twelve to fifteen chapters altogether in the village, each headed by a figure popularly known as *shaykh,* and officially as *naib,* since he deputizes for the *shaykh as-sijada* in Cairo and his representative in Asyut. The group headed by the *shaykh* is recruited locally according to networks of personal links. Membership is passed on from one generation to the next, and families are known for being Rifa'i or Shadhli. The individual chapter has more sociological reality than the links between Musha and the hierarchy in Asyut or Cairo. It is generally composed of a group of relatives, neighbors, and friends, at least insofar as its inner core is concerned. In addition to the *naib,* recognized roles include the *naqib* (second in charge), the *rais al-hadra* (in charge of the session and especially of the 'dancers' themselves), and the *munshid* (singer or reciter of the liturgy and of hymns). The ordinary members include the postulants (*murid*) and those who have received their first certificate (*ijaza*) and who are known as the *khalifas*.[6]

The social organization of the brotherhoods and the *dhikrs* faithfully reflects the village social hierarchy. The top roles mentioned above are occupied by fairly big landowners—not the very biggest, but those a rung down from the tractor-owning level.[7] The *shaykhs* usually have a finely-tuned consciousness of their elevation over their fellows. One Mirghani *shaykh,* encountered at a Rifa'i *dhikr,* commented with some disdain that those in attendance were "all *fallahin,* storekeepers or clerks"—in a word, ordinary people. The Shaykh I knew best was more concerned with the social than with the religious aspects of the role, which he had inherited from his father and grandfather. Shaykh Mohammed was apt, for instance, when calling an end to an evening, to remind everyone that they all had to work in the fields the next day. The ordinary members are likely to be drawn from the poor, the landless, the day workers and the youth. Women are interested in the activities of the brotherhoods, but must be involved from afar—watching from the roof, preparing food, perhaps insisting on the observance in the first place, and more recently listening to cassettes of the better religious singers.

The chief activity is the *dhikr,* in principle according to the *wird* (liturgy) of the founder. The *dhikr* can be elaborate or brief. It may begin with the liturgy, then have a central portion led by the singer, and conclude with the collective prayer of the *fatiha* and other Koranic texts. Finally there are refreshments or a meal. Moreover, the spatial layout is distinctive. The singer stands facing two parallel lines of ordinary members who bow and sway to his rhythm. The leaders are likely to be sitting somewhat apart, together with spectators, honored visitors, and the like, but they are commonly situated so that the singer faces towards them. A smaller group of men stand behind the singer, and are moved by the rhythm without joining the two lines. Those in the parallel lines are said to be those who *yufaqirru wa yaqulu allah* ("perform the *dhikr* and say the name of God"). They sometimes become dizzy from the movement, but as far as I can judge most do not actually enter into trance: certainly not a heavy one since within a minute after stopping they converse lucidly. A few particularly susceptible individuals may enter trance, but everyone tries to prevent or control this.

Dhikrs are commonly held to celebrate marriages and circumcisions. Many families also sponsor an annual *dhikr* as a result of a vow (*nadhr*) taken in the past. The brotherhood chapter itself may perform a *dhikr* to help celebrate a religious holiday, especially the festival of Shaykh Abdelfettah, the *mawlid an-nabi,* or Mohammed's Ascension (27th day of Rajab). The brotherhood leaders try to attend the festivals of the main Cairo saints, such as Sayyidna Hussein and Sayyida Zeinab. By paying a call on the *shaykh as-sijada* at this time they reestablish relations and demonstrate their allegiance to the hierarchy of the order, from which they in turn derive their own legitimacy at the village level.

Overall, perhaps ten percent of the adult men are directly involved in the activities of the brotherhoods in one of the roles mentioned, but many more participate indirectly as sponsors of an "evening" in response to a vow or a life crisis rite, or simply as casual spectators. Others in the village oppose the brotherhoods, arguing that they are not according to the Sunna.[8] Most opposed, however, are those associated with the ideas of the Muslim brotherhood and the "Muslim groups," who regard these activities as little better than examples of superstition and unbelief (Guenena 1986). In turn, the adherents of these groups are criticized for their lack of tolerance and their tendency to interfere in the affairs of others.

The Celebration of Mawlid an-Nabi

The most elaborate celebration of the year in Musha commemorates the birthday of the Prophet, *mawlid an-nabi.* During the year I was in the field this fell in January. On this occasion, the chapters of the brotherhoods in Musha reinforce their own social organization by holding sessions which all members and supporters are supposed to attend. The sessions take place on three successive evenings, ending with the eve of the holiday itself. The Rifa'iya chapter that I knew best held its sessions in a reception room attached to the house of its *shaykh,* in the western part of Musha.[9]

On the evenings of the celebration, the members of the various chapters gather after the evening prayer to march through the town chanting their songs and carrying their banners. There is an element of competition in this. The parade ends up in the room where the chapter will then meet and perform the ritual. In the case of the Rifa'iya chapter, on the first two evenings, various singers sang religious hymns in succession while the simple members formed two lines in front of them to bob and sway to the rhythm. Ordinarily, there were from six to twelve *faqqar* (recitants) organized and synchronized by one of the minor leaders, though sometimes there would just be singing and recitation without dancing. Others stood behind the singers, keeping track of the rhythm and the text. Still others were bringing and serving tea. At the other end of the room sat the Shaykh Mohammed and his associates, including honored guests and the other men who were leaders in this group. The distinction between the two groups of men was largely maintained. Only two individuals moved from one group to the other, and they were both in principle members of the higher status group who played a functional role in the performance itself. Those around the Shaykh were sitting on benches and had a table in front of them, while those at the other end of the room, when sitting, had to sit on the floor, cross-legged or with their backs against the wall. The quantity and variety of refreshments offered was also greater at the honorable end of the room. The second of these two evenings was not as well attended as the first, and the session itself only lasted an hour. The Shaykh was clearly disappointed by this, for he made a little speech trying to put a brave face on it. He argued that a good small group was better than a lukewarm large one, and that a *tariqa* goes up and down anyway—the small gives birth to the large, and the large to the small.

As in the evenings held in the reception rooms of the large farmers, the senior man present must dominate and lead the conversation. In these religious gatherings, however, a favorite topic of conversation is to recount one's trips to the major shrines of Egypt, or even the pilgrimage to Mecca. Generally, however, the conversation turns around fairly mundane questions having to do with local affairs, agriculture, and so on. At this second evening there was a visitor from the upstream village of el-Atamna, and so some of the conversation turned around the plans for celebrating the festival in that part of the valley.

The third evening of the *mawlid* is in some ways the most important. In the case of this group, it was postponed a day following the death of Shaykh Mohammed's brother-in-law. Instead of a *hadra,* the singers sang various religious songs referring to Mohammed and to the different saints. As they sung, they were interrupted from time to time by people who gave money. The singers called out the donor's name and the names of those on whom the donor was calling blessings. Generally speaking, the ordinary members and visitors who gave money had lengthy lists of people whose memories they wished to invoke in this religious setting. The distinguished guests, those sitting on the benches with the Shaykh, largely gave money without providing any list of names for blessing. In this case, the singer would supply the donor's name, and then add, "and his wife and children." The distinguished guests, who had come to honor the Shaykh and indirectly to support the institution, included some of the larger farmers in the village. They did not sit for long, but paid their respects and left. At the end of the evening, Shaykh Mohammed took the money from the man who had been collecting it all evening, and divided it (or at least some of it) among the singers and those who had helped with the evening. Almost certainly there was a surplus for the chapter leaders. After all the money had been distributed, the *rais al-hadra* invited members of the inner core to his house for a midnight supper. The chief topic of conversation at this supper was to recall who had turned up to demonstrate his respect for the Shaykh and the Rifa'iya, and who had failed to do so.

Other ordinary *dhikr*s held in people's homes were likely to end with a supper prepared by the women and served by the hosts. Once I saw a young man deliver a sermon at a *dhikr* held in honor of Sayyida Zeinab.

Functions

The brotherhoods serve several functions. They are a religious expression that parallels and supports the hierarchy visible in the economic sphere. They establish a pattern of religious sociability that holds together a neighborhood or a clan, regardless of the hierarchical differences in status. This is symbolized by the common meal at the end of the *dhikr*—even if the order of serving repeats the hierarchy. The brotherhoods create links between communities that enable economic activity such as trade or labor recruiting to go on as well. To some extent they cure the sick and provide an outlet for the mad. They provide an income for those involved, particularly the *shaykh*s and the singers. By competing with each other, the brotherhoods reinvigorate village social organization and prevent entropy. This competition (carried out in part through warring loudspeakers) is a surrogate for direct political competition between big families that itself might prove too divisive.

Here we are interested primarily in the first of these functions. The social hierarchy of the brotherhoods serves as a metaphor for the social organization of the village. Those who run the brotherhoods belong to the class of farmers that hires labor fairly regularly; the simple members generally are the ones who are hired, whether in agriculture, in construction or in another domain. Thus the social control that is exercised over the latter by the former in this religious context can be assumed to extend somewhat to the economic domain. The domain of work is never very far from people's minds, as is demonstrated by the concern of the Shaykh lest too long a *dhikr* in the evening interfere with work on the morrow. The hierarchy in work that is necessary for the social control of labor is thus symbolized and repeated in the religious hierarchy of the brotherhoods. That there is some net flow of resources to the richer leaders adds to the piquancy of the situation. The analysis of the final evening of the celebration of the *mawlid an-nabi* shows the significance of the role of the big farmers who do not take part directly in the activities of the brotherhoods. By showing their respect for the *shaykh,* and contributing money to him for redistribution to his followers or for his own use, they participate in the functional role of the brotherhoods as supporters of the hierarchical control of labor through its transposition to the religious plane. By the same token, the role of the richer families in supporting the *mawlid* of Shaykh Abdelfettah, and, in particular, *laylat al-fuqara,* also has elements of mystification—stressing village solidarity and the hierarchy within it rather than the divisions along categorical or class lines.

The activities of the brotherhoods, and the celebrations of the festival of Shaykh Abdelfettah, are institutions that serve to reinforce the hierarchical control of labor in work situations both by deflecting people's attention away from those work situations and by presenting a religious justification for that hierarchy, in effect giving a religious dimension to the meaning of hierarchy itself.

A Culture of Deference

Throughout this chapter we have seen the importance of vertical relationships between men. This is manifested in the conversation groups that assemble in the houses of the important men, in the manner of resolving disputes by calling in high-status mediators, and in the elaborate hierarchy of the religious brotherhoods. Although the formal institutions of VC, LPC, and Cooperative are not structured along the same lines, interpersonal relations within them tend to follow the same principles of verticality.

Deference behavior is part of the stuff of life in Musha. This is evident in the code of visiting according to which the host appears superior to the guest—a rule that tends to confine the most important men in the village to their own homes and thus makes them reliant on the eyes and ears of others to gather information. It is evident in the constant use of honorific titles. To call someone by name without a title implies that he is of much lower status. Within the village the most neutral title is "uncle" (*'amm*); others range from *shaykh* to *ustadh,* from *hajj* to "doctor." Occasionally the circumlocutious teknonym, *abu fulan,* is used. Whenever men gather they must discover who will accept a cigarette from whom, since the giver has a higher status than the recipient. The constant jostling to demonstrate these nuances in status leads to a very high consumption of cigarettes, and a considerable part of the expenditure of the middle and higher ranking men goes for cigarettes.

The culture of deference combines with the pattern of socio-economic differentiation, as realized through the process of political action, to produce a patron-client type relational network. The most important social relations one has are with one's superiors and inferiors, seniors or juniors; there are few situations where one is absolutely among equals—and they are likely to be internal to the family or lineage. Thus success in politics as in life lies in knowing how to placate one's superiors and dominate one's inferiors. Village culture does not give much support for the development of notions based on common status. The school classroom, especially at the secondary school level when the young people go away to a strange town to school, is the best seedbed for such ideas. Even the work situation in Musha rarely brings together people of common status performing similar or identical tasks—adult Musha men are more likely to work alone or in small groups performing specific tasks. The presence of a supervisor means that the focus of attention is on the worker-supervisor relationship rather than the relationship between the workers. The final chapter spells out the implications of this structure of inequality, based both on an unequal distribution of control over resources and on a culture of deference.

Notes

1. The best recent account of village politics is that of Harik (1974). He analyzes a village in Beheira which he observed in 1966–68. Both the history and geography were quite different—this was an "agrarian reform" village, and the analysis took place when socialism was in flower. The Minufiya villages analyzed by Berque (1957) and Stauth (1983) seem closer to Musha, but the material is too incomplete to judge. Some sense of politics in the Daqahliya village of Tafahna is given by Saunders and Mehanna (1986), and in a Nubian transplanted village by Kennedy (1977) and Fahim (1983). Adams (1986) also gives some idea of politics in rural Minya governorate and in a land reform village in the northern Delta. See also the study by Abdelmo'ti (1977) on class struggle in several Minya villages; his analysis of conflict should be compared with that of Abou-Zeid (1965). For an overview, see Toth (1980).

2. The only two candidates known to me who were also civil servants were both among the losers.

3. Musha was one of the cases referred to in a series of articles in *al-Gumhuriya* newspaper in June 1968. These articles cited Musha along with nine other villages, including the home village of Sayyid Mara'i, as examples of the retention of the traditional power structure in the new guise of formal elective institutions. Of Musha it is said that the power of the *'umda* was undercut by the creation of a police station. The secretary of the cooperative (*katib*) is identified as a key figure; in Musha he was a former employee of the *'umda,* and he had managed to become a wealthy and prominent figure with ties to other villages. At the same time the cooperative secretary was blamed by the farmers for some shortcomings in the cooperative. See Baker (1979:208) and Springborg (1982:180).

4. Marital disputes are also common, notably in new marriages, but I was less able to gather data on these.

5. My research assistant who was from an Asyut village east of the Nile thought that it was characteristic that people in Musha used these elaborate peacemaking mechanisms for something as minor as land disputes. In his area, they would only have been brought into play in the case of shedding of blood in a quarrel or a feud.

6. See Gilsenan (1973) for an excellent analysis of the structure and functioning of one of the urban-based brotherhoods in Cairo and Alexandria. I appreciated this book much better after having come into contact with the Rifa'iya brotherhood in Musha. See also Reeves (1981).

7. In the cell I knew best, the *naib* is a farmer of 12 feddans, whose father and grandfather played the same role, and whose sons are now civil servants. The *naqib* is a farmer of about 50 feddans, who is said to neglect his farming (relatively) for religion, and is from the lineage of Beit 'Abdin. The *rais al-hadra* is a small farmer, a *hajj,* from the lineage of Awlad Hassan.

8. The contrast between different religious styles in village Egypt has been evoked by many writers. The examples frequently contrast a rigorous interpretation of religion emanating from urban Egypt and a somewhat more tolerant and folkloristic set of village beliefs. This debate in the villages of Egypt is thus nothing new. See, for instance, Ammar (1966:78), Berque (1957); Fahim (1973); and Kennedy (1977).

9. Characteristically, Ammar (1966:46) reports for Silwa that the celebration of *mawlid an-nabi* reinforces lineage solidarity, while here it reinforces the hierarchically organized brotherhoods.

11

Inequality, Class, and the State in Rural Egypt

The recent transformation of Egyptian agriculture has had important effects on village social organization and rural class structure, as well as on the role of the state in rural life. At the outset of this book, I contrasted two alternative models for the interpretation of these changes. The "Agrarian Transition" model emphasizes the transformation of the peasant into a wage laborer as a consequence of technological changes in agriculture, and stresses the similarity of the class hierarchy in agriculture to that generated by industry. The focus, in other words, is on the shift to a new mode of production. The "Labor Process" model reflects a contrasting emphasis. It is inductive rather than deductive, and directs our attention to the detailed changes in the social organization of production. The focus is on the hierarchical control of work, surplus extraction, and class as a process rather than a category.

The data presented in this book show that whereas the peasant may indeed have disappeared, the wage laborer has not entirely taken his place. Instead we find the petty commodity producing small farmer household. The analysis presented in this book suggests that the independence of these households is largely illusory. They are integrated into a mode of production which we can characterize as "capitalist" in that capital (in the form of machinery as well as land) and profit are essential for its reproduction. The small farmer households are linked into the capitalist system through their dependence on the owners of capital and through their integration into the market. The typical class situation thus involves access to capital rather than a conflict in the work place between capitalists and workers. In short, the "Labor Process" model gives us better data from which to tackle the problem of differentiation and class formation in rural Egypt.

In analyzing the community from the point of view of a production system based on capital, I have stressed the changing role of the household. The role of the state in the labor process is also substantial, and the representatives of the state have considerable influence. Village social interaction is a level of organization which is intermediate between the household and the state, and wields a certain influence on household and individual choices and strategies. Thus despite the predominance of the state, class analysis is possible at the local level, if one recognizes that some classes are not present there, but influence the local scene from afar.

Hierarchy and inequality permeate village social relations. The analysis of Musha shows that there is considerable difference in the amount of resources people control and in their ability to carry out economic and social activities in the village. Those who control more resources also dominate the lives of the less fortunate in various ways. This gross economic difference is reflected in, and reflects, cultural patterns stressing deference, which serve to link people together in a continuing social system (Scott 1985). The problem that I now raise by way of conclusion is how to conceptualize and characterize this hierarchy and inequality. I propose to approach this first of all from the standpoint of class.

Class

Class is of course a highly problematic concept. The approach to class here assumes that class is a *process*, not a "thing." "Class" should be, not a status word, but a process word like production, reproduction, accumulation, or exploitation. We are concerned not to reify class but to use the concept flexibly in the sense that different class configurations are appropriate for different analyses. Thus we are not concerned to identify and isolate a number of social classes as a part of a static system. This approach, which polarizes social classes into politically active groups with a fairly high degree of self-consciousness, cannot be a starting point for the analysis, though it might be the conclusion.

The understanding of social-economic organization, the overall structure of society, starts from an analysis of the labor process, the social relations that grow out of the work needed to transform the natural world (here through agriculture) into something of social use (cf. Marx 1967:I:183; Burawoy 1984:30). These social relations are dynamic in that they involve repetition of activities through time, and consequently reflect minute changes in the round of everyday life as well as gross changes caused by the introduction of new technologies such as irrigation and mechanized traction.

The notion of class used here implies a provisional aggregate of individuals whose life experience has been molded by the labor process; a change in the labor process may produce different life experiences and so a different pattern of class affiliation. This produces what Marx called a "class in itself." In order for a "class for itself," i.e., with political consciousness, to exist, there has to be a pattern of easy communication among class members, so that values, attitudes, experiences, and plans can be shared, and there has to be some more or less overt form of political organization. This political organization might begin by being contingent, that is, tied to a particular issue but without a permanent structure; later on, a structure may appear. Thus, in analyzing class relations in a Tunisian village, I argued that if a class is to be perceptible as a social group in conflict with its dialectically opposed class, it must be an aggregate of individuals whose life experience is shaped first of all by working conditions and second by struggle; these individuals must have a common perception of their material interests formed as a result of frequent and easy exchange of ideas, and a consciousness that implies a vocabulary or idiom for its verbal or symbolic expression. Each class, in other words, must have a structure and an idiom, a way of representing its consciousness which articulates conflict (Hopkins 1977:454–455).

The analysis of the labor process under petty agrarian capitalism in Musha shows the patterns of work relations, and the patterns of access to land, water and machinery, and how they reinforce inequality. Despite the considerable economic and social inequality between individuals and households, however, there is no evidence that the people of Musha think in those terms, or that class has any phenomenological reality. Class is present in work relations only but it is not evidently a fact of life at the cultural or symbolic level. Instead of class feeling or a sense of stratification, the social arrangements by which Musha lives reflect a culture of status, deference, and patron-client links (cf. Stauth 1983).

The lack of class consciousness in Musha, or indeed, in most Egyptian villages, reflects, in the first place, the general absence of political struggle that reflects the opposed interests of different potential classes (but see Schulze 1981). There has been no crucible within which class consciousness formed. Political conflict in the village tends to take the form of rivalry between different clans, lineages, sufi chapters, sections or quarters of the village (Abou-Zeid 1965), rather than the form of opposition between economic categories such as landowners and workers or large and small farmers (for an example from urban Cairo, see Taher 1986).

In the second place, the free and easy communication between members of the same (potential) class is largely absent. Again, patterns of social relations reflect vertical links such as kinship and clientship, or neighborly relations, rather than categorical relations based on occupancy of the same class position. In practice, work rarely associates large numbers of Musha men. The coffee shop is a partial exception for the working class, and evening gatherings in the home or reception area of the village's big men is a partial exception for the upper (capitalist) class. But the top village farmers do not meet each other very often, because of the absence of neutral sites for such meetings and concerns about precedence in visiting.

Furthermore, there is no political or social organization in the village apart from those generated by the hierarchical structures of the village itself or by the equally hierarchical state.

Classes ultimately imply a division of labor within a national framework, and hence some kind of absorption of the local community into the body politic regulated by the state. The state, whose existence probably initially reflects the urban and international political arenas most of all, tries to penetrate and "capture" the rural areas (and some urban areas), with various degrees of success. The state also intervenes in the production process, though its intervention is manipulated. This intervention falls short of penetration or control of the organization of labor, and so the presence of the state has minimal implications for class formation or the creation of class consciousness. Instead, the bureaucracy and political structure of the state reinforce the importance of hierarchy.

The social organization of agriculture is based on the formation of unequal relations between the state and the large farmer, between the large farmer and the small farmer, between the farmer and the laborer. There are opposing interests, and each party tries to improve its own position in competition with the others, thus providing the momentum that perpetuates the farming system. Looking at class as a process rather than as a "thing" leads to less concern with identifying strata in village society that have opposing interests, at least in principle, and more concern with the way in which the labor process creates interests opposing different socio-economic positions.

The social relations that underlie the genesis of class in Musha are thus: (1) hirer-hired (farmer-worker); (2) machine or capital owner-renter of machinery; (3) purchaser-producer (merchant-farmer); (4) state agent-private farmer. This situation can be summed up in terms of three or five active classes in the agrarian society of Musha. In the agrarian sector itself there are (1) the large capitalist farmers, (2) the small farmers, the small-scale commodity producers, and (3) the laborers, those who rely entirely on selling their labor power, not uniquely within agriculture. These represent three separate socio-economic positions, and to sum them in this way eludes the question of the precise boundaries between them. The fourth and fifth active classes are the merchants and traders on the one hand, and the civil servants on the other. Since many people in the first three classes also trade or work for the government, these are not entirely separate classes, but they are distinct socio-economic positions within the functional whole of the village. These relationships can be further clarified through an examination of the hierarchical control of work and the extraction of surplus.

Hierarchical Control of Work

The notion of the hierarchical control of work leads us to postulate that a class relation exists when one person or group of persons asserts control over the work of another. This is the case (in principle) when a farmer hires another person to work for him, or when the state, through its agents, intervenes in the production process. However, the implications of the hierarchical control of work for class are diminished by the decentralization of the control over labor characteristic of the labor process which this book has analyzed.

In the first place the effects of mechanization on the hierarchical control of work have been slight. The owners of machinery (capital) have not used their position to exert any control over the labor process itself, leaving each head of a farming household responsible for recruiting the labor he needs to carry out his tasks. The (small) farmer and not the capitalist is responsible for whatever degree of control actually exists.

O'Brien (1984:238) has recently made the same argument for the Gezira scheme in the Sudan:

> The foregoing analysis has attempted to demonstrate that debates over whether Gezira tenants are exploiters or disguised wage-earners have missed the historically most significant aspect of their position in irrigated agriculture in Sudan—their decentralized role in supervising the huge wage labor force. Thousands of tenants have each negotiated wage rates with, hired, supervised, and paid small numbers of wage laborers in their individual tenancies. At the same time, tenants could, to varying degrees, replace expensive wage labor with free or less expensive household labor whenever they experienced upward pressures on wage rates. This function of the tenantry in mediating labor relations has been of inestimable political and economic value to management and the state in maintaining the fragmentation of the wage labor force and keeping wage rates low.

In the second place, the work groups that are thus assembled are generally rather small and tend to be governed by interpersonal relations of long standing rather than the impersonal relations of role to role that are more likely to allow for an understanding of the relationship in class terms. Whenever larger work groups are assembled—typically for harvesting—they are handled in such a way as to reduce the class implications of the situation. In many cases, those hired are teenagers or children; sometimes they are from neighboring villages, so that the class relations are projected outside the community; sometimes, as in the wheat or cotton harvests, the payment of piece rate wages emphasizes competition among workers rather than solidarity.

For all these reasons, the hiring of labor and the hierarchical control of labor have not (yet) had the impact on the formation of class consciousness and thus on the overt existence of class relations that one might have expected. Situations involving the hierarchical control of work are few; and the workings of a market in labor, land, machinery, even water, enable people to avoid human situations that would sharpen people's sensitivity to class distinctions and to stratification.

Workers are separated from the productive process, control of which remains in the hands of the individual farmer-managers. Yet these farmer-managers are themselves not masters of the situation, for they have to call on the owners of machinery to perform essential tasks for them. Thus the lines of control and the movement of surplus value are quite different than in the archetypical industrial situation. The surplus value produced by the farmers-managers is absorbed, not by those who control their work, but by those who provide them a service.

The state is also ambitious to assert control over the labor process through a variety of means. The state created and guarantees the land tenure system, with its implications for differential control and access to land. It took the initiative in rebuilding the irrigation system. During the socialist period of the 1960s the state extended its ambitions for control through the creation of a mandatory cooperative system which claimed to oblige farmers to grow certain crops in certain fields at certain times, creating a mandatory crop rotation system, and doubling this with a complicated system of subsidized inputs and forced deliveries. Much of this still exists.

Surplus Extraction

For further clarification, I now turn to the problem of the extraction of surplus value. Because of the difficulty of gathering figures, I do not intend to suggest a rate of exploitation or extraction of surplus, but instead aim to point out the paths and contexts in which it is possible to speak of the extraction of surplus.

Wages in Musha had risen considerably prior to my fieldwork, and they have risen more since. However, there are many kinds of work that are paid differently, and at a higher rate: piece work in agriculture, construction, brick making, and so on. The wages were generally conventional for the village, and consequently were established by bargaining, particularly between the larger farmers and those available to work by the day. In order to argue that the wages were exploitative, i.e., that they offered the worker nothing beyond the amount needed for his reproduction and that of his family, I would have to possess a lot more detailed and reliable information about household accounts than I in fact have. As a general impression, one can say that wage earners were not worse off than small holders (say less than two feddans), so that in these cases, the relationship was one between equals. However, the larger employers were constantly seeking ways to reduce their wage bill, either by hiring teenagers instead of adults, or hiring workers from other villagers whose men were willing to work for lower wages than the men of Musha. The various alternatives had in general the effect of keeping wages somewhat lower than they might have been.

Here one can note that if women were to enter the labor market, this would be another factor having a depressing effect on wages, for the large farmers would soon justify or rationalize lower wages for women, and this would make them effective competitors against the men. Some men might then accept lower wages in order to compete for work against the women. For the moment, women ridicule the idea that they might work in the fields. As Mencher comments for agricultural work in South India (1978:206): "It is difficult back-breaking work, and if a woman can get out of doing it, she will." Thus it is the women who have the most obvious interest is maintaining the notion that it is shameful for a woman to work in the fields, and their refusal has an effect on men's wages.

More important as techniques for the extraction of surplus are the rental of machinery and (under some conditions) of land. Those who control capital in the form of farm machinery rent it on a piecemeal basis to others in exchange for a share of the income from agriculture. The profitability of machinery is enhanced by state subsidies for fuel, oil, and the purchase price of the tractor. Rental prices for tractors are set fairly high and have a tendency to rise. They reflect market factors—relative scarcity of machinery as well as at least tacit collusion among machine owners to keep rates high. Again, it may be hard in theory to determine a "fair" price. But it is evident that rental rates are not fixed on a "cost plus" basis but that owners charge what they think the market will bear. Their rates also reflect to some extent the existence of social relations between them and their customers—kin are often charged less, as are certain other categories.

Legal rents are controlled by the government, and do not reflect inflation. Thus they tend to appear relatively low. In most cases, the recipient of the rent is a small owner. In fact, the most common case occurs when one brother remains behind and "rents" the land of his siblings in order to assemble a "farm" of a few feddans in size while the "owners" migrate to the city, take government jobs, and so on. I suspect that in many such cases, no rent is actually paid; there is just an understanding that the absent owner has in principle something to come home to. "Free market" rents are frequently by the season (i.e., winter or summer) rather than annual, and they are several times higher than the legal rents. One large landowner estimated to me that he would make more money by renting out his land illegally in the summer than by cultivating it himself, whereas in the winter the reverse was true (because of the low labor requirements of the winter crops).

Marketing also is available as a mechanism for extracting surplus. The issue here is the "fairness" of the price which the centralizing merchant pays the farmer for his crop. Again, these prices fluctuate according to market conditions. They vary from season to season and from year to year. However, at least in some cases it is clear that the greater capital of the merchants gives them an advantage. They can afford to store a crop for a period of time while waiting for the right selling price, whereas the small farmer is more likely to want to trade his crop for cash right away.

The state has two methods for extracting surplus from the population, including both large and small farmers. In the first place, it taxes the land, albeit lightly. It is not certain that the state derives any real financial benefit from this, because inflation has eroded the value of the sum of money collected. In the second place, it controls the terms of trade for certain crops, presumably in its favor (cf. Abdel-Khalek and Tignor 1982; Adams 1986). It sets the "farmgate" price for cotton below the world market price, intending to reap a profit on the transaction. The relatively low fixed price for food crops helps subsidize the urban populations who buy the crop through urban consumer cooperatives. Again, it is not clear whether the state comes out ahead in these transactions, not least because the state also assumes responsibility for providing, financing, and maintaining the irrigation works, subsidized inputs, roads, and transportation system necessary for agriculture.

From the point of view of the (potential) class structure of the rural areas, the significance of the state's involvement lies in the creation of a bureaucracy to serve its ends. Most of the members of this bureaucracy are of rural origin, and many are officials in their native village, as in Musha. The existence of these posts offers certain families and individuals a chance to extend their prominent role in the village to a new area and to use the new structures to affirm an old dominance. Thus the analysis of class relations in the village has to take these new figures into account. They are an extension, at least in Musha, of the power of the traditional landed families. At the same time, government service is a path to upward mobility for many poor or middle families. There is also a sense, moreover, in which the government officials are the representatives in the local community of the national ruling class. They are charged with carrying out the various rules and regulations devised by the state and its ruling group to extend their influence at the village level. This is particularly expressed through the desire to control agriculture choices and work.

Power

If there is substantial inequality in Musha, to the point where it is possible to argue that class objectively exists, then what can explain the fact that there is so little class consciousness, so that people do not organize their behavior according to the construct of class differences and rivalries? A part, perhaps a large part, of the answer is that the dominant group—the large farmers and their allies in the bureaucracy, but mostly in this case the large farmers themselves—uses its position to create and enforce another model of society. In the *German Ideology* Marx and Engels (1970:64) noted:

> The ideas of the ruling class are in every epoch the ruling ideas. . . . The ruling ideas are nothing more than the ideal expression of the dominant material relationships, the dominant material relationships grasped as ideas; hence of the relationships which make the one class the ruling one, therefore, the ideas of its dominance.

To the extent that the model of the ruling class (the large farmers) guides and organizes people's behavior, there is no room for class-oriented behavior.

This alternative model stresses hierarchy, patron-client type relations, charity to the poor. It builds on an image of the (relatively) poor in the village as dependent on the big families for employment, charity, and mediation with the government bureaucracy. There are two main ways of achieving this. One is through the manipulation of Islamic values; the other is through successfully acting as brokers in a patron-client type vertical network.

The large families in the village encourage a certain kind of Islam—the Islam of the family mosques and the religious brotherhoods. What these two have in common is that they reflect and reinforce the patriarchal structure of family, kinship and neighborhood in the village. The family mosques are gathering places for prayer that serve a small neighborhood most of whose inhabitants are either members of the family or clients of it. The officials of the mosque tend to be the poorer relatives or clients, with the possible exception of the imam himself. Most mosques in Musha are of this type. The religious brotherhoods are also often based on one of the village neighborhoods, and we have seen that they incorporate a significant hierarchy that corresponds to that in the economic domain. An extension of this argument is that such religious movements as the Muslim brothers or the "Islamic groups" may represent the opposite logic, to the extent that they are based on a more egalitarian form of internal organization.

The custom of charity, and in particularly the annual celebration known as *laylat al-fuqara,* also reinforces these vertical links. At this annual festival held in honor of the "patron saint" of the village, meat from sacrificial animals donated for the most part by the big families of Musha is distributed to all the inhabitants of the village. This represents a symbolic redistribution of goods and benefits from the rich to the poor, and it is fairly self-consciously maintained by the rich in order to buttress this kind of relationship, a kind of clientele-like relationship (cf. Scott 1983:207).

Members of big families act as patrons in other ways, too. They intervene to help settle quarrels, using the weight of their position to encourage the disputants to reach a compromise. These quarrels range from marriage disputes to battles over land. They also act as intermediaries between their clients and the incomprehensible state, making sure that some of their poorer clients receive a share of cloth being sold at subsidized prices to the poor, for instance, or that the cooperative treats them right. The ability of the rich to act as patrons is symbolized by the fact that by and large they live scattered among the poor who are their clients. In many cases, the poor wait on the rich in the evening when the work is done, and form a "court" in their houses.

In various ways, the poor are thus dependent on the rich, and this is in no small measure responsible for the relatively slow emergence of class consciousness and class conflict. As long as the rich are careful to play the role of patron, and to sustain those institutions such as the religious ones that support this verticality, this model of society will continue to retain its prominence over a model built on the notion of strata or layers, which would then emerge into a true class consciousness model.

Agrarian Transformation in Egypt

Although the bulk of the evidence in this book is from a single village in Upper Egypt, it bears directly on the comprehension of the agrarian transformation in Egypt. This involves the transformation of "labor into wage-labor and the means of production into capital" (Marx 1967:III:885). In the analysis of the labor process in Musha the significance of both wage labor and the growth of capital in the form of agricultural machinery is evident. It should not, however, be imagined that the importance of either wage labor or capital is strikingly recent. Throughout this book the historical depth of the phenomenon has been underlined.

The farming system of Musha has several important internal dynamics. One of these is capital accumulation in the hands of the large farmers, a process that was perhaps interrupted by the socialist period in Egypt as a whole during the 1960s. Although Musha was little touched by agrarian reform, the threat of further reform discouraged people from investing in agriculture. The rich landowners in Musha invested in other areas, such as urban real estate and commerce. By 1980 a second echelon of farmers was filling in the gap behind the rich farmers of the 1930s. However, the emphasis in the 1980s was more on expanding control of machinery than on simple accumulation of land. Thus the relationship of the larger farmers to the smaller farmers around them was mediated through their control of the access to machinery more than through control of the access to land.

A class of large farmers continues to play an important role in Musha. The remaining majority of the population includes small farmers, laborers, and others. Many of these are subordinated to capital in the form of machinery, yet the organization of that subordination is based on a distinction between the extraction of surplus value and the hierarchical control of labor. The relative decentralization of control over labor, while it contrasts with the continued flow of surplus value to the large-scale operators, allows for the survival of some small and middle farmers. The continued presence of nominally independent small farmers is a structural part of the system, since it allows for much of the benefit from agriculture to end up in the hands of the few while eliminating the onerous task of supervising labor. The agrarian transformation of agriculture in Musha does not imply an extreme form of class differentation into a small group of capitalist farmers and a larger group of the proletarianized, but instead includes a wider range of possible socio-economic positions. Such proletarianization as exists is masked, and the case of Musha does not correspond to any of the possibilities enumerated by Keyder (1983) for Turkey—neither the polarization of the wheat-growing areas on the high plains of eastern Turkey nor the gradual creation of family-sized enterprises in the valleys of western Turkey.

The small farmers and the landless continue their struggle for survival, using various techniques to find the proper niche in the agrarian economy of Musha. The survival strategies of the small farmers rely to a great extent on the subsidies of the state, which provides agricultural inputs at reasonable cost—but at the expense of tying them more firmly to the state's policies in agriculture. The small farmers must thus evolve in the space left to them between the activities of the large farmers and the role of the state. Reliance on animal husbandry for the flexibility that agriculture itself does not allow is important (Fitch and Soliman 1983). The landless must seek a source of cash income, whether in the form of agricultural or construction wage labor or as a government employee.

But for the landless and the small farmers there is always the option of leaving Musha, either temporarily or permanently. In terms of the agrarian society of the village, this acts as a safety valve. The opportunity to migrate is also an old one, although it may be more of a positive choice and less a matter of sheer survival than it was a century ago. In any case, the flow of migration income into a village like Musha has historical antecedents. To some extent, small-scale agriculture is now subsidized by the income earned outside the village.

Working conditions themselves have been transformed by the modification of the irrigation system and the introduction of machinery. Jacques Berque (1957:23) pointed out that the changes in the irrigation system affect the very rhythm of the farmer's work. Instead of a slow rhythm determined by the annual flood, there is now the accelerated rhythm of the two week irrigation cycle in the canals, and the more demanding water requirements of the plants themselves, notably cotton. The existing tractors and threshing machines, and the seed drills and harvesters yet to come, impose a different kind of collective work on people—rather than small groups over a long period of time, now the requirement is for large groups working frenetically for a relatively brief period of time, and the consequence is more of a demand for hired labor.

The implications of this for the household are also substantial. Instead of a household organized for productive purposes, and incorporating within itself the sexual division of labor, there is now a household organized for managerial purposes. This is striking in the case of the farm households, large and small. The household itself provides less and less of the actual labor needed for agriculture, and instead has recourse to wage labor as a supplement. The role of the head of the household is more that of a manager, balancing out the need to deal with the government (the cooperative), to hire machinery, to assure a regular water supply, to engage the labor needed for certain tasks, and to look after the marketing of the produce. Along with this tendency is also the trend towards part-time farmers: more than a matter of having a son with a non-farm income, now many small farmers try to combine a government job of their own with continued management of their farm. This is only possible due to hired labor and the availability of machinery to accelerate key work processes.

What remains of the traditional involvement of the household in productive activity is to a great extent a matter of the role of women in the household in caring for animals or carrying out such tasks as cooking, cleaning, child care, etc. Thus the ideology of the traditional productive household serves to buttress a certain patriarchy, and is perhaps useful for a certain reproduction of the institution, even though the activities of the male household head are now more oriented towards manipulating the outside world than in mobilizing the forces within the productive unit.

The role of the state in agricultural production continues. It probably reached a kind of plateau in the socialist 1960s, and has neither advanced nor retreated from that plateau since then. However, whereas the trend in the 1960s was for the state to penetrate more and more into the organization of the productive process (the labor process), in the last decade, the state's tactic has been more to influence choices through manipulation of market mechanisms (the prices of inputs and crops) and through creation of improved infrastructure, such as canals and roads. The state also continues as the arbiter of the rural-urban dichotomy, particularly insofar as prices are concerned.

Thus each of the components of the agrarian farming system has a role to play in the reproduction of the system, its own internal dynamic—the household, the community, and the state; the large farmer, the small farmer, and the non-farmer. These internal dynamics are to some extent mutually reinforcing, as in the change of the economic position of the small farmer household and the introduction of machinery. They are also to some extent contradictory, as in the accumulation of capital by the larger farmers and the continued viability of the small farmer household, or the balance between the financial attractions of migration and the social balance of the community. The gradual shift in the level of agricultural technology will have an effect on the social organization of agriculture; and change there will place the organization of work at variance with the kinds of image that farmers and workers make of their own society. From this creative tension comes further change.

Writers on Egypt for the past century have frequently stressed the rapid process of change which the countryside is undergoing. To talk of transformation is not to imply that there is a solid beginning point and a finite end. We are recording one moment in a long transition. The present shows a movement away from a household-based agriculture using traditional animal-powered technology and towards one rooted more in community processes (such as a village-based labor and marchinery market) and relying on mechanical traction and water lifting. The role of capital, for both large and small, rich and poor, is expanding, with consequences for the organization of society. This transition is simultaneous with the continued spread of a market for agricultural produce, so that more and more the farmers are producing (not just cotton but all crops) for the market, and purchasing more and more of what they need from the market. At the lower end of the scale, this movement away from subsistence farming may represent an impoverishment, yet it is required both by the demands of the state and the profits of the large capitalist farmers. The pressure in agrarian society towards concentration of resources in the hands of relatively few enterprises (whether large private farmers or other alternatives such as state-run production cooperatives) is constant. The introduction of more labor-saving machinery will increase this pressure. The state favors the trend to the extent that it increases total productivity. Yet what will the consequences be for the small farmers and the non-farmers? The balance between equity and productivity is dynamic and cannot be established once and for all. The analysis of the social organization of agricultural work through a study of the labor process reveals some of the issues involved, and may contribute towards a better understanding of that dynamic balance.

Bibliography

Abdel-Fadil, Mahmoud. 1975. *Development, Income Distribution and Social Change in Rural Egypt, 1952–1970.* Cambridge, Cambridge University Press.

Abdel-Khalek, Gouda, and Robert Tignor. 1982. *The Political Economy of Income Distribution in Egypt.* New York, Holmes and Meier.

Abdelmo'ti, Abdelbasset. 1977. *Al-sira' al-tabaqi fi al-qariyah al-misriyah.* Cairo, Dar al-Thaqafa al-Jadida.

Abul-Ata, A. Azim. 1977. "The conversion of basin irrigation to perennial systems in Egypt." In *Arid Land Irrigation in Developing Countries,* edited by E. B. Worthington. Oxford, Pergamon, pp. 99–105.

Abou-Zeid, Ahmed. 1965. *Al-thar—Darasa anthropolojiya bi ahda qura al-sa'id.* Cairo, Dar al-Ma'aref.

Adams, Richard H., Jr. 1985. "Development and Structural Change in Rural Egypt, 1952 to 1982." *World Development* 13 (6):705–723.

———. 1986. *Development and Social Change in Rural Egypt.* Syracuse, Syracuse University Press.

Al-Sayyid-Marsot, Afaf Lutfi. 1977. *Egypt's Liberal Experiment: 1922–1936.* Berkeley, University of California Press.

———. 1984. *Egypt in the Reign of Muhammed Ali.* Cambridge, Cambridge University Press.

Amélineau, E. 1893. *La géographie de l'Egypte à l'époque copte.* Paris, Imprimerie Nationale.

Ammar, Hamed. 1966. *Growing Up in an Egyptian Village.* New York, Octagon Books.

Ayrout, Henry Habib. 1952. *Fellahs d'Egypte.* Cairo, Editions du Sphynx.

———. 1963. *The Egyptian Peasant.* Boston, Beacon Press.

Baer, Gabriel. 1962. *A History of Landownership in Modern Egypt, 1800–1950.* London, Oxford University Press.

———. 1969. *Studies in the Social History of Modern Egypt.* Chicago, University of Chicago Press.

———. 1982. *Fellah and Townsman in the Middle East.* London, Frank Cass.

Baker, Raymond W. 1978. *Egypt's Uncertain Revolution under Nasser and Sadat.* Cambridge, Harvard University Press.

Barclay, Harold B. 1971. "The Nile Valley." In *The Central Middle East,* edited by Louise E. Sweet. New Haven, HRAF Press, pp. 1–77.

Barois, Julien. 1889. *Irrigation in Egypt.* Washington, Government Printing Office. The Miscellaneous Documents of the House of Representatives for the 2d Session of the Fiftieth Congress, 1888-1889, volume 9, Washington, GPO, 1890 (translated from the original French edition of 1887).

______. 1911. *Les irrigations en Egypte.* 2e ed. Paris, Beranger.

Bennett, John. 1969. *Northern Plainsmen: Adaptive Strategy and Agrarian Life.* Chicago, Aldine.

Berger, Morroe. 1970. *Islam in Egypt Today: Social and Political Aspects of Popular Religion.* Cambridge, Cambridge University Press.

Berque, Jacques. 1955a. "Sur la structure sociale de quelques villages égyptiens." *Annales Economies-Sociétés-Civilisations* 10(2):199–215.

______. 1955b. "Dans le delta du Nil." *Annales de Géographie* 64 (#344):277–290.

______. 1955c. "Dans le delta du Nil: le village et l'histoire." *Studia Islamica* 4:91–109.

______. 1957. *Histoire sociale d'un village égyptien au XXième siècle.* Paris, Mouton.

Binder, Leonard. 1978. *In a Moment of Enthusiasm: Political Power and the Second Stratum in Egypt.* Chicago, University of Chicago Press.

Blackman, Winifred S. 1968. *The Fellahin of Upper Egypt.* London, Frank Cass.

Bösl, Karl. 1984. "Musha: Struktur und Entwicklung eines ägyptischen Dorfes." *Geographische Rundschau* 36:248–255.

Braverman, Harry. 1974. *Labor and Monopoly Capital: The Degradation of Work in the Twentieth Century.* New York, Monthly Review Press.

Bremer, Jennifer Ann. 1982. *Alternatives for Mechanization: Public Cooperatives and the Private Sector in Egypt's Agriculture.* Ph.D. thesis, Kennedy School of Government, Harvard University.

Brunhes, Jean. 1902. *L'Irrigation, ses conditions géographiques, ses modes et son organisation dans la péninsule ibérique et dans l'Afrique du Nord.* Paris, C. Naud.

Burawoy, Michael. 1979. *Manufacturing Consent.* Chicago, University of Chicago Press.

______. 1984. "The Contours of Production Politics." In *Labor in the Capitalist World-Economy,* edited by Charles Bergquist. Beverly Hills, Sage Publications, 23–47.

Butzer, Karl W. 1976. *Early Hydraulic Civilization in Egypt.* Chicago, University of Chicago Press.

Byres, T.J. 1977. "Agrarian Transition and the Agrarian Question." *Journal of Peasant Studies* 4(3):258–274.

Commander, Simon, and Aly Abdullah Hadhoud. 1986. "From Labour Surplus to Labour Scarcity? The Agricultural Labour Market in Egypt." *Development Policy Review* 4(2):161–180.

Crary, Douglas D. 1949. "Irrigation and Land Use in Zeiniya Bahari, Upper Egypt." *Geographical Review* 39:568–583.

Demangeon, A. 1926. "Problèmes actuels et aspects nouveaux de la vie rurale en Egypte." *Annales de Géographie* 35:135–173.

Dessouki, Ali E. Hillal. 1982. "The Shift in Egypt's Migration Policy: 1952–1978." *Middle Eastern Studies* 18(1):53–68.

Diraz, Hamed Abdel-Maguid. 1968. "Taxation and Agricultural Development in the United Arab Republic (Egypt)." Ph.D. dissertation in Business and Applied Economics (Finance), University of Pennsylvania.

Eigner, Diethelm. 1984. *Ländliche Architektur und Siedlungsformen im Aegypten der Gegenwart.* Vienna, Veröffentlichungen der Institute für Afrikanistik und Aegyptologie der Universität Wien, Nr. 30.

El-Kholy, Heba Aziz. 1985. *Property Relations and Irrigation Organizations: A Case Study of Water-Lifting Devices in an Egyptian Village in the Delta.* M.Sc. Thesis, Cornell University.

El-Messiri, Sawsan. 1983. "*Tarahil* Laborers in Egypt." In *Migration, Mechanization, and Agricultural Labor Markets in Egypt,* edited by Alan Richards and Philip Martin. Boulder, Westview, pp. 79–100.

El-Shagi, El-Shagi. 1969. *Neuordnung der Bodennutzung in Aegypten.* Munich, Weltforum Verlag (IFO-Institut für Wirtschaftsforschung München, Afrika-Studien 36).

ERA 2000. 1979. *Further Mechanization of Egyptian Agriculture.* Gaithersburg, Md., Report to USAID.

Evetts, B.T.A. (translator). 1895. *The Churches and Monasteries of Egypt and Some Neighbouring Countries, Attributed to Abu Salih, the Armenian.* Oxford, at the Clarendon Press.

Fahim, Hussein M. 1973. "Change in Religion in a Resettled Nubian Community in Upper Egypt." *International Journal of Middle East Studies* 4:163–177.

———. 1983. *Egyptian Nubians: Resettlement and Years of Coping.* Salt Lake City, University of Utah Press.

Fitch, James B., and Ibrahim A. Soliman. 1983. "Livestock and Small Farmer Labor Supply." In *Migration, Mechanization, and Agricultural Labor Markets in Egypt,* edited by Alan Richards and Philip Martin. Boulder, Westview, pp. 45–78.

Friedland, William H., Amy E. Barton and Robert J. Thomas. 1981. *Manufacturing Green Gold: Capital, Labor, and Technology in the Lettuce Industry.* Cambridge, Cambridge University Press.

Gadalla, Saad M. 1962. *Land Reform in Relation to Social Development, Egypt.* Columbia, University of Missouri Press.

———. 1977. "The Influence of Reproduction Norms on Family Size and Fertility Behavior in Rural Egypt." In *Arab Society in Transition,* edited by Saad Eddin Ibrahim and Nicholas S. Hopkins. Cairo, American University in Cairo, pp. 323–342.

———. 1985. "Shanawan Experimental Development Project." Report to USAID.

Geertz, Clifford. 1979. "Suq: The Bazaar Economy in Sefrou." In *Meaning and Order in Moroccan Society,* edited by Clifford Geertz, Hildred Geertz, and Lawrence Rosen. Cambridge, Cambridge University Press, pp. 123–310.

Gilsenan, Michael. 1973. *Saint and Sufi in Modern Egypt.* Oxford, at the Clarendon Press.

———. 1983. *Recognizing Islam: Religion and Society in the Modern Arab World.* New York, Pantheon Books.

Glavanis, Kathy R. B., and Pandeli M. Glavanis. 1983. "The Sociology of Agrarian Relations in the Middle East: The Persistence of Household Production." *Current Sociology* 31(2):1–109.

Goodman, David, and Michael Redclift. 1982. *From Peasant to Proletarian: Capitalist Development and Agrarian Transition.* New York, St. Martin's Press.

Gotsch, Carl H., and Wayne M. Dyer. 1982. "Rhetoric and Reason in the Egyptian 'New Lands' Debate." *Food Research Institute Studies* 18(2):129–147.

Guenena, Nemat. 1986. *The 'Jihad': An 'Islamic Alternative' in Egypt.* In *Cairo Papers in Social Science* 9, #2.

Harik, Iliya. 1974. *The Political Mobilization of Peasants: A Study of an Egyptian Community.* Bloomington, Indiana University Press.

______. 1979. *Distribution of Land, Employment and Income in Rural Egypt.* Ithaca (N.Y.), Cornell University Rural Development Committee (Center for International Studies), Special Series on Landlessness and Near-Landlessness #5 (with Susan Randolph).

Hart, Keith. 1982. *The Political Economy of West African Agriculture.* Cambridge, Cambridge University Press.

Hopkins, Nicholas S. 1977. "The Emergence of Class in a Tunisian Town." *International Journal of Middle East Studies* 8:453–491.

______. 1978. "The Articulation of the Modes of Production: Tailoring in Tunisia." *American Ethnologist* 5(3):468–483.

______. 1983. "The Social Impact of Mechanization." In *Migration, Mechanization, and Agricultural Labor Markets in Egypt,* edited by Alan Richards and Philip Martin. Boulder, Westview, pp. 181–197.

______ et al. 1980. "Animal Husbandry and the Household Economy in Two Egyptian Villages." Manuscript report, Catholic Relief Services/USAID, Cairo (with co-authors).

______ and Sohair Mehanna. 1981. "Egyptian Village Studies." Cairo, Agricultural Development Systems Project, Economics Working Paper #42.

______, Sohair Mehanna and Bahgat Abdelmaksoud. 1982. *The State of Agricultural Mechanization in Egypt: Results of a Survey, 1982.* Cairo, Ministry of Agriculture.

Hussein, Mahmoud. 1973. *Class Conflict in Egypt: 1945–1970.* New York, Monthly Review Press.

Ibrahim, Ahmed Hassan. 1982. "Impact of Agricultural Policies on Income Distribution." In *The Political Economy of Income Distribution in Egypt,* edited by Gouda Abdel-Khalek and Robert Tignor. New York, Holmes and Meier, pp. 198–235.

Ibrahim, Saad Eddin. 1982. *The New Arab Social Order: A Study of the Social Impact of Oil Wealth.* Boulder, Westview.

Idiart, Pierre. 1961. "Métayage et régimes fonciers dans la région du Faguibine (Cercle de Goundam—Soudan)." *Etudes Rurales* 1(2):37–59 and 1(3):21–44.

de Janvry, Alain. 1981. *The Agrarian Question and Reformism in Latin America.* Baltimore, Johns Hopkins University Press.

______ and K. Subbarao. 1983. "Wages, Prices, and Farm Mechanization in Egypt: The Need for an Integrated Policy." In *Migration, Mechanization, and Agricultural Labor Markets in Egypt,* edited by Alan Richards and Philip Martin. Boulder, Westview, pp. 237–264.

Johnson, Pamela R., et al. 1983. *Egypt: The Egyptian American Rural Improvement Service, A Point Four Project, 1952–63.* Washington, USAID Project Impact Evaluation Report No. 43.

Kelley, Allen C., Atef M. Khalifa, and M. Nabil El-Khorazaty. 1982. *Population and Development in Rural Egypt.* Durham, Duke University Press. Duke Press Policy Series, Studies in Social and Economic Demography #5.

Kennedy, John G. 1977. *Struggle for Change in a Nubian Community: An Individual in Society and History.* Palo Alto, Mayfield. (with Hussein Fahim).

Kepel, Gilles. 1984. *Le prophète et pharaon: les mouvements islamistes dans l'Egypte contemporaine.* Paris, La Découverte.

Keyder, Caglar. 1983. "Paths of Rural Transformation in Turkey." *Journal of Peasant Studies* 11:34–49.

Khafagi, Fatma. 1983. "Socio-economic Impact of Emigration from a Giza Village." In *Migration, Mechanization, and Agricultural Labor Markets in Egypt,* edited by Alan Richards and Philip Martin. Boulder, Westview Press, pp. 135–156.

———. 1984. "Women and Labor Migration: One Village in Egypt." *MERIP Reports,* #124, pp. 17–21.

Landau, Jacob M. 1953. *Parliaments and Parties in Egypt.* Tel Aviv, Israel Publishing House.

Larson, Barbara K. 1980. Parts IV and V of the Village Flocks section of the "Final Report: Poultry Improvement Project—Egypt." vol. II, pp. 234–317. Report by Mathtech, Inc. to USAID.

———. 1982. "Periodic Markets in Egypt and Tunisia Compared." *Peasant Studies* 10(1):49–58.

Leaf, Murray J. 1983. "The Green Revolution and Cultural Change in a Punjab Village, 1965–1978." *Economic Development and Cultural Change* 31:227–270.

Lee, David R. 1970. "The Location of Land Use Types: the Nile Valley in Northern Sudan." *Economic Geography* 46:53–62.

Lenin, V.I. 1960 (originally 1899). *The Development of Capitalism in Russia.* London, Lawrence and Wishart. Collected Works, vol. 3.

Lozach, Jean, and G. Hug. 1930. *L'habitat rural en Egypte.* Cairo, Imprimerie de l'IFAO.

Lyons, H.G. 1908. *The Cadastral Survey of Egypt: 1892–1907.* Cairo, Survey Department, Ministry of Finance.

Marglin, Stephen A. 1982. "What do Bosses do? The Origins and Functions of Hierarchy in Capitalist Production." In *Classes, Power, and Conflict,* edited by Anthony Giddens and David Held. Berkeley, University of California Press, pp. 285–298.

Marx, Karl. 1963 (originally 1852). *The Eighteenth Brumaire of Louis Bonaparte.* New York, International Publishers.

———. 1967 (originally 1867). *Capital.* New York, International Publishers. 3 volumes.

Marx, Karl, and Frederick Engels. 1970. *The German Ideology.* New York, International Publishers.

Mayfield, James. 1971. *Rural Politics in Nasser's Egypt: A Quest for Legitimacy.* Austin, University of Texas Press.

Mehanna, Sohair, Richard Huntington and Rachad Antonious. 1984. *Irrigation and Society in Rural Egypt, Cairo Papers in Social Science.* vol. 7, monograph 4.

Meillassoux, Claude. 1964. *Anthropologie économique des Gouro de Côte d'Ivoire.* Paris and The Hague, Mouton.

———. 1975. *Femmes, greniers et capitaux.* Paris, Maspero.

Meinardus, Otto. 1969. "The Upper Egyptian Practice of the Making of Eunuchs in the XVIIIth and XIXth Century." *Zeitschrift für Ethnologie* 94:47–58.

Mencher, Joan P. 1978. *Agriculture and Social Structure in Tamil Nadu.* New Delhi, Allied.

MetaMetrics. 1981. "Rural Sanitation in the Arab Republic of Egypt." Washington, D.C., report to USAID.

Meyer, Günter. 1978. "Erschliessung und Entwicklung der Aegyptischen Neulandgebiete." *Erdkunde* 32(3):212–227.

Mickelwait, Donald R., David Stanfield, Ibrahim Abbas Omar and Gary Eilerts. 1980. "Monitoring and Evaluating Decentralization: The Basic Village Services Program in Egypt." Washington, Development Alternatives, Inc., for USAID/Cairo.

Nadim, Asaad. 1979. "The Role of the Village Bank in the Rural Community." Report for the International Islamic Center for Population Studies and Research, al-Azhar University, and USAID.

Netting, Robert M., Richard Wilk and Eric Arnould. 1984. *Households: Comparative and Historical Studies of the Domestic Group.* Berkeley, University of California Press.

O'Brien, Jay. 1984. "The Social Reproduction of Tenant Cultivators and Class Formation in the Gezira Scheme, Sudan." *Research in Economic Anthropology* 6:217–241.

Owen, Roger. 1969. *Cotton and the Egyptian Economy, 1820–1914: A Study in Trade and Development.* London, Oxford University Press.

Radwan, Samir. 1977. *Agrarian Reform and Rural Poverty, 1952–1975.* Geneva, International Labor Office.

Reeves, Edward Bradley. 1981. *The Wali Complex at Tanta, Egypt: An Ethnographic Approach to Popular Islam.* Ph.D. thesis, University of Kentucky.

______. 1983. "Farm Systems Research and Village Shopkeepers in North Kordofan, Sudan." *Practicing Anthropology* 5(3):8–9.

Richards, Alan. 1980. "The Agricultural Crisis in Egypt." *The Journal of Development Studies* 16:301–321.

______. 1981. "Agricultural Mechanization in Egypt: Hopes and Fears." *International Journal of Middle East Studies* 13:409–425.

______. 1982. *Egypt's Agricultural Development, 1800–1980: Technical and Social Change.* Boulder, CO, Westview Press.

Richards, Alan, and Philip Martin. 1983. *Migration, Mechanization, and Agricultural Labor Markets in Egypt.* Boulder, Westview.

Richards, Alan, Philip Martin and Rifaat Nagaar. 1983. "Labor Shortages in Egyptian Agriculture." In *Migration, Mechanization, and Agricultural Labor Markets in Egypt,* edited by Alan Richards and Philip Martin. Boulder, Westview, pp. 21–44.

Rizqallah, Fawzeya, and Kamel Rizqallah. 1978. *La préparation du pain dans un village du delta égyptien (Province de Charqia).* Cairo, Institut Français d'Archéologie Orientale.

de la Roncière, Charles. 1931. "La géographie d'Egypte à travers les âges." in *Histoire de la nation égyptienne,* edited by Gabriel Hanotaux, vol. 1. Paris, Plon.

Ross, Justin C. 1892. *Notes on the Distribution and Maintenance of Works in the Basin System of Upper Egypt.* Cairo, National Printing Office.

______. 1893. "Irrigation and Agriculture in Egypt." *The Scottish Geographical Magazine* 9:169–193.

Roumasset, James R., and Joyotee Smith. 1981. "Population, Technological Change, and the Evolution of Labor Markets." *Population and Development Review* 7(3):401–419.

Rugh, Andrea. 1984. *Family in Contemporary Egypt.* Syracuse, Syracuse University Press.

Saab, Gabriel. 1960. *Motorisation de l'agriculture et développement agricole au Proche-Orient.* Paris, SEDES.

———. 1967. *The Egyptian Agrarian Reform 1952–1962.* London, Oxford University Press.

Sahlins, Marshall. 1972. *Stone Age Economics.* Chicago, Aldine-Atherton.

Sandes, E.W.C. 1937. *The Royal Engineers in Egypt and the Sudan.* Chatham, The Institution of Royal Engineers.

Saunders, Lucie Wood, and Soheir Mehanna. 1986. "Village Entrepreneurs: An Egyptian Case." *Ethnology* 25(1):75–88.

Schulze, Reinhard. 1981. *Die Rebellion der ägyptischen Fallahin 1919: Zum Konflikt zwischen der agrarisch—orientalischen Gesellschaft und dem kolonialen Staat in Aegypten 1820–1919.* Berlin, Baalbek Verlag.

Scott, James C. 1983. "Small Arms Fire in the Class War: Rich and Poor in a Malay Village." *Political Anthropology* vol. 2, *Culture and Political Change,* pp. 189–215.

———. 1985. *Weapons of the Weak.* New Haven, Yale University Press.

Seddon, David. 1978. *Relations of Production.* London, Frank Cass.

Silvestre de Sacy, Baron Antoine Isaac. 1810. *Relation de l'Egypte par Abd-allatif, médecin arabe de Baghdad, suivie de divers extraits d'écrivains orientaux, et d'un état des provinces et des villages de l'Egypte dans le XIVe siècle.* Paris, Imprimerie Impériale.

Springborg, Robert. 1979. "Patrimonialism and Policy Making in Egypt: Nasser and Sadat and the Tenure Policy for Reclaimed Lands." *Middle Eastern Studies* 15:49–69.

———. 1982. *Family, Power, and Politics in Egypt.* Philadelphia, U. of Pennsylvania Press.

Stauth, Georg. 1983. *Die Fellachen im Nildelta: Zur Struktur des Konflikts zwischen Subsistenz- und Warenproduktion im ländlichen Aegypten.* Wiesbaden, Franz Steiner Verlag.

Tadros, Helmi Ragheb. 1984. *Social Security and the Family in Egypt.* In *Cairo Papers in Social Science.* 7, #1.

Taher, Nadia Adel. 1986. *Social Identity and Class in a Cairo Neighborhood.* In *Cairo Papers in Social Science.* 9, #4.

Tignor, Robert. 1982. "Equality in Egypt's Recent Past: 1945–1952." In *The Political Economy of Income Distribution in Egypt,* edited by Gouda Abdel-Khalek and Robert Tignor. New York, Holmes and Meier, pp. 20–54.

Toth, James F. 1980. "Class Development in Rural Egypt, 1945–1979." In *Processes of the World-System,* edited by Terence K. Hopkins and Immanuel Wallerstein. Beverly Hills and London, Sage, pp. 127–147.

Treydte, Klaus Peter. 1979. *Agrarreform und Entwicklung: Ziele, Strategien und Effekte der Agrarreform in den Ländern Nordafrikas, Analyse aus entwicklungspolitischer Sicht.* Bonn, Verlag Neue Gesellschaft.

Wallerstein, Immanuel. 1974. *The Modern World-System: Capitalist Agriculture and the Origins of the European World Economy in the Sixteenth Century.* New York, Academic Press.

Walz, Terence. 1978a. *Trade between Egypt and Bilad as-Sudan, 1700–1820*. Cairo, Institut Français d'Archéologie Orientale.

______. 1978b. "Asyut in the 1260's (1844–53)." *Journal of the American Research Center in Egypt* 15:113–126.

Warriner, Doreen. 1962. *Land Reform and Development in the Middle East: A Study of Egypt, Syria, and Iraq*. 2d ed. London, Oxford University Press.

Waterbury, John. 1983. *The Egypt of Nasser and Sadat: The Political Economy of Two Regimes*. Princeton, Princeton University Press.

Weber, Max. 1978. *Weber: Selections in Translation*, edited by W.G. Runciman. Cambridge, Cambridge University Press.

Willcocks, William. 1889. *Egyptian Irrigation*. London and New York, E. & F.N. Spon.

______. 1935. *Sixty Years in the East*. Edinburgh and London, William Blackwood and Sons.

Winkler, Hans Alexander. 1934. *Bauern zwischen Wasser und Wüste: Volkskundliches aus dem Dorfe Kiman in Oberägypten*. Stuttgart, Kohlhammer.

______. 1936. *Aegyptische Volkskunde*. Stuttgart, Kohlhammer.

Wolf, Eric R. 1981. "The Mills of Inequality: A Marxian Approach." In *Social Inequality: Comparative and Historical Approaches*, edited by Gerald D. Berreman. New York, Academic Press, pp. 41–57.

Zimmermann, Sonja D. 1982a. *The Women of Kafr al Bahr*. Leiden, Research Center Women and Development, University of Leiden.

______. 1982b. *The Cheese-makers of Kafr al Bahr: The Role of Egyptian Women in Animal Husbandry and Dairy Production*. Leiden, Research Center Women and Development, University of Leiden.

Index